Why Feminism?

WHY FEMINISM?

Gender, Psychology, Politics

LYNNE SEGAL

Polity Press

Reprinted 2002, 2005

Polity Press
65 Bridge Street
Cambridge CB2 1UR, UK

Polity Press
350 Main Street
Malden, MA 02148, USA

ISBN 0-7456-2346-8
ISBN 0-7456-2347-6 (pbk)

A catalogue record for this book is available from the British Library.

Typeset in 11 on 13 pt Berling
by Ace Filmsetting Ltd, Frome, Somerset
Printed and bound in Great Britain by Marston Book Services Limited, Oxford

This book is printed on acid-free paper.

For further information on Polity, visit our website: www.polity.co.uk

05434020

Contents

Acknowledgements   viii

Introduction: Why Feminism?   1

1 Generations of Feminism   9
    Acts of Memory   10
    Dubious Contrasts   12
    Rowbotham's 'Seventies' Feminism   17
    The Collapse of a Vision   21
    A New Fundamentalism   27
    The Turn to 'Theory'   29
    Political Agendas   33

2 Gender to Queer, and Back Again   38
    The Rise of Gender Theory   39
    The Allure of Difference   43
    The Romance of Otherness   49
    The Joys of Queer   55
    Transgender Dialogues   60
    Back to Gender?   66
    The Future of Gender   70

3 Genes and Gender: The Return to Darwin   78
    Science versus Culture?   79
    Survival and Sexual Selection   81

Evolutionary Psychology: The New Contender 86
The Tale of the Female Ape 94
Theoretical Pluralists: The Enemy Within 100
Gene Talk versus Social Change 104
For Epistemic Diversity 111

4 Psychic Life and its Scandals 116

Tricks of Memory 117
Dilemmas of Science 120
Troubled Vision 123
Feminist Denunciations 124
Fantasy versus Trauma 127
Models of Memory 133
Memory as Narrative 137
Betrayal versus Abuse? 141
Narratives in Context 145

5 Gender Anxieties at the Limits of Psychology 149

Feminism Enters the Academy 150
Still Searching for Sex Differences 152
Feminist Psychology and Social Constructionism 154
Openness to Gender Heterodoxy 156
The Predicament of Men 160
Projects for Reforming Masculinity 164
Deconstructing Gender 170
Subjectivity and Change 171

6 Cautionary Tales: Between Freud and Feminism 174

Opening Skirmishes 176
Imagining the Void 179
Oedipal Dramas and the Crisis of Paternal Authority 185
The First Bond and its Consequences 190
Retrenchment versus Renewal? 193
Sexual Difference versus Gender: Accepting Ambiguity 195

7 Only Contradictions on Offer: Feminism at the
   Millennium   200

    Snapshots of Gender   201
    The Subject of Dependency   206
    Family Values   209
    Sweeping Anti-statism   211
    Switching to the Subject   215
    Activist Challenges   217
    Disciplinary Feminism   220
    Cultural Imperatives   223
    Feminism without Politics   225
    Political Futures   229

Notes   233

Index   274

Acknowledgements

Fewer people than usual helped me with this book, which says something about these times. As pressures to publish from within the administration of academic space encounter the shrinking possibilities for cross-over writing with mainstream publishers, and the fractiousness between feminists is matched by the decline in collective political engagements, I wasn't confident I could manage to write at all any more: no longer sure of whom I would be writing for, or why. But I am still lucky enough to find myself within networks in which feminism, and often even socialism, are lifetime commitments, which continue to inspire me. I would like to thank John Fletcher, Catherine Hall, Katherine Johnson, Cora Kaplan, Loretta Loach, Mandy Merck, David Newson, Sheila Rowbotham, Alan Sinfield, Barbara Taylor, Ruth Thackeray and Leonore Tiefer for advice, assistance or encouragement. I am very grateful for the support of my editor David Held. Above all, I value the love, generosity and rigorous red pen of Peter Osborne, without whom . . .

Introduction:
Why Feminism?

Why is feminism still so contentious? Feminism grew too big for its marching boots in the closing years of the 1970s; since then, many of its exponents have taken a more reflexive turn. But the anxiety it generates has far from dissipated. Indeed, feminists even frighten each other. Today, maverick voices emerge on all sides, rebuking a politics they claim to espouse. 'Many a monster can march about flying the banner of "freedom" or "feminism"', philosopher Jean Bethke Elshtain alleges from the USA – condemning women who do not subordinate their own rights to the welfare of their children.[1] In these pages, I try to make sense of the *mélange* of contemporary feminism. I wonder whether we can still look to it for a confrontational and broadly transformative politics and culture, or whether it has become little more than a blip in the march of economic neo-liberalism.

It is hard to avoid either idealizing or trashing one's past, feeding the unruly envy between and within political generations. It is harder still, and obviously foolhardy, to engage in any form of futurology. In all social movements, once the excitement of finding a new collective identity begins to ebb, everyday politics becomes a more discouraging, even tedious affair; a matter of competing interests and conflicting alliances. It never remains the revelation which first inspired new levels of self-confidence and hope, as it was when women's liberation erupted into the lives of many women at the close of the 1960s. Yesterday's visionaries are today's scapegoats, when not newly tamed and domesticated.

The declining passion for politics evident in many veteran feminists, accompanying the frank rejection of feminism by many young women, is part of a wider 'exhaustion of utopian energies' since the 1980s, a time often described as 'post-socialist', if not 'post-political'.[2] There is a firm consensus at the close of the twentieth century that little, if anything, remains of a socialist left capable of winning popular support for its vision of a more egalitarian future. The verdict on feminism, and its now diverse aspirations, is more ambivalent. Its promotion of women's interests is usually endorsed in mainstream politics, while still anxiously traduced on every side. But the inequalities and divisions between women themselves have dramatically deepened, while many of the problems which energized feminists into collective action in the 1970s everywhere persist. This is both despite, and because of, the many gains achieved by women throughout the century. Some were consciously fought for; others were the more ambiguous, unintended consequences of changes in capitalism – pushing women into the future first, as exemplary low-paid, flexible workers.[3]

Indeed, current debates are obsessed with gender contrasts and conflicts, often packaged as slanging matches between feminists themselves: 'movement' feminists, like British old-timer Bea Campbell, are pitted against American 'celebrity' feminists/anti-feminists, like Camille Paglia. Here women's political differences can be made to service antithetical desires: serious interest in gender issues *and* the satisfaction of misogynist expectation. However dubious its delivery, though, there is no doubting the continuing social centrality of gender anxieties – whether triggered by family breakdown, new 'laddism', teenage pregnancy or some other form of sexual or social panic. This means that as a feminist it is hard to remain detached from the political arena, whether or not one feels able to preserve or refashion one's political visions or, harder still, one's collective engagements.

Yet, we must persist, why *feminism*? Is the time for the renewal of feminism not long past, given the remarkable shifts in gender relations? Gender disruptions are indeed ubiquitous, as I illustrate throughout this book, but surely men are now often its victims, whether in the classroom, the workplace or the divorce courts. Moreover, publishers (especially feminist ones) have been suggesting that 'there is no market any more for specifically feminist books'.[4] But that is only part of the story. Books about women? That is quite another matter. They are in huge demand.[5] Never has more been written about the concerns of women. Nor has so much anxiety been manifest on the threat they pose to the serenity of men. At a time when gender distinctions have been disrupted and denaturalized everywhere, through the combined forces of economic, political and quite literal biomedical interventions, the question of women's difference and distinctive dispositions remains paramount. The dismantling of gender archetypes provokes their perpetual rearticulation, as I show in chapter 2. With feminism posed against women, and gender posed against politics, what in the world do we make of 'feminism' today?

A mere generation ago, it caused little surprise when the American poet Adrienne Rich declared feminism a renaissance 'far more extraordinary and influential' in shifting perspectives than the effects of the move from theology to humanism in the European Renaissance.[6] Partisan, for sure. But the decades of resurgent feminism did fundamentally transform our perceptions of both present and past. They threw up some revolutionary conceptions of the future in the process. Today, that word – the new 'f-word' – is in free fall, often arousing little more than a yawn. 'Feminism is boring', the British journalist Polly Toynbee moans, summing up the abiding apprehensions of her peers, women influential in the mainstream media.[7] Boring, perhaps, but still capable of stirring up enormous animosity, and never left to rest in peace.

Suitably distanced from feminism's supposedly dour defenders, Toynbee herself proceeds to produce a thoughtful summary of why women need feminism: continuing inequalities in their earnings, the difficulties of being torn between careers and children, their greater vulnerability to domestic violence and rape, especially when most financially dependent on a man – as the mothers of young children. Passé, predictable, prosaic; yet the common sense of our age. Who wants yesterday's slogans? Who wants yesterday's woman? In fact, it is not just feminism, but participation in the public terrain of politics itself which is now commonly dismissed as 'boring', or assumed to be motivated by an exclusive self-interest, in a world where individualism has intensified with an awesome vengeance, demolishing most of its erstwhile critics; or at least, those whose politics cannot be reduced to the vivid provocation of rebellious lifestyles. The irony is that current forms of feminism display an extraordinary endurance and diversity; so varied, indeed, that common ground can be hard to find.

What is feminism? Who is a feminist? Contention rather than accord is what we must explore in answering such questions today. This is a perplexing situation for those who identified with a movement which, during its activist peak, preferred to operate through consensus. Moving on from the burning questions, bonfires and street parades, the change in the self-conception of the women's movement was the beginning of an always ambivalent slide into the cultural mainstream: goodbye to 'Women's Liberation', with its clenched fist, its militant slogans and joyful songs ('The Women's Army is Marching'); hello to 'feminism', with its diffuse theoretical underpinnings and performative uncertainties ('doing feminism', 'doing gender'). 'Could you please say a few sentences without using the word "struggle"?', interviewers of feminists in the mid-1970s used to ask, when we held forth on our goals and aspirations, believing that we could work to better the lives of women everywhere. 'Could you please tell me what your struggle for health, housing, clean water, union recognition [or some other bread-and-butter issue], has to do with feminism?', one might easily hear today.

The difference is context. As I explore in my opening chapter, the women's liberation movement emerged at the close of the 1960s in critical dialogue with a broader left movement fighting for a more egalitarian world. Even in the USA, where more conventionally liberal movements, like the National Organization of Women, were always stronger than in Britain, one prominent wing of the movement was militantly leftist and radical. In the three decades of second-wave feminism, as I trace out in subsequent chapters, one can discern the successive dominance of three distinct styles and viewpoints, although earlier outlooks continue – often angrily – to contest more modish replacements. During the foundation and spread of the women's movement in the 1970s, there was an emphasis on women's shared needs, and struggles to end gender inequalities and cultural subordination. This turned into a dual and contradictory prioritizing of women's distinct 'difference' alongside recognition of multiple differences between women in the 1980s, accompanying the entrenchment of divisions within feminism itself. Subsequently, there has been a shift towards discursive analyses of the instability of *all* identities and differences, as feminist theory found a home in the post-structuralist academy of the 1990s.

One explanation of the shift in feminist consciousness and priorities suggests that the early women's liberationist search for social transformation came up against women's own subjective resistance to change.[8] Women's internalized submissiveness or nurturing sensitivities may, or may not, prove genuine enough. But the turn inward, often to psychoanalysis, was part of something wider. It was never going to be easy to persuade individual men to change, but it was going to be far harder to undermine the interconnecting worlds of home, jobs and cultural and public life which overwhelmingly reflect the principle of male authority. Nevertheless, in my view, feminism's distinct legacy still lies in its potential, however complex and difficult, to connect personal and cultural issues to economic and political affairs. This is why in this book I move back and forth between explorations of gender dynamics at the social and political level and attempts to theorize differences, identities and subjectivities in the psychological and symbolic domains. Throughout, I am seeking ways of negotiating the increasingly bitter tension between feminist activisms and academic feminisms – often misleadingly reduced to clashes between the economic versus the cultural; maldistribution versus misrecognition.

In my lifetime, feminists have always been interested in the autobiographies of women, hunting down the words of their foremothers and constructing their own tales of personal struggle and survival, whether in the quest for self-enlightenment or for solidarity with other women. In the most recent flowering of the genre, women academics have taken to writing their memoirs. And if their narratives display somewhat less disadvantage and hardship than many that preceded them, their proliferation carries its own story of the contradictions of feminism at the close of the twentieth century. These are times in which a woman – even, or perhaps especially, a fem-inist – can be accused of abusing her institutionalized power: an authority which she wields, not so much in the familiar female sphere of the family, as in the once seamlessly male world of the academy, or some other public position. The autobiographical writing of that most ostentatiously undutiful daughter of feminism, Jane Gallop, *Feminist Accused of Sexual Harassment* (1997), springs immediately to mind. But she is joined by a host of other women memoirists of the 1990s, whose world is the university: today's most prestigious stronghold of feminist practice.[9] What the feminist academic memoir brings to that world is a focus on the personal. Ironically, the more some women seem to be winning old gender battles, power-dressing for their jobs in the professional world, and narrowing the gender differences affecting their daily lives, the stronger the affirmation of women's unique affiliation to personal life. As Calista Flockhart – pocketing her millions from portraying the winsome, emotionally wobbly, lawyer, Ally McBeal – assures us, women can't 'have it all': 'I don't think there's an answer here, just anxiety and conflict'.[10]

Women can't have it all, no doubt; and the political never did reduce to such dreams of personal transcendence. But in exploring the paradoxes of gender in this book I seek to promote a combination of theoretical questioning and political engagements which might enable more women to share in the self-questioning, the pleasures and, above all, the solidarities and egalitarian settlements that feminism, at its most generous, regards as the birthright of women everywhere.

Using conflicts over 'gender' as my key symbolic site, I see the cultural fluidities of sexual and gender identity celebrated in recent post-structuralist and queer feminist readings mocked by the return of a Darwinian fundamentalism and the rise of genetic determinism in popular culture and much of the social sciences. Fierce controversies over memory and trauma return us to the promise and the perils of relying upon the light that Freud seemed to shine on the strange working of the mind: rarely matched, however, by attention to the power relations and normative frames in which the language of desire is acquired, suppressed and distorted. In the 1970s feminists demanded public recognition of the extent of child sexual abuse; today, saturated with sensationalized tales of victimhood and abuse, some now deplore the curiously depoliticized fate of their protests when exploited by the media, or used to consolidate the need for expert advice and healing.

Mainstream culture has found many ways of accommodating feminism, ranging from the endorsement of women as sexually vulnerable and abused, through the managerial appropriation of equal opportunities to hypocritical applause for women's supposed caring virtues and values. What we have yet to see is movement towards fairer and more caring societies, whatever the rhetoric of New Labour in Britain or the machinations of Clinton in Washington. Approaching the millennium, media outlets select their favourite figures to assess the impact of three decades of feminism, hoping for simple messages which can be repackaged as new and contentious. They are easy to find. From one side, Germaine Greer wades in to announce that women today are regularly, even increasingly, demeaned and damaged, especially in sex with men: 'For all our liberation talk, rich, modern, western woman is continually, repeatedly mutilated'.[11] She echoes the enthusiastically embraced gloom of another populist, white, Western feminist, drowning us in her rhetoric of the destruction of women's achievements in the twenty-first century: 'Feminists will be visible only in pornographic scenarios as stereotypically cartoonish uppity women, made happy and normal through rape'.[12] From the opposite side, Rosalind Coward contends that it is time for Western feminists to stop viewing women as oppressed, because she sees instead 'situations where men are really becoming vulnerable and women potent'.[13] In fact, feminism could still offer us something far richer than such simplistic gender-polarizing polemic.

As funding for welfare shrinks, the working day lengthens,

inequality deepens and political protest is everywhere muted, it is women and children in particular who remain at the cutting edge of the contradictions between work and welfare markets and morality. Certain groups of men are known to be 'failing' today, both at school and in the job market, with destructive consequences. These consequences are all the more destructive because of the effects of gender: the assumption that men should always be the dominant sex. When wider questions of social inequality and gender justice are posed alongside problems of identities and belonging, the domain of feminism immediately expands. It is such a feminism which I believe we still need: we need the continuing provocation which its inquiries can still arouse; we need its collective efforts to find solutions when the dreams and realities of specific groups of women and men are most awry; we need its potential, at its most thoughtful, to embrace complexity and conflict in the experiences of individual women and men, as the resilience of images of masculinity as power are shaken by the actualities of shifting gender dynamics and the fragilities of gendered and sexual identities. Drawing primarily on the Anglo–American experience, *Why Feminism?* attempts to lay out the potentialities and pitfalls of feminist consciousness for the century ahead.

1

Generations of Feminism

Politics makes comics of us all. Or we would weep.
Sheila Rowbotham, *Dreams and Dilemmas*

I have been thinking for some time now about relations between political generations and the enduring impact of those formative moments which first enable us to make some sense of the world, and our place within it – an unjust and shabby world, whatever our personal circumstances. Such moments remain all the more powerful if, like many of my own generation who became students in the 1960s, you have hoped – with whatever levels of scepticism and self-mockery – to participate in the making of history. They leave their mark, even as changing times cause one to rethink, perhaps even to renounce, one's former political presumptions. Yet what often leaves erstwhile political crusaders with little more than mournful and confusing feelings of loss and regret – whatever our capacities for irony – is the way in which new narratives emerge as collective memories fade, writing-over those which once incited our most passionate actions.

So it has been with Women's Liberation, that second wave of feminism which arose out of the upsurge of radical and socialist politics in the late 1960s. It grew rapidly as a mass social movement, peaking in the mid-1970s before dissolving as a coherent organization by the end of that decade. It affected the lives of millions of women. Over a quarter of a century later, however, the sparse amount of thoughtful scholarship analysing the distinctiveness of that upsurge of feminist activism must struggle for attention amidst a glut of texts delineating its contemporary academic progeny – largely scornful of its rougher parent, and the motley basements, living-rooms, workplaces and community centres in which it was hatched. This is not just a female Oedipal tale, as disobedient daughters distance themselves from their mothers' passions, seeking recognition for themselves. It is also a sibling affair, as feminists contend with each other; fearful, perhaps, of being overlooked should we fail to keep abreast of new theoretical fashions, or else unable to admit the inadequacies and contradictions of past attachments.

Acts of Memory

A small band of feminist historians, mostly in the USA, who *are* trying to recapture the diversity of the movement in which they participated, declare that they cannot recognize themselves, or others, in what they see as the distorting accounts of Women's Liberation circulating in contemporary feminism. Rosalyn Baxandall and Linda Gordon, for example, are gathering material for a multi-volume collection of literature from the movement in the USA. They are joined by others interested in archiving the local histories of Women's Liberation, such as Patricia Romney, documenting a group of fifty women of colour based in New York and Oakland, California, who – along with other black activists in the sixties and seventies – became the forgotten women who 'fell down the well' (as Carolyn Heilbrun puts it) in subsequent rewritings of women's liberation as exclusively white.[1] These historians are well aware of the dangers of their proximity to their own research, of how memories are muted or reshaped by subsequent perspectives and interests, whether one's own or those of younger recorders. At a recent symposium on the history of women's liberation in the USA, Margaret Strobel recounted that even when rereading her *own* diaries and letters she is amazed at their failure to match her current recollections of the events she recorded there.[2]

Reading our own histories through the interpretations of others can be more unsettling still. Awareness of the tricks of memory, and the dearth of thoughtful reflections on a re-

markable period of feminist activism fast being forgotten,
prompted two other veteran US feminists, Rachel DuPlessis
and Ann Snitow, to embark upon their own memoir project:
not in search of 'truth unmodified', but to seek out the ambiguities and ambivalences with which those who gave birth to
the movement would now recall their engagement in its past.
Open, questioning and self-critical, as they introduce the rich
and varied collection which ensues, they nevertheless argue
compellingly that caricature and forgetting is the greater
danger haunting women's political actions: 'For amnesia about
political movements is not only an innocent effect of general
forgetfulness, but is socially produced, packaged, promulgated,
and perpetuated.'[3] I agree. It is extraordinary – exciting and
troubling in equal measure – to read these distinct and divergent accounts from women whose lives were shaped by their
belief that collective action could (and, for a while, did) transform everything, from personal lives to workplace conditions,
social policy, the law and almost every aspect of culture. It is
important, if only to realize quite how strange their rhetoric
and sensibilities appear in the current political climate; the
words not so much of another generation, with less sophisticated ideas, as of another species.

As if foreseeing this impression, Meredith Tax mourns: 'I
feel like one of the last surviving members of a nearly extinct
species – the committed left-wing feminist'.[4] Although still
working successfully to promote women's writing and struggles through the international forum Women's WORLD
(Women's World Organization for Rights, Literature and Development) which she helped to found in the 1990s, Tax
knows she can no longer make her own voice heard at home.
A pointed reminder of changing times, at least for those aware
that it was she who published one of the earliest underground
classics of women's liberation, *Woman and her Mind: The Story
of Everyday Life* (1970), which sold 150,000 copies in pamphlet form around the world. I could quote from it to this day.

Contemporary texts reviewing recent feminist history provide sobering examples of how the past is read through the
concerns of the present: invalidating earlier meanings and
projects as well as erasing their heterogeneity. Moreover, the

displacement of former struggles and perspectives is all the
more disconcerting when contemporary theorists, starting off
from an abhorrence of binary logics and a scepticism about all
attempts to generalize, go on to draw false contrasts and make
reckless generalizations of their own. It is this which startles
me when I read accounts of the distance self-proclaimed 'nineties' feminism has travelled from women's liberation, and
what now appears neatly homogenized as 'seventies' feminism.

Dubious Contrasts

A distinguished British collection of feminist thought, edited by Michèle Barrett and Anne Phillips, *Destabilizing Theory*
(1992), highlights what it refers to as 'the gulf between feminist theory of the 1970s and 1990s'. It opens with the assertion: 'In the past twenty years the founding principles of
contemporary western feminism have been dramatically
changed, with previously shared assumptions and unques-
tioned orthodoxies relegated almost to history'.[5] Quite so.
But just what is being dispatched here? Was it all of a piece?
And is it equally anachronistic for contemporary feminists?

'Seventies' feminism is criticized for its 'false certainties';
its search for structural causes of women's oppression (indeed for its very notion of 'oppression'); its belief in women's
shared interests (indeed, its very attachment to the notion of
'women' or 'woman'), and so forth.[6] 'Nineties' feminism, in
contrast, has replaced what is seen as the naive search for the
social or material causes of women's oppression by complex
elaborations of the discursively produced, hierarchical constitution of an array of key concepts: sexual difference in particular, binary oppositions in general, and the hetero/sexualized
mapping of the body as a whole. *Destabilizing Theory* rejects
what it proclaims to be the assumptions of 'Enlightenment'
thought: 'a notion of a powerful and self-conscious political
subject, a belief in reason and rationality, in social and political progress, in the possibility of grand schemes of social reform'. It is impressively cautious about the 'ambiguous status

of theory', yet it still risks a few generalizations of its own: tending towards a totalizing dismissal of 'seventies' feminism, and the reduction of *dissimilar projects* to common ground: 'Feminists have moved from grand theory to local studies, from cross-cultural analysis of patriarchy to the complex and historical interplay of sex, race and class, from notions of a female identity or the interests of women towards the instability of female identity and the active creation and re-creation of women's needs and concerns.'[7]

A comparable tension can be found in an American collection aiming 'to call into question and problematize the presumptions of some feminist discourse': *Feminists Theorize the Political* (1992), edited by Judith Butler and Joan Scott.[8] Its introductory essay is also cautious about drawing comparisons between different phases of feminism, aware that contrasting 'post-modern' feminism with an earlier 'modernist' feminism buys into precisely the conceits of modernity itself, sharing all its enthusiasm for identification with the 'new' and over-confident renunciation of the 'old'. (Although it is surely a strange hostage to fortune to insist, on its opening page, that '"post-structuralism" indicates a field of critical practices that cannot be totalized'.[9]) Circumspect and equivocal as Butler characteristically is, habitually preferring the interrogative to the more vulnerable affirmative mode, her influential writing is always *read* as primarily deconstructive, privileging regulatory semiotic or semantic issues around 'subjectivity', 'identity' and 'agency'. Here, she insists that: 'To recast the referent as the signified, and to authorize or safeguard the category of women as a site of possible resignifications is to expand the possibilities of what it means to be a woman and in this sense to condition and enable an enhanced sense of agency'.[10] Butler is certainly right to stress that 'what women signify has been taken for granted for too long'. But, in calling for 'the conditions to *mobilize the signifier* in the service of an alternative production', she delineates a project which is distinctly different from the close attention to social *structures*, *relations* and *practices* which an earlier feminist project prioritized in pursuit of political-economic restructuring, and the transformation of public life and welfare.

When women joined campaigns in support of demands for nurseries, reproductive rights, education and skill training; to assist women fighting low pay, discrimination and 'harassment' at work, violence and sexual abuse at home, militarism worldwide; to fight racism, legacies of imperialism and work within Third World development projects; found the women's health movement, and so on and so forth, they were engaged in 'an alternative production'. The sudden collectively confident embrace, or alarming display, of hitherto demeaned descriptions of womanhood – gaudily paraded on countless banners, T-shirts and badges – was certainly very much part of the process: 'The category "women", so fresh and surprising on that fictive but evocative Day One of the Second Wave, is familiar now, to some an oversimplification, to others banality'.[11] The way representation carves out reality and moulds action is central to all political activity. None the less, a feminism which *begins* with the textual practice of re-theorizing signifiers of subjectivity is one which is *incommensurate* with, as well as distanced from, the perspectives and practices of Women's Liberation. It is simply not the same project, however sympathetic to many of those earlier goals someone like Butler clearly is.[12] As others have noticed, the commitment to heterogeneity, multiplicity and difference underlying recent feminist theorizing can anomalously disguise a hegemonizing dismissal of theoretical frameworks not *explicitly* informed by post-stucturalism.[13] Joan Scott, at times, seems to exemplify this form of exclusion of theoretical diversity when she attacks 'resistance to poststructuralist theory' as resistance to 'theory' itself: 'Since it is in the nature of feminism to disturb the ground it stands on, even its own ground, *the resistance to theory* is a resistance to the most radical effects of feminism itself'.[14]

Here is the problem: contemporary feminist theorizing rarely acknowledges the time and the place of political ideas. It addresses only abstract *theories* and their refutation. It operates with an idea of the history of feminism as the evolution of academic theory and debate. Tellingly, both the British and North American feminist collections I have mentioned offer their readers a full index of *names* – in which, inciden-

tally, extraordinarily few of the influential feminist names of
the 1970s appear – but no index of *topics*. In the Blackwell
textbook *Feminist Thought,* by Patricia Clough, dedicated to
'Women around the World Resisting Oppression, Domination, and Exploitation', there *is* a context index, but interestingly neither hint nor whisper of abortion or reproductive
rights, housework, childcare, nurseries, welfare provision,
immigration, marriage, the family, poverty, the state, employment, trade unions, healthcare or violence against women.
There is pornography, autobiography, film theory, literary
criticism, Woman, Native, Other. However you cross-reference
it, just a few aspects of women's actual resistance 'around
the world' seem to have gone missing in this nineties text.[15]
Almost no effort is made to refer back to the activities and
goals of Women's Liberation in these books, only an attempt
to contrast theoretical positions as ideal types.

The reason is, of course, that this is an easy way to *teach*
feminism as an academic topic. But you cannot translate the
time of theory and its fashions into political history, without
absurd caricature: concealing conflicting perceptions and nuances with each categorical tag. Thus early Women's Liberation becomes, for example, a 'feminism of the subject', when
it was not a theory about subjectivity at all – however much it
concerned women struggling to make themselves visible in
quite new ways. It is almost always described as a theory of
'equality', rather than of 'difference', when it was neither of
these things – the one usually presented as merely an inversion
of the other. Both of these descriptions miss the point. Wom-
en's Liberation in its heyday was a *theory and practice of social
transformation*: full of all the embroiled and messy actions,
hostilities and compromises of collective political engagement.
For the most part, it manoeuvred within a broader culture
of the left: refusing to separate women off from wider struggles against inequality and subordination, but fighting the
perpetual marginalization or neglect of what were often wom-
en's most specific interests and concerns. It endlessly debated
questions of priorities, organization and alliances in the attempt to enrich women's lives and connect with other radical
projects (heatedly discussing the varied – often opposed –

interests of different groups of women, especially the most vulnerable). In the process, it transformed the very concept of the 'political', giving women a central place within it.

My sense of the recent history of feminism, in particular of the socialist-feminist strand of Women's Liberation flourishing in Britain in the early seventies, conflicts with Julia Kristeva's often cited stagist mapping of three generations of feminist thought, in her famous essay 'Women's Time', first published in 1979. There she depicts the first wave of feminism as a time when women, using a 'logic of identification', pursued liberal, egalitarian ends, followed by the emergence of a militant second phase, which rejected all 'patriarchal' thought and practice, attempting to create 'counter-societies' constructed around mythical notions of womanhood. This is the now familiar erection of a binary division between 'equality' feminism, followed by its opposite, 'difference' feminism: women first seek inclusion in, and later exclusion from, the masculine symbolic order. Drawing upon Derrida, Kristeva proposes a *third* generation of feminism, which is critical of the binary of sexual difference itself, since 'it is now possible to gain some distance on these two preceding generations of women'.[16] Toril Moi would later label and promote Kristeva's three stages as 'liberal', 'radical' and 'post-' feminism, again criticizing what she identified as the humanistic and essentialist errors of the first two stages of feminism, in order to advocate the theoretical work of post-feminist deconstruction.[17]

Yet, as I hope to show, although they never used the rhetoric of deconstruction, the third stage now being labelled 'post-feminism' is not so removed from where many second-wave feminists came in. Attempting to avoid the problems of straightforward inclusion in, or exclusion from, the masculine symbolic order and a world organized primarily around men's interests was the problem many feminists tried to tackle all along (although using different conceptual tools, some borrowed from Sartre and de Beauvoir; some from Marx, Freud, Reich, Gramsci or Marcuse). The contrasts are not always as significant as recent re-tellings suggest. Here are the words of one feminist writer and activist who was for a few years tremendously influential as an inaugurator of *'stage one'* of second-wave feminism, looking at her own first attempt to articulate feminism, thirty years on: 'When I read it over, despite all that has happened since, the intensity of loneliness returns. It was like walking over a moor in the mist, trying to speak, with the words sticking half formed in your throat. Such difficulty finding appropriate words, really a new political language, is not so surprising.' But then this writer, as we shall see, also knows how easily simplistic readings overwrite earlier formulations: 'perceptions can be there one minute, and gone the next'; 'as the years go by, what was once a contemporary account comes to reveal a particular historical moment, not simply because of what is said but in the very way it is written'.[18]

Rowbotham's 'Seventies' Feminism

In my view, the most useful – and perhaps the only meaningful – way to think about the similarities and differences between different generations of feminism is by reflecting upon what defines a political generation and what smashes its hopes and dreams. On an International Women's Day march in the early seventies, Sheila Rowbotham carried a placard that read: **'Equal Pay is Not Enough. We want the Moon'**. (File under equal rights feminism? Perhaps not. Is the moon here a symbol of female difference? Not likely.) We got neither, as she wrote a decade later, but the radical heritage of Women's Liberation continues, she argued, whenever feminists work to realize the dream 'that all human beings can be *more* than present circumstances allow'.[19] That vision is not one of equal rights. It was called 'socialism' and it was being reshaped to service feminism.

I want to focus on Sheila Rowbotham's writing as she has been one of the most careful chroniclers (and continuing committed exponents) of Women's Liberation in Britain, in the hope that it may be, as she puts it, 'neither falsely valued nor undervalued', but that feminists might reflect back upon 'the hurly-burly of battle, draw clarity from real muddles and learn from our mistakes.'[20] Dream on!, one might feel, in these new comprehensively market-driven, mean-spirited times. Since memories find resonance only in pertinent contexts, Rowbotham adds, if you 'ignore the humdrum you fall into arrogance'. [21] Rowbotham was one of the many inspirational voices of seventies feminism consciously attempting to create 'a movement which is confident, gleeful, generous and loving', even while already knowing that any such oppositional activity can have costly overheads which drain and exhaust the spirit.[22] It was her lonely search to find the then unfamiliar words which could express her personal alienation, as one of the exceptionally few women trying to set down her thoughts in the sexist world of radical politics in the late 1960s, which resulted in the first pamphlet on Women's Liberation to be published in Britain – in January 1969. And it was she who proposed the first Women's Liberation conference in Britain, which occurred at Ruskin College in Oxford the following year. Most importantly, for my purposes here, it was her books which were read by tens of thousands of feminists throughout the world in the 1970s. They were hugely influential in the initial years of women's liberation. Moreover, Rowbotham would be criticized, early on, as representing a seventies feminism, unformed by psychoanalysis or structuralism.[23] Today, of course, her flaws would be seen as an inattention to post-structuralism or 'post-modernity' – that paradoxical twist of modernity, contrarily repudiating linear narratives while depending on one.

Joining the game of textual analysis, I recently re-read some of Rowbotham's books of the 1970s and early 1980s, something I do often to prevent my own long-term memories from dissolving (there seems nothing to be done about the crashing of short-term ones). Ironically, what is extraordinary about Rowbotham's writing is usually quite the reverse of what critics of seventies feminism imagine. It conveys an openness, chronic *lack* of certainty, an almost infuriating tentativeness, reiteratively asserting: 'What we have developed through action and ideas has always to be subject to reassessment'; or, 'I am too encumbered by the particular to move with grace and delicacy between subjective experience and the broad sweep of social relationships'.[24]

From her earliest reflections, Rowbotham describes the search for the roots of women's subordination as a 'perilous and uncertain quest'.[25] Her texts always stress what she calls 'the differing forms and historically specific manifestations of the power men hold over women in particular societies'.[26] They focus sharply on the diversity and situational specificity of women: whether of class, race, employment, domestic situation or (although not at first, as she herself soon notes self-critically) sexual orientation: 'Our own indications are only tentative and incomplete. . . . Women's liberation is too narrow in social composition to comprehend the differences between middle class and working class, black and white, young and old, married and unmarried, country and townswomen'. Moreover, she writes, in 1972, 'it is clear that most of the isolated gains we can make can be twisted against women and that many partial gains are often a means of silencing one group at the expense of another'.[27] She emphasizes the role of language as one of the crucial instruments of domination:

> As soon as we learn words we find ourselves outside them. . . .
> The underground language of people who have no power to define and determine themselves in the world develops its own density and precision. . . . But it restricts them by affirming their own dependence upon the words of the powerful. . . .
> There is a long inchoate period during which the struggle between the language of experience and the language of theory becomes a kind of agony.[28]

Ignorant of post-structuralism Rowbotham may have been, writing these words in her mid-twenties, but not so ignorant, I would suggest, of the issues they address. Moreover, her voice was not a lone one; it feels to me like the remembered buzz in the air, what the women I knew best were tuned in to.

She tussles (a favourite word) endlessly with the problems of relying on direct experience, seeing it as both a strength and weakness – again, not so unlike, if less theoretically fine-tuned, than the essay by Joan Scott on the topic in the collection from the USA mentioned above, written

twenty years later.[29] She continuously affirms the pointless-
ness of attempting to pin down the nature of either 'women'
or 'men', adding that: 'All revolutionary movements create
their own ways of seeing. . . . But this is a result of great
labour'.[30] Her writing, like the forces which drew many
women together in the early years of Women's Liberation,
reflects the radical left (largely Marxist) thought of the day:
'An emergent female consciousness is part of the specific
sexual and social conjuncture, which it seeks to control and
transform.'[31] So while questions of subjectivity and identity
are most definitely not ignored (and when they appear, are
quite as shifting, provisional and contingent as any post-
modernist might desire), the goal is always to transform
society, to make it a better place for all its members, especially its neediest and, in her words, 'gradually accumulate a
shared culture of agitation'. She writes:

> There is democracy in the making of theories which set out to
> rid the world of hierarchy, oppression and domination. The
> act of analysis requires more than concepts of sex and class,
> more than a theory of the subject, it demands that in the very
> process of thinking we transform the relations between thinker
> and thought about, theory and experience. . . . Analysis is not
> enough alone, for we enter the beings and worlds of other
> people through imagination, and it is through imagination
> that we glimpse how these might change.[32]

Many seventies feminists have recalled, like Rowbotham, the
imaginative leap when they first began to turn outwards to
other women, generating an almost open-ended desire for
solidarity with just those women they had hitherto distanced
themselves from: 'The mainspring of women's liberation was
not a generalised antagonism to men but the positive assertion of new relationships between women, sisterhood'.[33] Socialist feminists argued that while capitalist societies had
changed the relative power and privileges of men, they had
also consolidated women's inferior status, along with that of a
multitude of other historically subordinated groups – predominantly along racialized and ethnic lines. So while it was

not *inconceivable* that women might gain equality with men in existing capitalist societies, it was thought that this would require such deep levels of cultural, economic and political change that they would already have become societies which were fundamentally different from any we have known.[34]

The Collapse of a Vision

The state, in socialist-feminist analyses like those of Elizabeth Wilson or Mary McIntosh, was seen as not strictly 'patriarchal', but serving to regulate, and occasionally to restructure, the often contradictory and conflicting needs of a male-dominated market economy and the still intrinsically patriarchal arrangements of family life.[35] It was from such analyses that they set about shaking out and making visible the separate and distinct needs and interests of women (kept hidden by familial rhetoric); campaigned against state policies and discourses which defined and enforced women's dependence on men; demanded an end to the scandalous social neglect of women and children at risk from men's violence; fought for more and better social provision and community resources; all the while seeking alliances with other oppressed groups. Strategic priorities were usually paramount, whether making demands on the state or on the trade unions, and even when elaborating utopian visions of communities and workplaces compatible with choice and flexibility: where the needs of all dependent people would not be hidden away in idealized, yet neglected and isolated, often impoverished, family units.[36]

This socialist-feminist strand of Women's Liberation, chronicled in books like Rowbotham's *The Past Is Before Us*, remained an active and influential source of ideas and strategies for promoting women's interests until the mid-1980s, usually working in diverse radical and reformist coalitions with other progressive forces.[37] However, the frustration and defeats of a second term of Conservative rule (1983–7), targeting and weakening precisely those nooks and crannies in local government, resource centres and collective spaces which feminists and other radicals had managed to enter, gradually exhausted not only the political hopes, but even the dreams of many.

In recalling the early achievements of the women's movement in re-launching feminism, we also need to consider its limitations. The bustling energies and tight-knit friendships in the small groups most feminists liked to work within – even their principled structurelessness – could make women who didn't fit in feel all the more excluded from the imagined joys of 'sisterhood'.[38] The fierce commitment to ideals of complete equality not only created what could prove inefficient structures, but often triggered suspicion and hostility towards those seen as arrogant or ambitious. The disavowal of envy and competitiveness between women made its concealed expression all the more embittered: 'If you want to be a good feminist, then be a good girl and think about everybody but yourself', as New York feminist Muriel Dimen would later tease those who wrapped themselves in unrealistic feminist rectitude.[39] Above all, looking for shared experiences between women frequently meant disregarding the incongruous or divisive. Again, from the memoirs now emerging in the USA, Joan Nestle reflects how her embrace of feminism as a lesbian in the early 1970s made her a stronger person, who could properly value other women for the first time:

> I learned new ways of seeing my woman's life, new understandings of gender oppression, a new language, but I also learned the boundaries beyond which the politics could not go. . . . We could talk about sex [but] not about desire. We could talk about work, but not about class as it expressed itself in the groups, most of which were dominated by middle-class women.

True. But as Nestle quickly adds, these silences were made to be broken by the insights of feminism itself:

> I realized that my experiences as a sexual deviant had given me insights into certain issues like pornography, prostitution, and gender questioning that while not the prevailing ones in the lesbian feminist seventies and eighties were too important to be buried.[40]

Any myth of women's cosy unity, fighting the combined subordinations of sex, race, class and heterosexism, could never hold for long: to this day, however, many dream of its return, harshly denouncing differing traitors to the cause – from 'liberals' and 'careerists' to 'purists', 'pornographers' or 'identity fetishists' – for its absence. Race would prove an even more explosive issue than class and sexual orientation. Poverty and racism were constant preoccupations of women's liberation, both in theory and in practice (especially in the USA, where so many pioneering feminists had emerged out of the civil rights movement), but feminist groups remained overwhelmingly white, and predominantly middle class. Conflict was soon breaking out everywhere, as particular groups of women expressed their sense of exclusion within the movement itself. In the USA Toni Cade's anthology *The Black Woman* appeared in 1970, and the first National Black Feminist Organization and the Sisterhood of Black Single Mothers were both formed as early as 1973, although organizations of black women and women of colour did not reach their peak until the early 1980s. In Britain, the first black women's conference was held in 1979. As in the USA, the most painful clashes over race would occur in the second decade of resurgent feminism, with black women in both countries challenging the priorities of white feminist analysis over the previous decade: for privileging sexism over racism, and ignoring the particularities of ethnic difference.

Nevertheless, trying to learn to listen to, and act upon, black feminist perspectives was not initially a decisive factor in the fading of the socialist-feminist vision in Britain. On the contrary, black feminists then occupied the *same* political spaces, and pursued largely *similar* or *parallel* strategic campaigns for expanding the choice and resources open to black women and their families. The political limitations they saw in what they defined as 'Euro-American' feminism, at that time, as Valerie Amos, Gail Lewis, Amina Mama and Pratibha Parmar made clear in 1984, was that it has 'contributed to an improvement in the material situation of white middle-class women often at the expense of their black and working class "sisters." . . . The power of sisterhood stops at the point at which hard political decisions need to be made and political priorities decided'.[41] The problem, as Barbara Smith saw it in the USA, was similar: how to 'build a women's movement that addresses the life circumstances and priorities of all women', one she connected with grassroots activism.[42]

There were without doubt race and class-bound limitations, as well as unrecognized elitisms, prescriptive moralisms and self-policing, in the diverse perspectives and practices of Women's Liberation. But the precarious presumptions and faltering visions of many seventies feminists who yearned for a better world for all, including themselves, often had less to do with dogmatic certitudes, conceptual closure, binary thinking, identity politics or even false universalism, and much more to do with the floundering fortunes of grassroot or movement politics in harsh and unyielding times. The death knell of the seventies feminism I dwelt within was not simply the fall-out of internal conflict and divisions, whether over race, class or sexuality, although they did turn feminist political spaces into stressful combat zones. Rather, coming together as agitators, of whatever sex, race or ethnic specificity, to pursue goals which require, among other things, a more egalitarian and caring world, brought us up against a ferocious, if contradictory and erratic, political opponent. This is something a new generation of academically licensed theorists, turning inwards rather than outwards, often prefer to ignore.

In New York, veteran campaigner and author Vivian Gornick recalls: 'Then the unthinkable happened. Slowly, around 1980, feminist solidarity began to unravel. As the world had failed to change sufficiently to reflect our efforts, that which had separated all women before began to reassert itself now in us ... the discrepancy between desire and actuality was too large to overcome'.[43] Her contemporary trailblazer at the *Village Voice* is even more convinced that the shift in economic fortunes and political conversation meant that there was soon 'no legitimate public language in which to describe utopian vision and systemic opposition'.[44] In the end, the fundamental limitation of the utopian visions of feminist activists, hoping to transform both themselves and society as well, was our failure to see our own dependence on a wider left politics and social democratic consensus – whatever their shortcomings. As economic survival became more problematic for many more people, as the public mood shifted and an anti-government, market-driven culture became ever more hegemonic, the social world sustaining progressive thought and practice continued to wither.

Since the 1980s, the ever more deregulated, universalized, interests of global capital have produced deepening social inequalities, nationally and internationally. In the process, they have ensured a significant increase in the pressures of time on most women, and of poverty for some women, even as others, especially when child-free, seem to prosper in the spaces which have opened up for them in the expanding managerial, service and professional world. Some feminists have managed to remain determinedly politically engaged. Having moved on from campaigns into study groups or graduate training, they have helped to create or sustain more focused groups in defence of reproductive rights, fighting for legal change, social policy reform, human rights organizations and Third World women's groups or, especially in the USA, creating centres for training women organizers. In Britain, government institutions, the media, work in education at all levels, have each provided spaces for promoting specific feminist ideas and practices. Black feminists have continued to organize against white racism, and to oppose the rise of religious fundamentalism in some of their own communities, while feminists from diverse backgrounds remain active in fighting against or supporting the survivors of sexual and domestic violence.

Nevertheless, times have changed irrevocably. Around 1980 it would have been hard to find a single self-respecting feminist in Britain who had not trekked out to Grunwick's factory in west London, in support of the predominantly Asian women on strike, or at least considered such action. Two decades later, it would be hard to find a self-respecting feminist who had even *heard* of the predominantly Asian women on strike at Burnsall in Birmingham, as Melissa Benn has noted, over an almost identical set of issues: refusal of union recognition, low pay, and the use of dangerous chemicals; or who would have contemplated supportive action, if they had.[45] As I write, women care workers in Tameside, in Greater Manchester, enter their second year on strike, not just against their own appalling pay and conditions, but just as much to protect the interests of the very vulnerable elderly people who were in their care. Yet there is little national concern from anyone for issues which would once have rallied passionate feminist support. It is true that those women's liberationists with the freedom, time and confidence to plunge into action in support of women facing the harshest forms of exploitation had a certain naivety – which today would be labelled arrogance – concerning their own ability to bring about radical change. But, as Rowbotham would later reflect, this was not just self-delusion: 'There was considerable upheaval not only in Europe and the US but globally in these years – the first symptoms of the fundamental changes which were to take shape from the mid 1970s.'[46]

Looking at a world transformed by feminism, which usually pays lip-service to ideas of equality in both the workplace and the home, intransigent domestic inequalities still mean that 80 per cent of employed wives with young children continue to shoulder most of the burdens of housework. The idealism and audacity with which the young American housewife Alix Kates Shulman could get her husband to sign her detailed Marriage Agreement is something we sorely miss. Published in 1971 in the mainstream women's magazine *Redbook*, where it generated over 2000 letters of support (followed by front-page derision in the *New York Times Book Review* from people as eminent as Norman Mailer and Joan Didion), it began: 'We reject the notion that the work which brings in money is more valuable. The ability to earn money is a privilege which must not be compounded by enabling the larger earner to buy out his/her duties and put the burden either on the partner who earns less or on another person hired from outside.'[47] A different time, a different place. Yet, the failure of such a politics, which could collectively fight for the restructuring of the workplace as well as demand change on the home front, means that an ever expanding group of women add to their increasing overload of work the burden of deeply resenting their husbands, and finding their home lives an arena of conflict and strife. This was the report from the domestic front issued by Arlie Hochschild in her book *The Second Shift* (1989) and, even more forcefully, after the restructuring of the job-front, in *The Time Bind* (1997).[48] The legacy of seventies feminism, seen as a movement of social transformation aiming to increase the power and self-determination of women everywhere, is contradictory and diverse. But serious consideration of its successes and failures is grievously absent in most recent theoretical profiles.

A New Fundamentalism

There is another twist in this tale of two generations of feminism. In terms of the writing-over of earlier feminist narratives, the painful irony is that precisely when deconstruction and other forms of post-structuralism were imprinting themselves on academic feminism – promoting conceptual uncertainty, political indeterminacy and subjective fluidity – directly opposing discourses of female victimization, moral certainty and psychic essentialism now were entrenching themselves in a new form of feminist fundamentalism and contested activism in the 1980s. The voices of feminism which survived and gained followers internationally in the 1980s came from its best-known, North American, white spokeswomen, like Robin Morgan and Andrea Dworkin. These no longer expressed anything resembling socialist feminism, with its analysis of specific historical contexts, shifting institutional arrangements, particular social practices or the multiple discourses securing women's inequality and marginality. Rather, ideas denouncing the ageless dominance of 'masculine' values and behaviour were the ones most widely promulgated and seemingly accepted as the voice of feminism. A new and complacent romance around the feminine took precedence in the best-known forms of feminist thought, with women celebrated as essentially nurturing, non-violent and egalitarian; accompanying condemnation of the 'masculine' as ineluctably dominating, destructive and predatory.

It was this form of so-called 'cultural feminism' which I criticized in *Is the Future Female?* (1987). The original sub-title of my book, 'Arguments for Socialist Feminism', was rejected by my feminist publisher, Virago Press, as already too unpopular to promulgate, leading to the more neutral 'Troubled Thoughts' of its published subtitle.[49] The simplistic and reductive anti-pornography movement would soon emerge as the single most visible and highly funded feminist campaign of the 1980s – originating, and always most prominent, in the USA. In attempting (however defectively) to affiliate their gender politics with every other conceivable form of subordination, socialist feminism had generated cumbersome discourses, full of compositional complexities, caveats and uncertainties. Its rhetoric was a world apart from the fire and brimstone of the rising theoretician of anti-pornography feminism, Catharine MacKinnon, who was matched only by her comrade-at-arms, pornography's other foremost foe, Andrea Dworkin. Ironically, but far from coincidentally, the thing which pornographers and anti-pornographers most share is the desire to arouse: to pound an audience with their rhythmic, repetitive images – although it is only anti-pornographers who fixate on such exceptionally sadistic sexual imagery. The delivery of Dworkin and MacKinnon is evocative of puritan barnstorming down through the ages.

In my book *Straight Sex* (1994),I traced the rise of a more pessimistic sexual conservatism within feminist thinking from the close of the 1970s, which insisted, misleadingly, that sexuality was the single overriding cause and manifestation of men's oppression of women – sprouting from its roots in pornography. Catharine MacKinnon later summarized her contentious rewriting of feminist history: 'feminism is a theory of how the erotization of dominance and submission creates gender, creates woman and man in the social form in which we know them'.[50] Some feminists saw these moves, as I did, as part of a reaction to more conservative times, and the setbacks faced by many forms of feminist activism, especially in the USA, where it originated at the close of the 1970s. 'Pornography', Ann Snitow suggests, became a metaphor for women's defeat. Isolating sexuality and men's violence from other issues of women's poverty, social inequality and domestic overload was not only a defensive tactic for women, but one in perfect harmony with the rising tide of conservative backlash against radical politics more generally.[51] The right has always liked to demonize sexuality, and have us see it as the source of all our ills. This ensured that they would move swiftly into an alliance with anti-pornography feminism. And however vigorously we hear it denied, Dworkin's and MacKinnon's alliance with the moral right is well documented.[52]

Meanwhile, as the 1980s progressed, it was either those, like Catharine MacKinnon, who offered some version of an increasingly totalizing and sanctimonious feminism (clinging to the moral highground of women's marginality and helplessness), or others, like Camille Paglia, with equally totalizing inversions of this position (caricaturing feminism as prudish and puritanical) who found favour with the media. Neither offered any challenge to traditional gender discourses.

The Turn to 'Theory'

In contrast, at the cutting edge of the new feminist scholarship of the 1980s, these same gender discourses were being broken down and questioned. It is hard to summarize the illuminations and provocations of academic feminism's current embrace of post-structuralist critiques of universalizing thought and emancipatory narratives (to which I return, in one form or another, in most of the following chapters) without courting the danger of homogenizing contemporary theorizing, much as it has erased the complexities of seventies feminism. The appropriation of post-structuralist priorities would inspire what has become known as 'feminist postmodernism', although this conceptually confused and confusing label is not accepted by some of those placed under its banner – Judith Butler, for one.[53] At least three separate strands of thinking are usually lumped together under this heading – deriving from Jacques Lacan, Jacques Derrida and Michel Foucault, respectively – despite their very different implications for feminism.

The first and for a while the most influential post-Lacanian strand, often simply called, misleadingly, 'French feminism' (which is discussed most fully in chapter 6), restricts its focus to the idea of sexual difference effaced by the spurious unity or wholeness of the Western 'subject' (Man): the white, male bourgeois subject of history who hides behind the abstract universals of the philosophical tradition. It stresses the need to fracture the universal or humanist self through attentiveness to its repressed or marginalized other: 'feminine' difference. Subversively imagined and rewritten as positive, the decentred side of the silenced and repressed 'feminine' is thought to enable women to 'foresee the unforeseeable', and escape the dichotomous conceptual order in which men have enclosed them.[54] This new focus upon images of female corporeality has been seen by its exponents as presenting a fresh purchase on the old essentialism debate, transcending earlier forms of historical, sociological or psychoanalytic anti-essentialist arguments. The 'feminine feminine', Hélène Cixous and Luce Irigaray suggest, can emerge only once women find the courage to break out of the male imaginary and into a female one – once women begin to speak and write their sexuality, which is always plural, circular and aimless, in contrast to all existing singular, linear and phallocentric, masculine forms of symbolization.[55] Such feminist reclaiming of the body unfolds here as always culturally and psychically inscribed female experience, not anatomical destiny, and is perhaps best seen as a form of aestheticized, high modernist, 'avant-gardism'.[56] It is nevertheless still narrated in terms of a *universal* corporeal subjectivity for women.

The attraction of such difference theory, which encourages the feminist to speak 'as a woman', is obvious. The revaluing of those aspects of women's lives and experiences previously ignored or demeaned in male-centred theorizing was, and remains, crucial to feminist research and practice. But there is still a problem which it cannot easily tackle (even if we ride with its own cheerfully embraced contradictions), once we turn from the academic to the political realm. As I have argued elsewhere, it is precisely ideas of sexual difference encompassing the experiences supposedly inscribing our distinctive 'femaleness', which most dramatically *divide*, rather than unite, feminists attempting to fight for women's interests.[57] It is easier for women to join forces around issues on the currently unfashionable economic front (demanding parity in wages and training) or on social policy (demanding more and better publicly funded welfare resources) than it has ever been for women to unite around issues of sexuality and the meanings we attach to the female body. Creatively exciting as the project of re-imagining female corporeality has proved to be for some feminists,[58] its neglect of issues of class, race, ethnicity and other forms of marginality as equally constitutive of women's subjectivity and destiny has seemed exclusionary and disempowering to other feminists. Such criticism has been most forcefully expressed by black and ethnic minority feminist theoreticians: from Gayatri Spivak to Barbara Christian or Deborah McDowell.[59] Some academic feminists like to quote Gayatri Spivak in support of their view that women today must 'take "the risk of essence" in order to think really differently'.[60] However, Spivak herself has reconsidered her earlier suggestion for a 'strategic' use of a positive essentialism. Since such a move is viable only when it serves 'a scrupulously visible political interest', she now warns: 'The strategic use of essentialism can turn into an alibi for proselytizing academic essentialisms'.[61] And it has.

Spivak belongs to the second, more rigorous, Derridian strand of feminist post-structuralism, which is critical of the monolithic Lacanian version of difference theory. It questions all universalizing or totalizing theoretical tendencies, deconstructing every discursive patterning of the self, including that of 'woman'.[62] Here, in tune with the input of black, Third World, lesbian, and other feminisms, *every* generalization about women, including the feminist search for the causes of women's subordination or any generalized expressions of women's difference – whether seen in terms of responsibility for childrearing, reproductive and sexual experience, men's violence, phallogocentric language, a female imaginary, or whatever – is regarded with suspicion. This position is summed up by Donna Haraway:

> There is nothing about being "female" that naturally binds women. There is not even such a state as "being" female, itself a highly complex category constructed in contested sexual scientific discourses and social practices. . . . The feminist dream of a common language, like all dreams for a perfectly true language, of a perfectly faithful naming of experience, is a totalizing and imperialistic one.[63]

Haraway wants to replace this dream with her own one of 'a powerful infidel heteroglossia . . . building and destroying machines, identities, categories, relationships, spaces, stories', seeking a place for women in a future 'monstrous world without gender'.[64] Her dream is full of playful optimism about the future. For other more strictly deconstructive feminists, however, there is no theoretically defensible affirmative position, but only a reminder of the limits of concepts, as Spivak explains: 'the *absolutely* other cannot enter into *any* kind of foundational emancipatory project'.[65] Such a deconstructive feminism certainly avoids the perils of generalizations about female subjectivity. But it courts the danger that its own interest in endlessly proliferating particularities of difference, and the partial, contradictory nature of women's identities, endorses a relativity and indeterminacy which works to undermine political projects.

The third, Foucauldian, strand of post-structuralist feminism returns us to the body – to its 'sexuality' rather than to sexual difference – but only as a site or target of ubiquitous technologies of classification, surveillance and control. Foucault's warning that oppositional discourses are inevitably caught up in the relations of domination they resist has been important in highlighting the traps facing emancipatory movements: of reproducing rather than transcending traditional frameworks of subjection. And his arguments about meaning and representation have proved particularly productive for lesbian and gay theorists. Here, feminists can learn much from Foucault's insights about the genealogy of discursive regulation, but next to nothing about how organized resistance might impinge on such all-encompassing regimes of power, other than through the discursively disruptive, micro-political strategies favoured by some lesbian theorists.

Despite its influence on many feminists, especially via Judith Butler's suggestive ways of making 'gender trouble' by parody of the ties which bind the production of gender to hetero-sexual normativity, other feminists fear that a politics in which resistance is manifest primarily in individual performative sub-version of the symbolic domain is inevitably voluntaristic and elitist.[66] Moreover, while many 'Butlerians' still understand Butler as suggesting a type of individual transgressive 'per-formance' as the most relevant way of undermining existing gender dynamics, it is an interpretation she now rejects, for a more strategic engagement with 'the lived difficulty of politi-cal life'. Writing of cultural differences and the articulation of universal claims, she argues: 'What any of those terms will mean . . . will not be determinable outside the conflicts, insti-tutional arrangements, and historical conditions in which they occur'.[67] Quite so. Meanwhile, however, some feminists have used Foucault to reject earlier feminist analysis of power in relation to key structural and institutional sites. Again, the problem here is that it discourages analysis of just *where* and *how* women are best placed to combat the authority and privilege men commonly wield over them. This entails know-ledge of and collective action within those particular sites which are most advantageous to women or which have proved re-ceptive to change, while also pursuing strategies to under-mine or transform those which remain most rigid and resistant to change.[68]

Political Agendas

As discussed in later chapters, post-structuralism – especially in its Derridian and Foucauldian forms – has provided fem-inists with fresh conceptual tools for problematizing identities and social differences. It usefully emphasizes their hierarchi-cally imposed and coercive nature, and the multiplicity of intertwining, destabilizing and exclusionary discourses or narratives in which subjectivities are historically enmeshed. It suggests the possibility (however difficult) of categorical resignifications or reconfigurations, as well as the need for acceptance of paradox and contradiction in conceptualizing change. Feminists need to pay heed to the normativities and exclusions of discourse, especially as they construct differences between women. But in a world of intensifying inequality, any concern with either gender justice or the fate of women overall must also engage us in social struggle for economic redistribution, alongside (and inevitably enmeshed with) issues of identity involving cultural recognition and respect.[69] It is a socialist imaginary, combined with feminism, which has always stressed the sufferings caused by the material exploitation, deprivation and social marginalization of women and other oppressed groups around the world. These cannot be either superseded or replaced by battles over discursive marginalization and invalidation. The two objectives, though strategically distinct, are also intricately interwoven: the one turning feminists *outwards* towards women in struggle, the other directing us *inwards*, towards refiguring a hitherto abjected 'femininity'. Throughout this book I have aimed to keep both objectives in sight, pursuing theorizations sufficiently complex to embrace the intricacies of personal life, while refusing to give up on struggles for social justice and equality.

However plural and irreducibly complex our characterization of the social, any politics seeking the most inclusive transformation of socio-economic and cultural life must strive to challenge the major systems of domination. This means trying to figure out just what they are at this historical moment: uncovering why, and how, they persist, as well as their interaction with whatever specific location we occupy. Fearful of totalizing generalizations we may be, and cautious we must be, but the most central global axes of economic exploitation and cultural oppression continue to construct and reconstruct themselves in the interrelated terms of 'gender' (tied in with sexual orientation), 'class' (tied in with nationality and ethnicity) and 'race' (tied in with nationality, ethnicity and religion) within what is the currently *ever more* totalizing control of a transnational capitalist market. The invocation of specific differences can serve broadly based transformative ends, but only as part of *some wider political project* seeking to dismantle these basic structures of domination.

The Anglo-American reception of post-structuralism, with its central place in nineties feminist theory, came to prominence at a political moment far removed from the one which generated the confident hopes that Women's Liberation took to the streets. Ironically, some explications and critiques of post-modernism present it as responsible for *installing* feminism on the political agenda, as in Terry Eagleton's *The Illusions of Postmodernism*;[70] while others would see its influence as quite the reverse. Often distrustful, when not dismissive, of traditional forms of collective action and reformist political agendas, especially when class based, academic feminism faces an uphill task in describing how either attention to the discursive specificity of 'feminine' difference, or the proliferation of categorical heterogeneity and transgressive display, might ever again bring women together in any widely shared transformative feminist project. As Anne Phillips worries, introducing her own book *Democracy and Difference*, when feminist theoretical work shifted from broadly social concerns to the more abstractly cultural, there was no settling of previous disputes: 'It was as if earlier debates had shunted themselves into a forlorn and deserted siding. Later journeys set off from a different station.'[71] In particular, the more the attention to a language of difference, the less the interest in the effects of the continuing inequalities of class.

We need to remember that the word 'feminist' has a history. Sometimes feminists have focused directly on issues of sexual difference, at other times feminism has been more a movement for the transformation of the whole of society. At the close of the nineteenth century, 'feminism' first appeared in English to describe the movement of women campaigning for the right to vote, but within a few decades the concept had expanded to include a variety of different types of moral, economic, social and political campaigns waged by women.[72] The second wave of Western feminism has similarly drawn upon different meanings, at times stressing common goals and social transformation (especially in its early days), at others emphasizing women's particularity or difference, often moving on to the embrace of political heterogeneity and conceptual fragmentation. The difficulties of generalizing from women's experiences (or 'corporeal existence', through whatever mode of representation) are not hard to document. Nevertheless, in ways I develop in chapter 2, it is premature to downplay the significance of gender in favour of a plurality of equivalent differences. The tenacity of men's power over women means feminists must just as tenaciously seek to emphasize the diverse and multiple effects of gender hierarchy on the lives and experiences of women. But if feminism is to address the problems of the many women who need it most, it must see that the specificities of women's lives do not reduce to gender, which means working in alliance with other progressive forces combating class, racialized, ethnic and other entrenched social hierarchies.

Interestingly, one of the continuing threads between seventies and nineties feminisms (and there are many such threads, although we may not read about them in a significant number of nineties texts) is the continuing growth and vision of the international human rights movements, now often in the form of NGOs.[73] However, even there, as Suzanne Gibson and Laura Flanders have described, it has proved far easier for women to get their demands taken seriously by the United Nations when they address gender-specific, apparently more politically acceptable issues like rape and violence against women, than when they address employment rights, illiteracy or poverty.[74] Back in Britain, there will be little significant change in the situation of the women who are worst off until public resources are shifted to provide greater welfare provision, without the constraints of market considerations. Yet today's Foucauldian feminists who write about the state reject earlier feminist analysis of its structures and functions arguing that: 'In post-structuralist accounts of the state, "discourse" and "subjectivity" rather than structures and interests become the key terms'.[75] In my view, such re-theorizing threatens to lead us further away from any analysis of the state itself, and the way in which it has been changing. The state now embraces market forces in most of the areas from which they were previously excluded, against the interests of, in particular, women with primary caring responsibilities, children and all dependent people.

Britain, like North America, has been moving as fast as it can in quite the opposite direction from that which might assist those women in greatest need of economic and social support. This is why I remain a socialist feminist: still hoping for more dialogue than I find at present between different generations of feminism. Sometimes, as one of my colleagues writes when recalling his own formative moments in Northern Ireland, it is helpful if, without nostalgia, we summon up the 'courage of our anachronisms'.[76]

2

Gender to Queer, and Back Again

Gendered self-consciousness has, mercifully, a flickering flame.
Denise Riley, *Am I that Name*

Gender and second-wave feminism were born together, at the close of the 1960s. At least, gender has been used as an analytical category, rather than just a grammatical one, only since that time.[1] Breaking out of the confines of what had been deemed women's biological fate, gender would explain the social construction of 'femininity', and the maintenance of men's power and privileges relative to women. Gender was the name for all the acquired, culturally diverse and hence mutable ways of becoming a woman – or a man. However, with 'man' the universal linguistic norm of humanity, it was overwhelmingly women who were seen as marked by gender, rather than men. Men and masculinity were not for some time studied by feminists in their own right. To begin with, all attention was focused on the position and the particularities of women and femininity.

Yet sorting through the differing costumes of gender, and the fashioning of them, would itself eventually come to be seen as limiting: only another way of confining women within their all too familiar enclosures – whether in aprons, negligées or nursemaid's caps. First, the nature and extent of gender similarities and differences (as distinct from biological, especially anatomical, *sex* differences) provoked extensive feminist conflict. Next, attempts to fix the limits of the social and the psychic origins of gender difference came under scrutiny. Finally, the most extravagant trouble for gender theory would emerge from its ties to that third term to which both 'sex' and 'gender' have long been wedded: 'sexuality'. Nevertheless, some feminists fear that to abandon gender as a central category of analysis is ultimately to abandon feminism: born together, they will be buried together.

The Rise of Gender Theory

'One is not born, but becomes, a woman'.[2] With these fighting words delivered in 1949 in *The Second Sex*, Simone de Beauvoir inspired almost all the newly emerging feminist writers two decades later to draw a distinction between sex and gender – at least in the Anglophone movement. In Britain, when such social scientists as Ann Oakley first stressed the distinction between biological 'sex' and socialized 'gender', they had in mind the secure internalization of contrasting patterns of behaviour. The initial purpose of 'gender' was thus to displace the role of biology in determining 'masculinity' and 'femininity'. Gender referred to apparently stable differences between men and women, but differences 'ineradicably over-ridden by cultural learning'.[3] Its immediate consequence was to deny or minimize the existence of any fundamental differences between the sexes.

Feminists in the 1970s developed the rudiments of gender analysis by introducing sociological notions of 'sex roles' and 'sex-role stereotyping' to explore the multitude of social forces operating throughout a person's lifetime to produce appropriate gender patterns. They studied the internal workings of the nursery, school and job market, as well as the broader structures of family life, sexuality, culture and politics.[4] Gender was thus being used to refer both to the differences between men and women, and to the culturally diverse stereotypes or norms which were thought to determine those differences. Moreover, in seeing women as products of sexist culture, the dictates of 'femininity' were seen, for the most part, as subordinating and oppressive: 'Sexism has made of women a race of children, a class of human beings utterly deprived of self-hood, of autonomy, of confidence – worst of all, *it has made the false come true.*'[5] The young women who flocked to Women's Liberation at the close of the 1960s were unhappy with women's secondary status in society, and quickly produced a sea of statistics suggesting that women – to a greater or lesser extent depending on their circumstances – *suffered* from their identity and role as women, both physically and mentally.

The notion of gender was soon put to multiple uses, depending on who was investigating it. To feminists in psychology, gender was primarily a set of personality characteristics or predispositions, although in 1974 North American gender theorist Sandra Bem would expeditiously provide a way of measuring 'androgyny', suggesting that many individuals shared both feminine and masculine traits. Affirming an optimistic idea, then current in feminism, that a more androgynous future offered one way out of the old restrictions of gender, in her early research Bem proposed that androgynous individuals were more adaptable than those who were sex-typed.[6] A decade later (see chapter 5), some feminist psychologists, including Bem herself, had rejected their early focus on gender-related personality attributes or self-conceptions to stress instead of the acquisition of cognitive structures for organizing or framing perceptions in line with external 'gender schema', which ubiquitously emphasize gender dichotomy.[7] Meanwhile, sociologists and anthropologists were studying gender at the structural rather than the individual or subjective level, often referring to what Gayle Rubin had labelled the 'sex/gender system' to account for the systematic ways in which any particular society conceives and organizes kinship, reproduction, sexuality and its overall institutional practices and divisions of labour governing relations between the sexes.[8]

At the same time, feminists in literary fields were busy analysing the symbolic construction of gender in forms of speech and other representational genres and practices. Wherever they looked, and whatever they studied – from high culture to pornography – they confirmed de Beauvoir's belief that women exist as 'the Other' in a male-centred world: 'defined and differentiated with reference to man and not he with reference to her'.[9] Three decades on, de Beauvoir's compatriot Monique Wittig was reworking these ideas from the same foundation: 'The universal has been, and is, continually at every moment, appropriated by men.'[10] Summarizing this insight in the USA, Elaine Showalter, the original doyenne of feminist literary criticism, would write: 'all speech is necessarily talk about gender, since in every language gender is a grammatical category, and the masculine is the linguistic norm'.[11]

The shifting application of gender concepts, variously referring to individuals, social structures and symbolic systems, produced many of the puzzles and conflicts which continue to shadow it, both within and outside feminism. What is the connection between subjectivity and the socio-cultural relations of gender? Is gender neutrality possible, or are dominance and subordination intrinsic to gender differences? Were feminists aiming to eradicate gender, or merely to reform it? Does gender need to be refashioned to fit changing times? Is there some universal grounding, or set of determining factors, behind the transhistoric, global presence of men's greater access to power and privilege relative to women? How do changes in gender relations occur? How central or significant is gender in shaping women's and men's lives and experiences? What are the intersections of gender with other hierarchies of power and privilege?

In popular usage (and certain versions of what is known as 'liberal feminism'), there is no necessary relation between gender and power. Indeed, it is this potential symmetry between the two genders which leads French 'sexual difference theorists' to reject the concept altogether, as discussed below. Psychologists and clinicians, for the most part, see gender as involving harmony (or discord) between internalized concepts of self, biological sex and heterosexual object choice, with no reference to power. It is the psychoanalyst Robert Stoller who is usually credited with introducing 'gender' as an explanatory concept into the social sciences in 1968.[12] With fellow clinicians in California, Stoller pioneered research on and treatment for gender-related problems. There is now a mushrooming medical interest in gender 'disorders', resulting in the diagnostic category of 'Gender Identity Disorder' entering the official list of psychopathologies in the USA (*DSM -111*) in 1980, an affliction seen as manifest in cross-dressing and repeated desire to be the other sex.[13]

However, most feminists have always linked gender and power: indeed, were the two disconnected, there would be no need for feminism. Gender, as feminists have repeatedly demonstrated, is a central dynamic through which power is articulated: masculinity symbolizes power and authority; political power and moral authority is monopolized by men across all societies. Yet many men have little or no purchase on the power that is supposed to be the prerogative of their sex, while a significant minority of women have access to considerable power and privilege. Gender binaries never exist in pristine form. Women and men are always already inserted in contexts of race, class, age, sexual orientation and multiple other belongings: each with their deeply entrenched connections to power and authority, or the lack of it.

It is the difficulty of addressing the many questions surrounding gender, not least that of men's shifting and uneven purchase on power over others – including the women in closest proximity to them – which produced the more complex attempts to refigure 'gender theory' in the 1980s. Theorists searched for elaborations of gender broad enough to encompass its diverse social, psychological and cultural dynamics, mostly by stressing its intersections with class, race and other axes of power. Trying to analyse the different sites of gendered experiences and practices, feminists, in their more sophisticated formulations, began to theorize gender as an analytic tool for understanding cultural reality: seeing it as a category which operates in every sphere of human society, but in disparate ways which are neither fixed nor unitary. The historian Joan Scott, for example, distinguished four always interlinked but nevertheless distinct elements of gender, each forming part of the production of the perceived differences between the sexes in any specific context: (i) culturally available symbols which evoke multiple, often contradictory, representations; (ii) normative concepts for interpreting and using such symbols; (iii) social institutions and organizations; (iv) subjective identity.[14] In line with the bulk of feminist reflection, Scott also emphasized that gender operates as a primary way of signifying relations of power: authority, strength, power are everywhere coded as masculine; dependence, weakness, the alien, subversive and bizarre, as feminine. Moreover, their metaphorical utilization is always intensified in times of crisis, or in the consolidation of new regimes of power.

Even more hesitantly, the philosopher and psychotherapist Jane Flax argues that gender is not an object or set of objects, but rather that 'gendering' is always a complex and over-determined, often conflicting, set of processes, which 'are provisional and must be reproduced and reworked throughout our lives.'[15] From within sociology, Bob Connell has worked for many years to provide a 'systemic social theory of gender' which can encompass the movement, diversities, and personal and collective struggles encircling gender practices.[16] Devoting slightly less time to cultural symbols and their discursive framings, he analyses the interplay between three central dynamics shaping and reshaping gender practices: sexual divisions of *labour* in the home and the workplace; men's hold on state, juridical and all key sites of institutional *power*; the patterns of *desire*, or cathexis, first forged in the earliest relational bonds.

However, it has not proved easy for feminists, or anyone else, to keep the complexities of the psychic, the social and the symbolic in play when trying to understand how the perceived differences and social exchanges between women and men are best understood. Pressures to simplify and collapse gender into individual sex differences, contrasting identities or fixed social roles feed the abiding tensions between those who stress the psychic life of difference, and those who study the social dynamics of the gender order.

The Allure of Difference

One is not born a woman; and Simone de Beauvoir, as feminists quickly noticed, seemed to dismiss as demeaning the most distinctive ways of becoming one. The veneration for men and masculinity pervading the *The Second Sex* led many a feminist to distance herself from de Beauvoir, nowhere more passionately than in France itself. Nevertheless, with their account of a socially constructed 'femininity' as humbling and inhibiting women, second-wave feminists had early on been accused by others (and would often accuse each other) of playing down the differences between women and men and accepting the dominant dismissals of the feminine. The strident rebirth of feminism had focused first upon family life and women's dependent, undervalued, and not infrequently isolated and depressed domestic lives, especially when engaged in full-time mothering. From the USA, Ann Snitow would later trace feminists' repudiation of what came to be seen as the 'demon texts' of those early years.[17] Most notorious was Shulamith Firestone's *The Dialectic of Sex*, published in 1970, with its startling suggestion that feminism should 'free' women from their biology through technologies of artificial reproduction (a view immediately dismissed by most other feminists as hopelessly flawed).[18] The iconoclastic view which nearly all early women's liberationists had in fact voiced was merely a challenge to the coercive norm of motherhood as women's defining destiny, the sole route to female happines: but that, of course, was in itself to prove incendiary, for women as much as for men.[19]

By the mid-1970s the surge of interest in affirming women's lives in the face of rampant misogyny, feeding into the growth of women's studies in academic institutions and the rise of 'cultural feminism' in the wider women's movement, had begun to turn around earlier suspicions of the idea of women's distinctive characteristics, in favour of an appreciation of specific female experience. As early as 1973 Jane Alpert's essay 'Mother Right' appeared in the North American magazine *Ms.*, arguing for a feminist 'matriarchal reorganization' of society as the alternative to a socialist vision.[20] Soon afterwards more charismatic feminists, like the American poet Adrienne Rich, were writing lyrically of the revolutionary potential of women's bodies, and maternal experience – differentiating 'mothering' from existing patriarchal institutions of motherhood.[21] Rich's work also reflected a powerful strand of lesbian theorizing of the 1970s. In an influential essay published in 1980, she spoke of the role of 'compulsory heterosexuality' in erasing lesbian consciousness from women's experience. Rich located 'lesbian existence' in the love and tenderness women have shown towards each other throughout history, identifying it as the building block of 'female power'. For Rich, the 'lesbian continuum' exists, if subterraneously, in all 'women-identified' women. In what would prove a controversial desexualization, Rich's lesbian continuum ranges from genital sexual activity to the gentle nurturing ways of women, who have provided for other women from the cradle to the grave.[22]

An alternative critique of motherhood came from Nancy Chodorow's description of the effects of women's monopoly of parenting in the production of polarized and unequal gender identities: boys who are fearful of intimacy; girls who define themselves only in relation to others.[23] Chodorow argued for change in, rather than celebration of, existing patterns of parenting. But the mothering themes of Rich and Chodorow helped inspire a new celebration of 'maternal thinking' and 'maternal practices', quickly evident in feminist writing at the close of the 1970s. To the dismay of some other feminists, it was one which largely ignored evidence of the frustration, aggression and intense ambivalence also present in women's mothering experiences.[24]

The affirmation of gender difference was everywhere in feminist scholarship throughout the following decade, nowhere more strongly than in the USA where women's studies first set sail. From the widely acclaimed emphasis on women's separate styles of moral reasoning propounded by Carol Gilligan (who would eventually assume the first Chair of Gender Studies at Harvard University) to studies suggesting basic cognitive differences between women and men arising from women's separate 'ways of knowing', women were positioned in their own distinct, and supposedly shared, gendered space.[25]

Meanwhile, radical feminists in the USA extended this approach to singling out contrasts between male and female sexual practices (supposedly institutionalized through pornography) as pivotal to men's global dominance. In Catharine

MacKinnon's influential theory, gender consolidates itself through eroticized domination and submission: 'the social relation between the sexes is organized so that men may dominate and women must submit and this relation is sexual – in fact, is sex'.[26] MacKinnon, however, denies the existence of sexual difference as other than that of sexual domination (male) and sexual violation (female). The condition of coerced sexual subordination, or 'whore', constitutes the social meaning of 'woman' in the 'sexist social order' of heterosexuality: 'women are unimaginable without the violation and validation of the male touch'; 'What I've learned from women's experience with sexuality is that exploitation and degradation produce grateful complicity in exchange for survival'.[27] Moreover, as discussed in the previous chapter, the popular appeal of MacKinnon-style anti-pornography feminism, in offering cheap and simplistic solutions to the endemic and seemingly increasing problem of men's violence, meant that her theory and political agenda was soon being promoted as the imprimatur of feminism by much of the media.

At its best, gender analysis aimed to highlight a complex array of shifting, often contradictory, sites of compliance or struggle around men's power and authority across symbolic, psychic and institutional realms. But what the very different understandings of gender I have cited have in common is their attempt to make a single site of gender regulation stand in for all the others, in order to consolidate gender contrasts, and assign them universal causes. The most structurally static of all the theories of gender, the MacKinnonite equation of gender with sexual coercion (and its related demand for state regulation to protect women from victimization in pornography) was sadly, as I have indicated, also the one which would capture media attention, and be broadcast as paradigmatic of feminism. Germaine Greer is receiving unprecedented media promotion to disseminate this very same message even as I write, insisting that anyone who refuses to see that domination is intrinsic to heterosexual genital penetration is 'in denial'.[28] Meanwhile, throughout the reign of far right governments in Britain and the USA in the 1980s, best-selling books appeared from women calling themselves feminists which were overtly scornful of every aspect of the earlier feminist search for women's social and political equality with men, including their campaign in the USA for the Equal Rights Amendment, concurrently being derailed by Reagan.[29] The pull of what is called 'difference theory', relating to women's distinctive bodily and social experiences, thus took centre stage in the most influential forms of Anglo-American feminism. Yet this very prioritizing of gender difference occurred alongside a sharply contrasting rejoinder to the disentangling of difference: attention to divisions between women themselves.

The flowering of black and other particularizing feminist voices in the 1980s launched an upsurge of anger at the false universality in previous feminist accounts of women's supposedly special qualities which, they argued, merely represented the experiences of white, middle-class, Western women. In the haunting words of Audre Lorde, who knew that 'all women do not suffer the same oppression simply because they are women', or Alice Walker, who declared it 'apparently, inconvenient, if not downright mind straining, for white women scholars to think of black women as women', black feminists challenged white women's failure to prioritize racism, poverty or ethnic specificities in their celebration of women's identity.[30] Barbara Smith, one of the editors of the powerful anthology by American 'women of colour', *All the Women are White, All the Blacks are Men, But some of Us are Brave*, published in 1982, declared that unless the vision of feminism was one which 'struggles to free *all* women', it becomes 'merely female self aggrandizement'.[31] Another of its editors, the influential Chicano writer Gloria Anzaldúa, would later develop the notion of the 'mestiza', to describe the predicament of people who occupy 'the borderlands' between cultures (like the Chicana, or Mexicans, in the USA).[32]

Attentive to cultural location, and its barely visible articulation, these women of colour nevertheless tended to adopt a strongly materialist feminism, stressing economic and structural oppression alongside what would soon emerge as a more fashionable, near exclusive, focus upon the complexities of linguistic and discursive hierarchies of subordination and abjection. In Britain, as in the USA, black women throughout the 1980s were equally insistent that 'white, mainstream feminist theory . . . does not speak to the experiences of Black Women and where it attempts to do so it is often from a racist perspective and reasoning'.[33] Numerous Third World feminists, like Chandra Mohanty in her essay 'Under Western Eyes', now regularly spelt out the colonial presumptions in Western feminism's attempted universalization of women's subordination, emphasizing that the structuring of gender is always strongly marked by racial, cultural and other geopolitical relations of power.[34]

The synchronicity of accounts of women's distinctive gender difference offered by some theorists in the 1980s and the forceful feminist assertion of a multiplicity of 'differences' (most crucially around race and ethnicity, alongside the celebration of lesbian consciousness) was a peculiarly volatile coexistence. It would lead many feminists to endorse a type of pragmatic, yet somewhat contradictory, pluralism towards issues of 'difference': their centrality and significance always in threat from their collision and proliferation. For example, while many nineties feminist texts equate a 'politics of difference' with attention to 'the specificity of black women's experience and the racism of white feminists', many of the black and Third World feminists they consider themselves to be embracing remain more ambivalent about the contemporary feminist focus on questions of subjectivity and difference.[35] A confusion is at once apparent in the repeated affirmation that 'since the 1980s an erstwhile politics of identity has largely been superseded by a politics of difference'.[36] It is unclear how the one concept is supposed to replace the other, when the two concepts are mutually constitutive: no identity without difference, and no difference without some kind of identification. This is particularly evident if we look at the next twist in the increasingly tangled tale of the move to 'difference theory' in the 1980s.

The Romance of Otherness

Feminist scholars, influenced by developments in European philosophy, began using the tools of post-structuralist and psychoanalytic theory to challenge the reliance upon the category of experience in accounts of identity, or claims to difference. They were dismissive of most Anglo-American gender theory as mere sociological reductionism. Derrida's 'deconstructive' method of studying texts was used to uncover the metaphysical error of assuming that knowledge is grounded in some foundational experience, rather than in the shifting heterogeneity of discourses which serve to produce meaning. Following Ferdinand de Saussure's structural linguistics, meaning is seen here as constructed through the operation of linguistic contrasts or oppositions, rather than through correspondence with objects in the world.[37] In Derridian theory, 'différance' does not refer specifically to sexual difference, but rather to the endless dispersal of subjectivity and the inevitable deferral of meaning consequent upon the multiple applications and chronic instabilities of mutually interdepedendent, but nevertheless always hierarchical, binaries. The dominant 'masculine' term presupposes its 'feminine' underside, for instance, and vice versa. It is not just the case that these pervasive dichotomies cannot securely be held apart. Derrida also points to the set of exclusions necessary for their production: all that is outside the dialectic of negation cannot be represented in intelligent discourse. Nevertheless, within the snares of the binaries underpinning Western metaphysics – identity/difference, presence/absence, universality/ particularity – the 'feminine' appears only as the underside, the negative, the perennial representative of 'otherness', in feminist appropriations of deconstruction.

In contrast, sexual difference is central to the whole order of representation in psychoanalytic post-structuralism. With little interest in sociological theories of gender, feminist psychoanalytic literature influenced by Lacan addressed the central place of sexual difference at the heart of psychic life. In this view, gender theorists have mistakenly focused on social and material aspects of women's subordination, ignoring the deeper *asymmetry* between the sexes: the semiotic and symbolic structures which place women outside its categories of representation, irrespective of specific social and political arrangements. Here, it is argued that feminists need to begin from the emergence of subjectivity, or psychic individuality, which occurs in and through language, via entry into the Symbolic domain in which the phallus always already exists as the 'privileged signifier'. This ensures women's negative entry into culture.[38] Women are constituted in terms of lack, and men – since the phallus is not the penis – in terms of the constant threat of lack.

Most significantly, in this account, femininity is never securely acquired or completed. In Jacqueline Rose's well-known summary: 'the unconscious constantly reveals the failure of identity'.[39] (This perspective differs from that of 'object-relations' psychoanalysis, like that of the early Chodorow, where women's mothering ensures that daughters successfully internalize a nurturing and receptive femininity.) But, if sexual difference is a site of instability and failure at the individual unconscious level, it is nevertheless presented as a permanent structure in the timeless Symbolic. Inescapable antagonism between the sexes is thus inscribed within the Lacanian formation of subjectivity, as I discuss more fully in chapter 6.

More surprisingly, it was precisely the imperious rejection of any possibility of affirming the feminine in Lacan's structuralist account of phallocentric culture which would lure post-Lacanian feminists to do just that: attempt to delineate the feminine in terms of its seditious 'Otherness', an imagined subterranean existence outside the phallogocentric laws of Man or God. The most sophisticated, indeed esoteric, forms of difference theory were expounded in the work of those who claimed the name of 'French Feminism'. Hélène Cixous and Luce Irigaray fought the erasure of the feminine in the Symbolic order by producing their dissident poetics of the 'feminine feminine' and, with Julia Kristeva, celebrated the subversive potential of the tactile, rhythmic semiosis of the pre-Oedipal, pre-symbolic, maternal murmurings and communications, in disordering the Symbolic order. Although accused by other equally prominent theorists, for example Gayatri Spivak, of Eurocentric essentialism in their exclusive convergence upon *sexual* difference as the definitive difference constituting subjectivity (however devoid of fixity) French Feminism was nevertheless to prove highly influential in feminist scholarship.[40] In a new type of romanticized 'feminist myth of origins', a nostalgia for the imaginary symbiosis of the lost (pre-Oedipal) mother-child bond came to serve as a crucial psychic space for articulating the feminine, as Mary Jacobus reflected in the late 1980s.[41]

Hoping to bypass accusations of bias and exclusion, more recent sexual difference theorists have insisted upon the infinite heterogeneity, the absolute alterity, and complete absence of *any* distinctive qualities in the 'feminine imaginary' they seek to liberate from the shackles of inescapable phallocentrism. In the words of Drucilla Cornell: 'Feminism demands nothing less than the unleashing of the feminine imaginary made possible, paradoxically, by the lack of grounding of the feminine in any of the identifications we know and imagine as Woman'.[42] Speaking what they declare unspeakable, opposing all binaries by pitching the 'wholly Other' against phallogocentrism, privileging the opposition they aim to deprivilege, theorists of sexual difference have been straining conceptual coherence and intelligibility, along with political pertinence.

Rita Felski summarizes many of the incongruities others have noticed in these abstruse renditions in her essay 'The Doxa of Difference'.[43] If it were the case that language and human culture has been an exclusively male creation, why should contemporary feminists be any more successful at freeing themselves from the inescapable grip of phallocentric thought than their predecessors, whom they judge to have failed? In fabricating an avant-garde semiotics of difference, other feminist struggles are frequently dismissed as merely superficial reforms complicit with the masculine symbolic. As Felski concludes: 'A vision of femininity as pure otherness cannot speak to the messy blend of tradition and innovation, of recuperation and recreation, of borrowing from the past and imagining the future, that shapes feminist practise.'[44] Indeed, disdain for women's collective action separate from the delineation of feminine difference has accompanied French psychoanalytic feminism almost from its inception. 'We try not to be political', Julia Kristeva notoriously declared in an interview on British television in 1984.[45] More menacingly, Irigaray attacked other feminists fighting for equality, rather than asserting the importance of sexual difference, with the apocalyptic warning: 'To want to abolish sexual difference is to call for a more complete genocide than every other destruction in history'.[46]

There is an unbridgeable gap here between post-Lacanian difference theorists and those working, however critically, with more sociological applications of gender theory. Feminists, like me, who write about gender, cannot accept the idea that the overriding contradiction for feminists lies in an irreducible and irreversible asymmetry in the symbolic domain, unaffected by socio-historical shifts and pressures. The primary political point of gender theory, as I would choose to use it, is to explore the ways in which gendered identities are mutable cultural and historical productions, subjectively experienced as both precarious yet fundamental – with that precariousness most evident in men's uncertain hold on phallic masculinity.[47] The experiences and practices which stabilize as gender identity operate at diverse and shifting levels: from the most uniquely constituted inner recesses of the psyche, through the more flexible familial or occupational organizations of daily life, to enduring gender hierarchies embedded in symbolic configurations and ruling cultural and political elites. Changes at one level (like the visibility of strong and confident women, with authority in the home, the workplace and public life) create ruptures and fissures which can begin to effect change at other levels. Moreover, gender identities and practices are always themselves permeated by the effects of class, race, ethnicity and nationality.

In contrast, difference theorists, as Rosi Braidotti explains, believe that gender theory deradicalizes feminism and ignores its central task, that of 'empowering a female feminist subject': 'The whole point of taking the trouble to define, analyse, and act on sexual difference as a project aiming at the symbolic empowerment of the feminine (defined as "the other of the other") is to turn it into a platform of political action for and by women.' Later, Braidotti, via Deleuze, tries to illustrate how this 'other of the other', the feminine desiring subject, might 'find the exit from the prison-house of phallogocentric language': 'To achieve this, we need a quiet, molecular, viral, and therefore unstoppable revolution within the self, multiplied over a multitude of different selves acting as historical agents of change.'[48] For me, at least, these two political projects are not in dialogue. Simply put, with my own theoretical presuppositions, I am unable to provide an adequate account of Braidotti's position, since I can make scant sense of it as a politics.

Not surprisingly, many feminists who were aware of, but often did not participate in, the never-ending battles over sameness versus difference, gender parity versus deconstruction/rewriting of the feminine subject, were wearied and confused by these relentless theoretical reworkings, leading some to speak of an 'identity crisis in feminist theory'.[49] More judiciously, others counselled acceptance of both sides of the binary of 'being' and 'not being' a woman, since the divide exists as a marker of women's equivocal entry into modernity, both offering and withholding the inclusion of women in its vision of the freedom and equality it promises the straight, white, male, as subject of his own estate.

In what remains for me the most perceptive and enlightening of all the reflections on identity, Ann Snitow's 'Gender Diary', written at the close of the 1980s, records her own chronically anxious personal and theoretical oscillations over needing to value and organize around being a 'woman', and needing to reject the very category 'woman', and all its baggage. She argues persuasively that feminists can no more finally choose between the two positions than they can avoid *having* to choose within the twists and turns of ongoing political endeavour. Moreover, the divide always returns, in grassroots activism as well as in theory production, even though the issues propelling women into solidarity movements with other women are often not specifically gender issues. The grassroots women's movements she and other activist-oriented feminist scholars supported and studied, like the Mothers of the Plaza de Mayo in Argentina (demonstrating against the state over the deaths of their kidnapped and murdered children), often fractured over the political remit of their struggle, beyond that of the expression of maternal outrage.

The fluctuations over minimizing or maximizing difference seem inevitable, at all levels of the intersecting realms of the biological, the psychological, the social and the symbolic. Snitow concludes that there can be no transcendence of gender: the paradoxical desires to express, and to escape from, the feminine (like the particular significance of the many other forces governing women's lives) will shift only through historical change, they will not be resolved through theoretical revisions.[50]

> From moment to moment we perform subtle psychological and social negotiations about just how gendered we choose to be. . . . One can be recalled to "woman" any time – by things as terrible as rape, as trivial as a rude shout in the street – but one can never stay inside "woman", because it keeps moving. We constantly find ourselves beyond its familiar cover.[51]

Her words echo those of the British theorist and poet Denise Riley, who similarly notes the fluctuations of gendered identity while arguing that the history of feminism has been a struggle against 'over-zealous identifications' of what women are supposed to be: 'feminism must negotiate the quicksands of "women" which will not allow it to settle on either identities or counter-identities, but which condemn it to an incessant striving for a brief foothold'.[52] From this perspective, feminists can neither close down, nor retreat from, the questions gender raises: whether examining the myriad discourses in which it appears, or seeking equity in the diverse social relations it helps to structure.

The Joys of Queer

Some feminists have come to accept the inevitability of living with the paradoxes of gender, wanting to assert difference inside sameness, and sameness inside difference.[53] Others have sought nothing short of complete deliverance from its trappings. After the excitement and the anger which feminism once generated had dissipated – through internal conflicts and the recessionary tempo of the early 1980s – a fresh upsurge of political and theoretical ebullience emerged from lesbian and gay activists and scholars at the close of the decade. Feminism was a decisive influence on the emergence of gay and lesbian studies and activities (since the maintenance of the power and privileges of straight men was seen as pivotal to the policing of homosexuality), but its influence here had significantly declined, if not reversed, by the 1990s.

The inspiration for much of the new lesbian and gay agenda was the desire for an analytic and political separation of the category of sexuality from that of gender. Gayle Rubin's argument in 'Thinking Sex' (1984) is usually cited as the seminal influence; she departs from her earlier essay on the sex/gender system to argue that the power relations of 'sexuality' cannot be reduced to those of 'gender'.[54] Building on this distinction, Eve Kosofsky Sedgwick suggests that working with sexuality offers more space for deconstructive work on identity and its constraints, given 'its far greater potential for re-arrangement, ambiguity, and representational doubleness', than does working with 'gender', since 'virtually all people are publicly and unalterably [sic] assigned to one or other gender, and from birth'.[55] Illustrating the growing appeal of this analytic separation, the editors of the most comprehensive North American lesbian and gay anthology, published in 1993, suggest: 'Lesbian/gay studies does for *sex* and *sexuality* approximately what women's studies does for gender'.[56]

Catapulted into action by the calamity of death and suffering from AIDS (which decimated gay subcultures in the 1980s), armed with the diverse tools of discourse theory, deconstruction and psychoanalysis, a new flowering of lesbian and gay scholarship emerged under the banner of Queer Theory. Kicking off what some saw as the exclusionary and strictly gendered identities of 'lesbian' and 'gay', queer politics embraces every possible form of dissident sexualities, each demanding visibility in the straight world – not mere tolerance (at best), when closeted behind closed doors. 'What's Queer?', Sedgwick asks, and provides as part of her answer:

> The experimental linguistic, epistemological, representational, political adventures attaching to the very many of us who may at times be moved to describe ourselves as (among other things) pushy femmes, radical faeries, fantasists, drags, clones, leatherfolk, ladies in tuxedoes, feminist women or feminist men, masturbators, bulldaggers, divas, Snap! queens, butch bottoms, storytellers, transsexuals, aunties, wannabes, lesbian-identified men or lesbians who sleep with men, or . . . people able to relish, learn from, or identify with such.[57]

With that colourful sweep, almost anybody, it seemed, who was sufficiently stylish, could jump onto the queer platform, which was fast emerging as the cutting edge of fashion in some of the largest Western academic, political and art forums of the 1990s. 'For this', as British sociologist Ken Plummer observes, 'is the Golden Age of gay and lesbian studies'.[58] In a brilliant outpouring of texts, many of these confident new sexual outlaws set about the final trashing of gender, via the dismantling of the hetero/homosexual hierarchy.[59]

The addition of Foucault's writings to the arsenal of deconstructions of identity (as the alien, incoherent and unstable effect of discourse) would inspire more strategies of resistance to bodily inscriptions of gender. In his account of the history of sexuality, the discourses constructing and regulating the body and its activities are the primary site for the operation of power in modern societies. This form of domination is no longer primarily manifest in repressive decrees issuing from on high, but rather through the far more pervasive, subtle and elusive micro-practices for making sense of daily life. For the last two centuries, it has been sexuality (the body as metaphor for the soul) which increasingly grounded the truth of who and what we are: 'the project of a science of the subject has gravitated, in ever narrower circles, around the question of sex'.[60] Here, sexual identities are implanted by professional discourses which have their origins in regulatory fictions organized around the heterosexual/homosexual divide, tied to the masculine/feminine, active/passive polarities of gender.

Appropriating Foucault for feminism, Judith Butler (who would quickly emerge as the single most cited feminist theorist of the 1990s) calls into question the need for a stable 'female' identity for feminist practice, and instead examines the potential of a radical critique of categories of identity in her book *Gender Trouble: Feminism and the Subversion of Identity*.[61] Here, she suggests that the three concepts of 'sex', 'gender' and 'sexuality' are established in discourse only through a process of reiteration, or enactment in repeated cultural performances, that congeal over time to produce the effect of identity.[62] Gender performativity is not seen as a choice, but rather gender identities acquire what stability and coherence they have through a range of discourses available for delineating the body, all of which are framed within the coercive context of the 'heterosexual matrix' (a notion drawn from the work of Monique Wittig[63]). Identities are always normative and hence exclusionary.

Women are *neither* born *nor* made; but our actions are rendered intelligible only by the involuntary performance (or flouting) of heteronormative cultural discourses. However, Butler sees possible subversive effects or potential for resignifications in performative display which exposes the *artificiality* or constructedness of the oppositional markers of heterosexuality. Dissident sexual acts make 'trouble' for gender categories, disturbing the heterosexual matrix which secures sex and gender binaries: male/female to active/passive. The proliferation of sexual acts performed in non-heterosexual contexts thus disrupt and weaken normative gender framings.[64] From diesel dykes to lipstick lesbians, drag queens to muscle men, perverse sexualities potentially reinscribe or resignify sex and gender categories through their

transgressive mimicry or, in Butler's words, 'subversive repetition', of the heterosexual 'original', which is itself culturally crafted. Articulating what would become a founding
statement of queer theory, Butler concluded: '*In imitating
gender, drag implicitly reveals the imitative structure of gender
itself – as well as its contingency.*'[65] Though Butler herself would
soon strike a cautionary note, her ideas encouraged an upsurge of delighted followers – even a *JUDY* fanzine in California – among those who felt they could at last radically free
themselves from the constraints of gender. Via a kind of im-
provisational theatrics for remaking the body, her fans were
busy putting on, and off, the stylized practices and markings
of gender, in non-normative or queer framings.[66]

What is so striking, and to some feminists was so disturbing, about the engagement of lesbian feminists with queer
theory in the 1990s is its strategic reversal of the women-
centred identity politics so forcefully expressed by the directly preceding, and still overlapping, generation of lesbian
feminists. In terms of queer politics – not to mention the
classical conception of perverse sexuality as deriving from
gender inversion – the 'woman-identified-feminist' earlier
celebrated by writers like Adrienne Rich (in what was called
'cultural feminism') was a very 'straight' sort of lesbian: a
gender *conformist* rather than a gender dissident, albeit outside sexual exchange with men. These rising lesbian rebels
tended to exaggerate the homogeneity and rigidities of their
feminist predecessors, but they issued a decisive challenge
to what had become the increasingly restrictive moralisms
of significant strands of radical, lesbian and cultural feminisms:
sharing new norms of acceptable 'feminist' sexuality, mod-
elled on an ideal of 'lesbian' sex.[67] This involved the denunciation of the 'patriarchal' act of penetration, dildoes,
exhibitionism, power plays, pornography, and any hint or
echoes of what were seen as definitively oppressive 'heterosexual' fantasies and practices. As many lesbians would later
conclude (and some already said back in the 1970s and
1980s), this was a period when the 'lesbian' was desexualized, to be presented as a political prototype in line with the
dubious exhortation, 'Feminism is the theory; lesbianism is

the practice':[68] 'For five years I was terrified of getting my fingers near a vagina, lest they engage in a politically incorrect act. . . . We thought our sexuality was oceanic in those days, more transcendent than transgressive', queer theorist and AIDS activist Cindy Patton recalled in 1989.[69] 'I survived lesbian feminism and still desire women', a Butler enthusiast would proudly inform her new mentor.[70]

Of course, quite a number of lesbian feminists had always resisted what they saw as a compulsory 'feminist sexuality', a few choosing instead to explore the lavishly diverse range of consensual desires, fantasies, pleasures and practices, most brilliantly memorialized in the sexual stories and pornographic fictions of Joan Nestle.[71] However, queer emphasis on the political significance of sexual and bodily ambiguities encouraged far wider lesbian and feminist exploration of the profoundly perplexing nature of much sexual fantasy and practice, which had previously been muffled, if not actually censored. It similarly triggered awareness of the hitherto often repudiated links between power and desire; as indeed, had certain psychoanalytic feminisms, before it. More uniquely, it brought a host of once marginalized – often derided – agents to the forefront of queer analysis to unsettle or denaturalize the binary categories of gender, and to expand the possibilities for bodily experience. As Butler clarifies, hoping to reassure those feminists for whom her own political trajectory remains alien: 'To conceive of bodies differently seems to me part of the conceptual and philosophical struggle that feminism involves'.[72] I agree.

With the eruption of new sexual agents, theoretically tooled for 'resistance to regimes of the normal', queer politics eagerly highlighted the deviant, disowned, often anonymous, sex acts which occur in the subterranean world of public life (in parks, clubs and toilets), as Michael Warner celebrates in his introduction to *Fear of a Queer Planet*, (1993).[73] Occasionally, queer helped to fashion the resistance of hitherto completely quarantined and invisible sexual groupings, as in the formation of the Intersex Society of North America in 1992, for individuals born with 'ambiguous' genitals. More often, it consolidated the rebellion of those once most marginalized within older lesbian and gay (not to mention 'straight') communities. No longer simply the object of medical and social surveillance and management, in compliance with heterosexualizing gender imperatives, the body became the site of resistance for those who felt newly empowered to engage in self-formation and self-fashioning, placing choice and flexibility at the centre of their lives. Ironically, the anti-identity project of Foucault, Butler and post-modern discourse generally, was helping to provide the motivation for a crafting of *new* identities. The body was now the transcendent cultural metaphor for the blurring of boundaries between authenticity and artifice, material and virtual reality, our all-too-solid flesh and endlessly refurbishing machines.[74]

Transgender Dialogues

It was what Robert Stoller saw as the pathological plight of transsexuals – desiring bodily modifications to align their genitals with their sense of self – which had prompted him to promulgate the notion of 'gender' as the core category of identity. With neat irony, today, transsexuals are embraced as part of a queer vanguard able to disturb and unsettle, if not transcend, that very category (although by no means all transsexuals see themselves as transgressive). 'I am a transsexual by choice, not by pathology', the ebullient Kate Bornstein affirms in her engaging book *Gender Outlaw: On Men, Women, and the Rest of Us*.[75] Identifying as a transsexual lesbian, the thespian Bornstein argues that transsexuals who identify as 'transgendered' (a term recently coined to refer to all who *choose* to engage in cross-gender practices) can be seen as finding a means of escape from the rigidly bipolar gender system: the cultural imperative to be either a man or a woman. Wittily teasing all those separatist feminists who make her so unwelcome, she boasts: 'I'm *probably* the only lesbian to have successfully castrated a man and gone on to laugh about it on stage, in print and on national television'.[76] More prosaically, Anne Bolin, in her essay on male-to-female transsexuals, published in 1994, argues that transgenderism has the potential to undermine and transcend the gender system by refusing the connections between biological sexual signifiers and performances of gender.[77]

But this line of escape from gender would prove contentious, and not just (although, for sure) with homophobic or defensive heterosexuals, and straight or lesbian separatist feminists. In proclaiming the indeterminacy of gender, via dissident sexual practices, there is the danger of becoming more, rather than less, obsessed with its endless permutations.[78] Exemplifying a cavalcade of queer self-presentations in the USA, Judith Halberstam applauds: 'The drag king can be male or female; she can be transgendered; she can be butch or femme.'[79] That is so, and there is real pleasure and excitement in embodying (and for many in viewing) such transgressive figurations, which both mock and magnify the ways in which sex, gender and sexuality are habitually conceived and enacted. But, however parodic and pluralistic, to what extent is transsexualism an 'escape' from gender? How often is it read as emancipatory or subversive?

Icons of mass culture, from Mae West to Madonna, Valentino to Michael Jackson, have always thrived on forms of sexual ambiguity which suggest the seductive appeal of a transgressive or perverse dynamic at the very heart of heterosexist culture.[80] But with drag and queer display as popular (or unpopular) with reactionary as with radical audiences, its ability to unsettle and subvert normative structures of gender and sexuality seems no more powerful than its ability to mirror and to legitimate them. The uncanny strength of conventional sexual and gender binaries is their ability to triumph over the repeated attempts, both theoretical and performative, to dismantle and deconstruct them; to survive the copious evidence that behind heterosexual normality lies polymorphous perversion (as Freud is still loathed for telling us). As I explored in *Straight Sex*, the braided hierarchies of sexuality and gender have a remarkable capacity to thrive precisely on their own contradictions.[81]

It is not just that it can all be such very hard work (and very painful) trying to escape from one's assigned gender, striving to match one's appearance to whatever transgendered bodies seem to accord better with one's own feelings and fantasies of bodily authenticity – whether or not with a sense of freedom, or of drastic compulsion. It is also that the old gender markings are still *in place* in transgendered bodies, as Mandy Merck spells out: 'Drag fascinates in its simultaneous display of contradictory sexual meanings, not in their resolution or dispersal. It no more transcends gender than Michael Jackson's surgically altered appearance transcends race'.[82] Rather than transcending gender, the current fashionability of and preoccupation with transsexuality and bisexuality, cross-dressing and all the other attempts to combine and repackage gender and sexual signifiers, might be thought to keep us all the more in thrall to their now multiply exhausting demands and anxieties, fears and pleasures.

As Roger Lancaster ponders (after studying a variety of transgender practices in Latin America): 'Is male, phallic hegemony made, unmade, or re-made in this queer theatre of gender?'[83] It could be any of these three, depending on the nature and context of its audience, and the understandings they bring to bear on it. The 'black queer diva' Marlon Riggs expresses 'his' own suspicions of transgressive performances (not to mention the incongruous readings which back his personal self-imagining!): 'Le Butch-Girl wonders, for instance, if her/his permission to say gender-fuck is contingent upon knowing and articulating Fanon, Foucault, Gates, Gilroy, hooks, Hall, West, and the rest as well'.[84] Indeed, Butler herself has repeatedly made such statements as: 'I don't think drag is a paradigm for the subversion of gender. I don't think that if we were all more dragged out gender life would be more expansive and less restrictive';[85] and '[Transgender practices] can work to destabilize *or* to retrench dominant notions of gender, and they can work to link normative gender with normative heterosexuality, *or* to sever them from one another'.[86]

Lancaster and Butler thus agree that transgenderism may have both radical and conservative, transgressive and conformist, ramifications. However, faithful to Foucauldian formulations, they also agree that it is no more 'fraudulent' than any other enactment of gender. This is what they see as its strength in providing a *commentary* on gender, whether or not it is one which is decipherable by others. This perception leads Lancaster to reflect on the potential challenges to gender identity posed by heterosexuality itself.

> The "deceptions" of the transvestites are different from those of "real women" in degree rather than in kind. Nor is the precarious posturing of their "masculine" partners so different from that of other "men". The "real" man in a relationship with a biological woman is no less vulnerable to the sudden revelation that his partner is more a "man" than he.[87]

The latter point is one I have myself frequently illustrated, in both *Slow Motion* and *Straight Sex*, suggesting that although heterosexual engagement is quintessential to the confirmation of masculinity, it may also serve as its undoing.

Yet for all its commentary on gender and sexuality (available to those already enlightened), self-styled post-modern performances of flexible self-invention become more problematic, the closer the inspection of them. *The consummation of transsexual desire is the most decisive form of gender consolidation, notwithstanding its literal enactment of gender construction.* It is a perfect illustration of the fact that an awareness that gender is 'socially', 'performatively' or 'discursively' constructed, is very far from a dismantling of gender. Thus, while some queer theorists, as I have suggested, see transsexualism as the apogee of liberated sex, which has 'refused its imprisonment in the phallocentric orbit of gender',[88] there are other queer theorists who emphasize that it merely literalizes and thereby 'works to stabilize the old sex/gender system'.[89] In the most nuanced study of transsexualism I have seen, Jay Prosser rejects the transgressive/ literalizing binary to suggest instead that we simply listen carefully to transsexual and transgendered narratives for what they tell us about the continuing cultural force of feelings of biological embodiedness, and related gender belonging. These narratives, he suggests, 'produce not the revelation of the fictionality of gendered categories but the sobering realization of their ongoing foundational power'.[90]

Curiously, given the extraordinary degree of human reconstruction it involves, I suspect it is in its testimony to the continuing force of gender figurations that we can best explain why transsexualism is today, surprisingly, becoming *more* acceptable, at this time of widespread anxiety over upheavals in gender relations. In both Britain and the USA, upmarket broadsheets have recently been seeking out and publicizing the most sympathetic articles and news commentary on transsexuals. Significantly, however, the people they cover have all slotted into the more traditional transsexual (as distinct from transgender) narrative of being 'born with the wrong body'. Here it is gender, rather than sex, which is seen as the fixed and fundamental category, and the genitals are seen as a type of 'mask' that doesn't fit: 'I do not have a psychological condition', Claire reports (who before her sex change operation had chosen the surprisingly 'manly' job of policeman), 'I never chose to be like this. I was born like this, it is not a whim. It is a medical condition.' These transsexuals describe themselves as 'nature's mistakes'.[91] It is not so surprising, therefore, that the scientists who feel they know all about 'nature' (and are in tune with the *Zeitgeist* in mainstream biological and social sciences) persevered until one of their number managed to come up with a correlation to enable journalists to rush into print to report that in one foetus in 10,000 the 'area of the brain responsible for gender develops in contradiction with the external sex organs'.[92] It is an area of the brain which has mysteriously managed to escape the attention of other biological scientists, despite their obsessive, hundred-year search for it!

Whether the pursuit of bodily transformation is seen as dictated by 'nature', conditioned by family and cultural experiences, or simply a form of freely chosen self-expression in selecting one's body of 'choice', the blurring which occurs is *not* one between genders so much as one between subversive rebellion against, and conservative accommodation to, oppositional gender binaries. Moreover, self-construction resonates perfectly with the comprehensive commodification of contemporary capitalism. The prosthetic body becomes merely the latest, enormously profitable, consumer product, whether via cosmetic surgery, drugs, implants, or whatever the roving biomedical and fashion industry can come up with to accommodate individual fantasy to its new commercial technologies. More generally, as Alan Sinfield worries, queer theorists can be seen as 'particularly complicit' with an oppressive economic and political system: 'They celebrate the fluidity of the subject, which suits the marketing business very well; they present the moment-to-moment desperation of capitalism as analagous to gay cruising and as the best kind of life; they glamourise the "risk" in S/M practices in the language of stock-market trading in derivatives.'[93]

A final problem with queer theory's programme of exposing the volatility and constraints of gender identity lies in its characteristic disdain for the psychic pain, fear and potential disintegration which so often accompanies gender uncertainties – outside the protective boundaries of academic or theatrical engagement. As the British psychoanalyst Adam Phillips remarks: 'Being blithe about transgression quickly becomes a way of forgetting that people actually suffer, and so of putting the (moral) emphasis in the wrong place.'[94] That suffering, it is certainly true, is produced and constantly exacerbated by the invasive and pathologizing cruelties of heteronormativity. But that is not all there is to say about people's desire for a sense of identity and belonging. All identities provide a necessary coherence and stability, a familiar place from which to act. Indeed, as Jonathan Dollimore suggests, identity serves as a constant protection *against* desire. However dissident, identities provide not only refuge and solidarity, but a way of disowning unwanted, disconcerting or embarrassing desires. Dollimore recounts the reflections of a gay man who is completely horrified to find that he desires a straight black woman, only to express his enormous satisfaction on learning that the object of his desire is reassuringly 'all-man': 'Oh god, the relief, the blessed relief!'[95] After feminism, after gender theory, after queer theory, after all the flaunting of the inherent instabilities or fluidities of gender and sexuality, the problem remains: we still live in a world haunted by cultural and personal fixations on sexual opposition. As Prosser shows us, transsexual narratives 'return us to the complexities and difficulties that inevitably accompany real-life experiences of gender crossing and the personal costs of not simply being a man or a woman . . . [where] transition often proves a barely livable zone'.[96]

Back to Gender?

We are all transsexuals now, Jean Baudrillard declares, with his reliably hyperbolic rhetoric. Pessimistic conservative that he is, despite his bizarre elevation as post-modern hero, Baudrillard mourns this new flexibility of desires and pleasures. Today we are all '*symbolically* transsexuals', accelerating into a void where 'nothing is either masculine or feminine': 'Once the orgy has faded away, the liberation of sex will have had the effect of sending everybody in search of their "gender", their generic and sexual identity, with fewer and fewer answers given the circulation of signs and the multiplicity of pleasures'.[97] Despite welcoming rather than lamenting the spaces where gender flexibilities and sexual ambiguities are free to flourish, I see things differently. We have transcended neither gender nor sexual hierarchies, although their enactments have certainly been subject to considerable upheaval: some, the product of organized resistance and transgressive agitation; most, the product of unintended displacements and commercial possibilities.

At least among the cosmopolitan cultural elite, the emergence of queer rhetorics and confrontational politics enhanced awareness of the tenuousness of both gendered and sexual identities, and the discontinuities in the ties that supposedly bind them. They also mobilized new alliances in the face of the violence of persisting homophobia and the harsh policing of any challenges to heterosexual conformity which do not keep to their designated niches – on stage, vaudeville, in carnivalesque festivities, or wherever they are permitted for one brief moment to entertain and titillate, but not lead astray, the presumptively heterosexual milieu. Transgression can be part of a wider culture of oppositional consciousness (its often disturbing impact strongest when it is new and surprising), and can help to build the progressive political struggle on many fronts. But that broader struggle has become less and less visible in recent lesbian and gay texts, which, in the context of the withering away of left alliances and principles, are more concerned with post-modern literary theory.

The British AIDS activist and theorist Simon Watney asks why the recent lesbian and gay studies movement has had so little to say about the experience of living with the AIDS epidemic: 'often preferring to view [it] through the binoculars of arcane literary theory, rather than the perspective of establishing and fulfilling urgent, practical research needs.'[98] When such research is undertaken, of course, it immediately brings us back to all the ways (both symbolic and tangible) in which the now far less attractive issues of racialization and class are central to the formation and practices of sexuality, alongside gender and global relations of power. These include: the hugely diverse rates of longevity and suffering for those living with HIV and AIDS; the prospects or obstacles for sex education and safer-sex projects; the chronic sexual exploitation and abuse of particular groups of (mostly) young women and men; the detrimental biopolitics of multinational chemical corporations.

Watney's misgivings about queer erudition and its distance from broader political analysis and activism marks him as a radical from another era, with different hopes, and different dreams: 'It is terribly easy to pose as a romantic Outsider, forever "transgressing" against evil norms of liberal humanism ... it is rather more difficult to understand the real world, and the possibilities it provides both for growth and fulfilment and for misery'.[99] Yet, his despair is also the theme of a host of other feminists, gay men, race and gender theorists who compare older visions of collective social transformation with what they see as the fragilities of individualized trangression. In the world we know, sexuality is lived through gender, race, class and other axes of power. The writings of those theorists and activists who have struggled together to make that world a more democratic and egalitarian place signal common concerns: 'Just as political economy needs a better appreciation of the stubbornness of cultural difference', Dennis Altman argues, from Australia, 'so does queer theory require some basic knowledge of political institutions and an appreciation of the ways in which economic globalisation is creating a newly universal sense of homosexuality as the basis for identity and lifestyle, not mere behaviour'.[100] 'Rearranging the signs of gender too often becomes a substitute for challenging gender inequity', Suzanna Walter writes, from the USA: 'Wearing a dildo will not stop me from being raped as a woman or being harassed as a lesbian . . . it will not, short of "passing", keep me out of the ghettoes of female employment'.[101] '"Queer" activists focus on "queer" issues, and racism, sexual oppression and economic exploitation do not qualify, depite the fact that the majority of "queers" are people of color, female or working class', her black compatriot Barbara Smith agrees.[102] 'Transformation' not 'transgression', should be our watchword, Elizabeth Wilson, in Britain, insists.[103] Sexual dissidence, as Alan Sinfield has always argued, should not be separated from broader aspirations for a fairer world: 'The task is less to applaud and hasten the disintegration of residual identities – the market will take care of that – than to assess and exert some influence over the emergence of new ones.'[104]

However, it could be argued that the more tenuous ties of queer theory's symbolic politics to more traditional political practices, and even the recuperability of its transgressive representations by market forces or hegemonic reframings are, in themselves, unfortunate only to the extent that they stand *alone* as a politics. There is no intrinsic imperative to prevent multiple political engagements, other than the tendency of more aesthetic traditions to display a disdainful detachment from the inevitably compromising work of coalition (or even subcultural) building. It is a graver problem if, on its own terrain, queer perspectives miscontrue the punitive and restrictive production and regulation of gender and sexuality. Yet I suspect that this is the case. Queer theory's semiotically driven reflections rarely address the ways in which, throughout our lifetimes, we move in and out of the identifications, pleasures and vulnerabilities of gender settlements, structures of desire, and management of bodily capabilities: health,

age and a myriad other belongings and exclusions play a
central role. We are never simply subject to (or in rebellion
against) sexual and gender norms or normativities. Against
Foucauldian framings, the complexity of both psychic life
and bodily investments are not homologous with polarizing
gender discourses, or the social injunctions which render them
intelligible. On the one hand, psychic life has an autonomous
complexity which sexual difference, or gender identity, does
not exhaust – however firmly or precariously experienced at
conscious and unconscious levels. It is never fixed or even
consistent in its manifestations. On the other hand, the external namings and rules which solicit gender and sexual
performativity are not themselves seamless and unchanging.
It is here that I would return to the work of certain feminist
clinicians critically rethinking psychoanalysis as 'the discipline
most practiced in the art of uncertainty', as the New York
analyst Virginia Goldner put it.[105]

Like her colleagues Muriel Dimen, Arlene Harris or Jessica
Benjamin, these scholarly clinicians describe how gender operates as an identificatory vehicle to establish, reject or maintain relationships with others. Gender is not internalized as a
single entity, rather it operates subjectively within an array of
often conflicting mental representations and self-perceptions.
These are built up, first of all, as a consequence of powerful
identifications with parents, siblings and significant others.
But such identifications are stamped all over with the effects
of the symbolic hierarchy of sexual difference, and the still
widely prevalent – although domestically specific and individually unique – experience of contrasting gender expectations and personifications from mothers, fathers and other
providers of love and care: the first objects of desire. 'It is
these overdetermined, internally contradictory, deeply embedded relationship premises that are always at risk of collapsing under their own weight that constitute the pathogenic,
wobbly "bedrock" of gender', Goldner concludes.[106] Since the
cultural dynamics of gender mean that it is never simply an
elaboration of anatomical sexual difference, it will always be
possible to question the meaning of 'masculinity' and 'femininity', and point to their uncertain content, both psychically

and socially. The emancipatory point is, surely, the hope that we might feel better able to acknowledge and indulge real gender ambiguities, rather than feel driven to reify or eliminate them, whether in oneself or in others.

The Future of Gender

It is time to dwell upon the significance of these battles over gender, old and new, and to consider, finally, just what we want to do with gender. Repeatedly questioned about the materiality of the female body (as distinct from its forcible production in discourse), and in particular about its distinctive relation to pregnancy and childbirth, Butler responds by explaining that the very question itself is part of the discursive enforcement of a norm, which inevitably gives some women a sense of failure, loss, or inadequacy: 'If you are in your late twenties or your early thirties and you can't get pregnant for biological reasons, or maybe you don't want to, for social reasons – whatever it is – you are struggling with a norm that is regulating your sex'.[107] True enough. And if you are in your teens, and eager to avoid pregnancy at all costs when having sex with men outside marriage, you are struggling against another set of regulations that may make contraception inaccessible, alongside normatively produced psychological constraints that often deny you the confidence and assertiveness to insist upon risk-free sex. But it is not norms or discourses which incite conception (or not) following 'unprotected' genital heterosexual acts. A foetus is neither implanted by language, nor dissolved by resignifications, although in most cultures it *is* certainly emblematic of the most controlling and coercive regulations investing the female body. As Bob Connell writes: 'Bodies are not just the object of our will, whether individual or social, *they are also our fate.*'[108]

Of course, every aspect of the predicament of unplanned teenage pregnancy needs to be understood culturally and politically, not by closer inspection of female anatomy – except for researchers of effective contraception. We need to discern such things as the role of religion, sex education, access to contraception, girls' levels of self-assertiveness, relevant peer subcultures (of girls, and of boys), the life choices open to young women, and so on, and on. What we need here is not so much to study the historically specific and mutable sex/gender system, as the prevailing gender/sexuality regimes. Women with children have another set of needs which, apart from pregnancy, childbirth and breastfeeding, have next to nothing to do with female biology and, new reproductive technologies now permitting, possibly little to do with sexual engagement. Rather, they are almost all connected to the differing cultural arrangements for housework, childrearing and care in the home – which to date have been predominantly arranged along gendered lines. The question is whether, and if so how, it might be possible to register women's specific needs and interests in relation to current gender structures in the social, political and economic domain, while still rendering notions of gender less rather than more controlling. As I see it, this cannot be done without the closest possible attention to the ways in which gender and sexuality operate together at any historical moment, in all their psychic complexity, and as a structure of social relations and symbolic contrasts.

Such attention to complex and intricate detail is what gender theory, at its best, tried to offer: exploring the historicity of gender at all levels of analysis. At its best, I believe, it has the potential to help us envisage similarities and contrasts in gender practices which might serve to encourage the continuing production of more enabling, rather than constraining, forms of gender. Awareness of diversities in the operation of gender patterns at the social level has the potential to increase our tolerance of the ambiguities of gender identifications and internalizations at the psychic level. Writing of the latter, Muriel Dimen suggests that gender needs to be seen 'as an internally varied experience [which is] sometimes central and definitive, sometimes marginal and contingent'. It is this very contingency which, she argues, 'generates uncertainty, invites inquiry, and offers richness'.[109] We need images of gender which would, for sure, be flexible, playful and plural but still recognizable as pertaining to the lives of women and men: to types of people who potentially share almost everything, with just a few small differences which, at different times, in different ways, bear an enormous historical weight. For all the talk of the disappearance of gender, the regulation of what is seen and often experienced as women's distinctive potential remains politically as prominent as ever. This is even clearer if we look beyond the affluent West, at the gender-specific effects of hunger and famine worldwide, where we would need to consider the 'missing women' – approximately 100 million of them – who have died due to the effects of sex-selective infanticide and the lower levels of nutrition and healthcare received by girls and women compared with boys and men.[110] As Jacqueline Zita concludes: 'Against the intellectual anorexia of post-modernism, this ["sexed"] body with its biology and history stubbornly returns with a weight that defies the transcendental promises of postmodernist fantasy and its idealist mechanism.'[111]

One is not born a woman, but becomes one. However, quite what one becomes is always ambiguous, with only some of the signs of 'woman' to the fore, some of the time. This is where the interaction of gender and sexuality is at its most volatile. The way to fight the idea of sex, and its rigidly conceived ties to gender or sexuality as the *core* of our being, is not to negate or eliminate our own complex psychic investments and social negotiations as gendered and sexually desiring beings. It is rather to highlight their complexity, and potential fluidity. It is also to mobilize in support of diverse struggles at the different sites where gender functions to constrain or suppress us – in both social and symbolic domains. As feminist schemes and dreams surely already suggest, sexual difference can be re-conceived, and re-enacted, in ways which work to undermine, rather than to shore up, strictly hierarchical conceptions of gender centred on affirming active/heterosexual/masculine dominance (symbolized as phallic). For her part, Gayle Rubin has always been clear that while sexuality is not reducible to gender, it is hardly disassociated: 'I never claimed that sexuality and gender were always unconnected, only that their relationships are situational, not universal'.[112] While Butler, paradoxically, remains hostile to any attempt to draw too strong an analytic separation between gender and sexuality, given what she sees as their overlapping performative construction through regimes of heterosexuality – despite having inspired a generation of sexual dissidents into battle against existing gender significations.[113] This is why, far from suggesting that gender does not exist, Butler can herself be seen as 'the reigning "Queen" of Gender', in Rubin's affectionately teasing accolade.[114]

In the USA, just when queer theory and transgression gained academic modishness – when Donna Haraway was celebrating, dissidents flaunting and Baudrillard lamenting – the coming of a future 'monstrous world without gender', the most significant, most modest, most easily bestowed choices which might have been made available to young women entering adult sexual engagements were being systematically withdrawn. The encouragement of sexual self-confidence and knowledge, information about sexually transmitted diseases and reliable contraceptive resources were officially forbidden in the public arena of teenagers. In 1997 the Adolescent Family Life Act became federal law in the USA, making available a $100 million a year funding for 'sex education', with an exclusive 'abstinence only' focus. All fifty states in the USA agreed to its funding framework, which prohibited information about contraception or safer sex techniques, despite ample knowledge (even admitted by its promoters) that its chastity lessons meet none of its intended goals: to reduce teenage pregnancy and HIV transmission, and to raise the age at which young people become sexually active.[115] One survey reported that students enrolled in an abstinence-only programme engaged in *more* sex than those in a control group which, although publicized, failed to prevent the Clinton Administration from making such courses the single top priority of its National Campaign to Prevent Teen Pregnancy.[116] This is in line with figures from the Netherlands, where teenage pregnancy rates are over thirteen times lower than in the USA, and the average age of first intercourse is higher.[117]

Overwhelmingly targeting and intimidating young women, the transparent aim of abstinence-only sex education is to promote fear and ignorance about sexual activity: 'Pregnancy,

AIDS, guilt, herpes, inability to concentrate in school, syphilis, embarrassment, abortion, shotgun wedding, gonorrhoea,
selfishness, pelvic inflammatory disease, heartbreak, infertility, loneliness, loss of self-esteem, loss of reputation, being
used . . . ectopic pregnancy, sexual violence, loss of a sense
of responsibility toward others, loss of honesty, jealousy, depression, death', are listed as just *some* of the hazards of non-
marital sex in the Parent-Teacher's Guide to 'sex education',
called – believe it or not – *Sex Respect*. It threatens, this time
aiming at boys: 'There's no way to have premarital sex without hurting someone', fully aware that the age of marriage in
the USA is, on average, a good ten years after the first sexual
engagement with others.[118] Helpful advice!

In her chilling account of the injurious effects of these pro-
abstinence educational packages, Judith Levine illustrates their
chronic dishonesty, and the callous perpetuation of falsehoods
about the dangers of all contraceptives, and of even the safest
sexual practices (like kissing!). As she notes mournfully, the
desiring body, and pleasurable, consensual sex acts, are just
nowhere to be found in sex education in the USA in the
1990s. Their anti-sex message is matched only by their rigid
notion of gender roles: 'the peers who pressured were invariably male, and those who refused and delayed were female'.[119]
However transgressive they may wish to be, many young
American girls are still terrifyingly coerced by the necessity to
avoid pregnancy, and the scapegoating and potential financial
penalties they face should they choose to mother, alone.

The world, mercifully, does not incorporate wholesale the
worst excesses of the robust American right (hopefully recently forced into something of a retreat even in their own
disgracefully vengeful domain), although they have a very powerful way of intimidating, or eliminating, opposition – worldwide. Meanwhile, the teenage pregnancy rate in England and
Wales is only sightly lower than that in the USA: rivalling the
very poorest parts of Western Europe; a startling seven times
above that of the Netherlands, and far higher than any other
EU country. In Britain, as in the USA, social inequality and
inadequate sex education are a significant part of the problem,
as British politicians are just beginning to admit.[120]

While the signs of liberal tolerance for choice and freedom in lifestyles can be found in specific arenas, such tolerance is all but submerged by the far greater buttressing of gender traditionalisms in most others: a common thread to almost every television drama I have watched of late, most of them home-grown in the UK, has been that any woman who disrupts the heterosexual dyad has only one choice: she must die.[121] Not so much female transcendence as a waiting tomb – for you know whom. And just as issues of pregnancy and parenthood still invest female bodies and women's deliberation in ways that remain gender specific, although strongly stamped by race, ethnicity and class, so too gender segregation at work and lower wages have become even more entrenched for poorer women (as discussed in my final chapter).

We have not, yet, done away with gender. And in the currently foreseeable future it looks unlikely that we will, for all the visibility of pluralities and ambiguities of identities and desires. Well before queer theory, social construction theorists often hoped to see the end of gender and sexual categorizing, usually based on the fallacious presumption that what is culturally forged is conceptually fragile and unstable. 'We must use whatever means we have to give up on gender', Suzanne Kessler (one of the early social construction theorists in psychology) argues today. She reaches this conclusion after surveying the burdens and indignities which surgeons have inflicted upon the small but significant number of infants born with ambiguous genitals to enable them to construct unequivocal gender identities.[122] Babies with aberrant 'gender markers' have been scarred for life, and their erotic sensitivities ablated, by a medical profession committed to producing culturally approved binary sex and gender orthodoxies. These normalizing procedures, adopted by medical and psychological experts to construct the 'successful vagina' or the 'good enough penis', occur long before children are in any position to choose their gender, genitals or sexuality: a situation some of the (often erstwhile) 'intersexed' have contested during the 1990s.

Another pioneer of social construction theory, Ken Plummer, already foresees a fundamental shift in categories of sexuality and gender: 'In the late modern world, the very idea of "being gay" will be transformed into the idea of a multiplicity of sexual/gendered/relational/emotional, etc., beings in the world. . . . The separate genders and their separate sexualities cannot so clearly be sustained'.[123] Yet another pioneer, John Gagnon, writes similarly that a 'strong social constructionist position' should be seen as 'the first step in attempting to eliminate that gendering'.[124] These social constructionists are wary of any talk of mental life. Indeed, Gagnon goes on to attack the emphasis on childhood and early object relations as a weakness of psychoanalysis. Ideally, they argue, there should be no limits or constraints on the relational interactions any individual can make throughout their life course.

This is not quite how I see it. Now is not the time for us to be forgetting gender. There are too many constraints which follow from its many paradoxes; even in a post-phallic world, some forms of gendered bodily difference are likely to be marked, although in different ways, at different times. Sometimes central to our lives, sometimes marginal, the gendered identifications we have made (most likely with people of both sexes) and the existing social structures of gender will continue to affect our desires as well as the connections we make (or fail to make) for giving and receiving sexual attention, recognition, nurturance and love, or for choosing (or being forced into) parenting and other caring work. The battles we wage around gender might one day allow these choices to be made in a world in which images of gender are more equal and more flexible than the cultural imperative to position ourselves within an oppositional phallic hierarchy, with its related privileges and constraints, have hitherto allowed them to be. As the lesbian feminist Biddy Martin suggests:

> What we come to experience as our relation to sexual difference, our most deeply felt sense of gender is, in part, the consequence of reducing a complex set of articulations to a false unity under the sign of sex. . . . The goal, then, should not be to do away with gender, as if that were possible, or to leave it intact as though it were a state, or to override or contradict it with our more mobile desires. We might rather

value it as an aspect of the uniqueness of personalities without letting it bind and control qualities, experiences, behaviors that the culture divides up rigidly between two supposedly different sexes.[125]

I agree.

3

Genes and Gender: The Return to Darwin

There is something immensely beguiling about strict adaptationism – the dream of an underpinning simplicity for the
enormously complex and various world.

Stephen Jay Gould, *New York Review of Books*

In the previous chapter I described how some feminists react
to the constraints of gender by seeking deliverance from all its
trappings – biological or cultural. In this one, I chart the
opposite response to gender uncertainties, coming from writers who think they have found the true biological constraints
on gender and sexual fluidities: 'Feminists, meet Mr. Darwin!', their champion in the USA announces.[1] It is an odd
time for the return of such fundamentalism. But the stakes
are high. The goal is not just conceptual containment of potentially unlimited shifts in gender beliefs and practices. It is a
return to the allegedly more rigorous authority of the biological sciences of much that has recently been understood as
cultural. The hope is to defeat, once and for all, those cultural
theorists who assume that 'ideas that draw upon the authority of nature nearly always have their origin in ideas about
society'.[2] Gender is a key symbolic site of this conflict.

Back in the 1950s, in the era of the strictest observance of
the truths of science and its pronouncements about nature,
Roland Barthes began his semiological assault on the constant
transformation of 'history' into myths of 'nature'.[3] Forty years
later, and his work might seem to be done. He and his intellectual kind convinced a generation of scholars that to engage
in any search for the universal causes of human actions, or the
foundational origins of civilization – however we might describe them – was to engage in the most oppressive and foolhardy form of metaphysics. Belief in universal truths (now

derided as 'grand narratives') has broken down in Western culture, some of the most sophisticated theorists assure us, from the platforms of literary and cultural studies. Indeed, Britain's best-known scientist, Richard Dawkins, likes to protest, in language as poetic as he can muster, that scientists are made to 'feel like shabby curates among literary dukes'.[4] But they are all wrong. There is a new form of fundamentalism in the social sciences and media world, which only a minority of cultural theorists have taken seriously. Meanwhile, the glittering prizes bestowed on Dawkins tell their own truth about intellectual authority.[5]

By the late 1980s disillusionment with Marxism (following a decade of defeat for left agendas and campaigns in Britain and the USA) had expanded to include a critique of all the universalizing principles of the Western Enlightenment, among many former political idealists. Any belief in universal laws of human nature came to be seen as terminally suspect by those who designate these times 'post-modern'. Yet, not coincidentally, in the same period, a type of Darwinian fundamentalism was growing in strength and authority in both the physical and social sciences.

Science versus Culture?

Speaking from the most exalted academic platforms, with the authority of the Chair for the Public Understanding of Science, specifically created for him at Oxford University (by the Microsoft millionaire Charles Simonyi), Richard Dawkins pronounces as his first axiom of science: 'Plants and animals alike are all – in their immensely complicated, enmeshed ways doing the same fundamental thing, which is propagating genes.'[6] The eternal truths of Darwin's grand narrative have returned with a vengeance to reshape intellectual agendas this *fin de siècle*, just as strongly as they did the last. A generation ago, appeals to evolutionary biology to explain cultural practices or social hierarchy were denounced as mere justifications for conservative prejudices. Today, the most simplistic forms of evolutionary theory are advanced by actively committed liberals and social reformers: manifest in Britain in the Blair government's favourite think-tank, Demos, preparing a report delineating the implications of evolutionary psychology for the shaping of social policy, *Matters of Life and Death: The World View from Evolutionary Psychology*.[7] It is not the beneficiaries of Barthes, but the successors of C. P. Snow, who now win most of the media accolades in the revitalized and transformed 'Two Cultures' debate.[8]

Few things are more depressing for me to have to write about than the renaissance of a Darwinian fundamentalism, whether in mainstream media debate or in the most powerful strands of the social and biological sciences. The goal of life in this form of evolutionary theory is twofold: to survive and to mate. It is a goal, according to Dawkins, implanted in the genes of all living things – however redundantly the components of genes lie on most chromosomes, never once triggered into any action at all. True, Sigmund Freud saw the ability to love and to work as necessary for human happiness, and I have little difficulty accepting that he is highlighting two crucial sites of human activity. But accounts of 'loving' and 'working' direct us immediately towards quintessentially human narratives; 'surviving' and 'mating' strip away this human dimension. It is a barbed contrast for one such as me, and my long-standing friends, who saw the meaning of human life in collective co-operation in the shaping of history. Nevertheless, given its place in contemporary thought, we must look very seriously at this resurgence of Darwinian thinking.

I hope to show how Nature and History are once again being confused at every turn, to the great impoverishment of both. The latest 'science' versus 'humanities' wars have been undertaken not just to reassert the presumed neutrality and rigours of science over the spirited and capricious fantasies of the imagination, but more importantly to defeat those who insist upon greater complexity and epistemic diversity, whatever their theoretical tools. However, there are sceptics within *both* cultures, many of whom have been pointing for some time to the recurrent deployment of science to provide spurious legitimation for popular cultural convictions.

Survival and Sexual Selection

It is hard not to see the current return to Darwin as being fuelled, at least to some degree, by a reactive search to legitimize predestined gender and sexual distinctions in the face of the personal panic and social alarm generated by a combination of feminist challenges and the seemingly unstoppable institutional shifts in gender practices. In the late nineteenth century and the early twentieth, at a time of heightened imperial conflict, Darwin's ideas were appropriated by eugenic movements in many Western countries, using notions of inherited 'degeneracy', 'feeblemindedness' and the dangers of 'miscegenation', to justify all manner of class, 'race' and anti-immigrant restraints and prejudices.[9] Today, they usually serve a somewhat different cause – not so much racial as gendered – although one which has surfaced before in earlier gender battles.[10]

In *The Origin of Species* (1859) Darwin documented the extraordinary *variation* in living organisms, past and present. He surveyed the abundance of fossil records of species which had become extinct, and marvelled that from 'so simple a beginning endless forms most beautiful and most wonderful have been, and are being, evolved'.[11] His central idea was the assertion that all living things that have ever existed are related, and have descended from a common origin which emerged from inanimate materials as the simplest form of life – now thought to be about three billion years ago. Darwin originally referred to his central idea as a 'theory of descent with modification', rather than as a 'theory of evolution' (implying a notion of 'progress')[12], but the speedy advocacy of his ideas by Victorian scientists and eugenic enthusiasts encouraged him to speak of 'evolution' in his next book *The Descent of Man* (1871). Unlike many of those who pronounce in his name today, Darwin believed that 'the present is the key to the past' (just as Marx had earlier remarked that 'human anatomy is a key to the anatomy of the ape').[13] Darwin did not believe, like his contemporary publicists, that the past holds the key to the future, the solution to the meaning of human life. On the contrary, he wrote: 'I have nothing to do with the origin of the primary mental powers, any more than with life itself'.[14]

Species have appeared and disappeared over time, Darwin argued, through a causal mechanism of 'Natural Selection, or Survival of the Fittest', which ensured that only those forms of life best suited to survive and reproduce themselves in any specific habitat would continue to exist as a species.[15] Alongside the random process of 'natural selection' for survival, Darwin also wrote of 'sexual selection' for effective procreation in sexually reproducing species. The latter generated 'a struggle between the males for possession of the females', as well as choice and selection of males by females (although females were seen by Darwin as playing a more passive, secondary role in the process of evolution).[16] In line with the panorama of imperial England, Darwin himself saw sexual hierarchy conjoined with racial hierarchy (indeed his most famous book is subtitled *The Preservation of Favoured Races in the Struggle for Life*), producing white males at the pinnacle of evolution. However, today's Darwinians usually distance themselves, at least formally (although, as we shall find, not always effectively), from the Victorian racist dynamics of 'sexual selection', even as they enthusiastically affirm its sexist dynamics: males have an inherent advantage in the evolutionary 'arms race'.[17]

Even here, not all contemporary Darwinians are quite as explicit as the popular science writer Robert Wright, who throughout the 1990s has consistently ridiculed feminists seeking equality with men as doomed by their deliberate ignorance or foolish denial of the 'harsh Darwinian truths' about human nature: 'Feminists are right to dread some of the rhetorical resistance Darwinism will abet'.[18] Expressing specious concern that feminism may falter from its own 'doctrinal absurdities', he challenges them to face up to the evolutionary basis for 'the "natural" male impulse to control female sexuality', 'men's natural tendencies to greater promiscuity', 'natural selection' for men to make 'the Madonna-whore distinction': 'Human males', in short, 'are by nature oppressive, possessive, flesh-obsessed pigs'.[19] Wright admits that men are 'not beyond cultural improvement', but 'the bad news is [that] the average beer-drinking, two-timing, wife-beating lout isn't going to change his moral views': 'Some changes can't be made and others will come only at some cost'. As Wright likes to reassure himself and the many readers of his best-seller *The Moral Animal: Why We Are the Way We Are*, feminists have managed to procure legislation against sexual harassment, and even elements of affirmative action for women, but they will never share power with men because they lack men's genes for competitiveness and risk-taking behaviour.[20] The ideological motivation at stake here is as naked as the eponymous ape, adroitly summed up by three feminist biologists reviewing the book: 'This particular version of evolutionary psychology implies that affirmative action can only result in hiring or promoting inferior candidates. . . . Compared with amending the Constitution to assure equal rights for women, fighting our (allegedly) genetically determined bodies and minds is daunting indeed'.[21] Feminists, back off!

Ideological imbrication, enshrining both patriarchal precedent and capitalist market values, was embarrassingly prominent to many in the first blast of resurgent Darwinism with the publication of E. O. Wilson's *Sociobiology* in 1975 and Richard Dawkins's *The Selfish Gene* the next year, soon followed by other influential publications in the social sciences, such as David Barash's *The Whisperings Within* (1979), and *The Evolution of Human Sexuality* (1979), by the anthropologist Donald Symons.[22] (Following the publication of *Sociobiology*, the US magazine *Business Week* ran a series of articles on 'The Genetic Defence of the Free Market', celebrating the evolutionary origins of men's competitive self-interest.[23]) In the decade of resurgent feminism, these books offered a distinctive genetic underpinning for male dominance and aggression, female passivity and domestication, in terms of 'the optimizing of reproductive fitness' – albeit without any reference to actual genetic makeup. Sexual selection for competitive reproductive advantage was the particular Darwinian contribution to emerge as the fundamental postulate of sociobiology. It was an elaboration not so much of Darwin's own writing, as of its extension to accounts of differential

'parental investment' in offspring (in sperm, egg and the raising of progeny to reproductive age), first proposed by the
somewhat less prominent US biologist Robert Trivers in
1974.[24]

On this account, promiscuous male behaviour evolved in
accordance with the maximum spread of the continuous 'low-
cost' supply of copious sperm; prudent and passive female
behaviour was selected to accommodate the 'high-cost', time-
consuming, requirements for the monthly production, successful fertilization, gestation and survival to reproductive
age, of the far more limited supply of female eggs. Dawkins
reiterates the theme: 'The sex cells or "gametes" of males are
smaller and more numerous than the gametes of females',
concluding, 'it is possible to interpret *all* other differences
between the sexes as stemming from this one basic difference. . . . Female exploitation begins here'.[25] The search
for single overarching principles unifying all forms of knowledge drives this return to Darwin. All human behaviour,
E. O. Wilson echoes, 'faithfully' obeys this one biological
principle: 'It pays males to be aggressive, hasty, fickle and
undiscriminating . . . females to be coy, to hold back until
they can identify the male with the best genes'. Wilson mani-
fests the peculiarity of this tunnel vision when he equates 'an
American industrial city' in the late 1970s with 'a band of
hunter-gatherers in the Australian desert': 'During the day
the women and children remain in the residential area while
the men forage for game or its symbolic equivalent in the
form of barter or money.'[26] Dream on!

However, the Western media have carefully selected this
particular theory of immutable human nature for survival:
a picaresque, if impoverished, way of construing the issues
of the day. In the early 1980s the biologist Randy Thornhill
and his fellow workers, also in the USA, wrote of the 'rape-
adaptation hypothesis', explaining why human males will rape
when their capacity to reproduce successfully is thwarted.
Thornhill was generalizing from observations of the so-called
'rape' of female flies by 'frustrated' male flies (the scorpionfly),
leading him to conclude that 'high status men probably rarely
actually rape'.[27] We are offered not only an evolutionary ra-

tionale for the inevitability of male violence against women, but the added bonus of extenuating justification for the class and race dynamics of the very high acquittal rates of rich, white males accused of rape – like William Kennedy Smith – compared with the speedy sentencing of the huge numbers of poor, black Americans, languishing on death row. David Barash drew similar conclusions from his observations of 'rape' in ducks (the mallard duck).[28] It may be possible to tame men's proclivities to rape when denied status and resources, these sociobiologists admit, but they all hasten to add, like Symons before them, that any such attempts to go against nature 'might well entail a cure worse than the disease.'[29]

Inside the academy, the circular, anthropomorphic arguments of sociobiology were briefly held at bay by widespread and vigorous rebuttal issuing both from biological and social scientists, who highlighted sociobiologists' careful selection of particular animals on which to project, and supposedly thereby explain, categories of behaviour derived from human consciousness, culture and conduct.[30] Given that at this time sociobiologists could not even pretend to have direct knowledge of the nature or operation of their ontologically founding category – human genes – their designated units for natural selection (as distinct from the individual organism, or groups of living creatures), there could in principle be little, if any, convincing verification (and obviously no falsification) for those who doubted their uniform narrative of the causal origins of individual and collective behaviour. At this time, molecular biologists could not claim even a scrap of knowledge about any human genes which might bear the remotest relation to the specific universal activities they were supposed to explain: an awkward failing, one might have thought, for theorists whose mantra was scientific rigour and whose goal the defeat of loose or sentimental thought and language. (The situation is not so different today.)

Since the 1980s billions of dollars have been pouring into biotechnology, bringing together the latest micro-electronic processors with techniques of gene splicing in the hope of commodifying and patenting new procedures for the production and handling of plant, animal and – most controversially of all – human life. These new genetic and computer technologies were developed in the 1970s, creating widespread investment frenzies which revitalized old dreams of brave new worlds, under human control. Meanwhile, global agrichemical, pharmaceutical and computer giants have also been pouring huge investments into genetic research since the late 1980s. As Andrew Ross outlines, despite meagre profits and very little to show for the many billions invested, 'a chorus of investors, executives, and industry boosters intoned the mantras of molecular biology as if it were some new kind of alchemy'.[31] The 'genetic revolution' had arrived. It would usher in the multi-billion-dollar Human Genome Project, attempting to map and sequence all the genes of human DNA. In the USA, federal support for the project (originating from initiatives taken in the mid-1980s) was set at $200 million a year from 1988, with state support for genome research and sequencing also accelerating in Britain, France and Japan, trailed by other Western states.[32]

With the thralldrom to dreams of genetic utopianism encouraging a return to the grand theory which first pointed us in that direction, the spread of neo-Darwinian ideas would soon prove unstoppable. What we have today is the most bizarre and muddled mix of genetic determinisms: one minute being used to set *limits* on the potential for possible change in human affairs; the next minute promising us a *limitless* prosthetic future, where nothing is impossible. Nature has framed strange formulations in her time, but none quite so strange as this.

Evolutionary Psychology: The New Contender

The ambivalent pull of new Darwinian thinking is nowhere stronger than in mainstream psychology, some of whose scholars, swimming smoothly with wider currents, have moved effortlessly from earlier espousals of cultural explanations for explaining human 'social behaviour' to promoting the greater utility of modern Darwinism, or new evolutionary psychology, for the same purpose. One such prominent British psychologist, John Archer, in the forefront of emphasizing the acquisition of sex differences primarily in terms of social learning theory in the heyday of environmentalism in the 1970s, re-emerged two decades later arguing that 'evolutionary theory accounts much better for the overall patterns of sex differences and for their origins'. 'Social role theory', he has come to believe, 'accounts very poorly, if at all, for the patterns of sex differences identified by evolutionary psychologists'.[33]

Evolutionary psychology emerged as the most conspicuous 'new' theoretical perspective within the field of psychology during the 1990s. Eager to replace all rival psychological theories and systems, the most distinguished representatives, like Tooby and Cosmides, believe evolutionary psychology will finally unify psychology with hard science; while David Buss recommends it as the new paradigm for all the social sciences, under the conceptual framework of natural selection.[34] Similarly, Martin Daly and Margo Wilson assert: 'What evolutionary psychology aspires to become [*sic*] is a Kuhnian paradigm shift'.[35] Presumably by this they mean that they are aspiring to 'effect' such a shift – ironically, in the very discipline which helped inspire Thomas Kuhn himself to write his trail-blazing *The Structure of Scientific Revolutions* (1962) in the first place. (Kuhn reveals in its preface that he had never known what it was like to live within a science where there was so little agreement about what problems are worth pursuing, or which empirical findings are of lasting significance, until he had the experience of spending some time among academic psychologists.[36])

Nowadays, evolutionary psychologists are somewhat less reliant on animal studies than sociobiologists have been. They are on the lookout instead for any universals of human behaviour and, on finding any hint of them, at once assume an adapted genetic origin. From the close of the 1980s, there have been attempts to apply Darwinian ideas in mainstream cognitive, developmental, individual, social, psychiatric and clinical pyschology, as human cognitive functioning and social behaviour is explained in terms of adaptations which must have been 'selected for' because they were successful in human and pre-human evolution.[37] These 'selected' behaviour patterns are described by Archer, for example, as those which have produced 'individuals who are able to pursue the reproductive strategies appropriate for their own sex'.[38] However, as was the case with sociobiology, it is just such presumed sex-differentiated reproductive strategies which take us back to the issues most strongly disputed by those who have been contesting men's institutionalized dominance over women since the 1970s: the inevitability of men's sexual harassment and violence; the inequality of women's domestic burdens and parenting activities.

In an article published in 1998 in the *American Psychologist*, four evolutionary psychologists in the USA summarize achievements to date, after discussions and commentary with ten other leading thinkers in the field in both Europe and America. Their central concept of an evolutionary 'adaptation' is defined, somewhat more flexibly than by Archer, as an 'inherited and reliably developing characteristic that came into existence as a feature of a species through natural selection because it helped to directly or indirectly facilitate reproduction during the period of its evolution'.[39] They then list thirty empirical 'discoveries' about human behaviour allegedly generated by evolutionary theory, many of them explaining gender contrasts. These include: sexually dimorphic mating strategies; men's preference for younger mates; male risk-taking in intrasexual competition for mates; patterns of spousal and same-sex homicide; design of male sexual jealousy; women's desire for mates with resources; sex-linked shifts in mate selection across the lifespan; causes of conjugal dissolution; mate guarding as a function of female reproductive value; waist-to-hip ratio as a determinant of attractiveness judgements.[40]

The overview offered by Buss and his co-writers is one of the more cautious in arguing the case for evolutionary psychology – taking note, in particular, of one of its main critics, Stephen Jay Gould. However, it is not hard to suggest other explanations for the behaviour patterns they list, however widespread across differing cultures. One does not have to believe that evolution and genetics play no role in human affairs (indeed, it would be hard to make much sense of such a claim in describing the behaviour of any living organism), to point out that the apparent universality of certain practices does *not* entail a genetic origin. Thus, even if we choose to overlook the weight of historical, anthropological and sociological evidence for enormous variability in the area of human sexual conduct, it would still be the case that the claimed universality of sexually dimorphic behaviour patterns could as easily be seen as a cultural *effect*, rather than as an evolved adaptation operating as a *cause*, of the hitherto (though now often challenged) global configuration of men's greater access to economic resources and social power and privilege compared with that of women.

Buss himself has produced a plentiful body of research on what he calls 'mating strategies' in the USA, Britain, and thirty-five other cultures, all showing that men declare themselves to be far more promiscuous than women, and readier to have sex with any female strangers, so long as they are young and attractive. Women, in contrast, are said universally to report desiring (or having 'mating' preferences for) ambitious, industrious men, with good financial resources.[41] Buss is researching the same furrow as many other evolutionary psychologists, who also assure us of the reality of men's predetermined sexual promiscuity which (together with their greater predisposition for violence and risk-taking) is one of the most repeated claims of evolutionary theorists.[42] But this, of course, is precisely what those who stress the cultural rather than the biological basis of contrasting sexual conduct themselves predict, whether via individually based 'learning theory' or discursively mediated 'social construction' perspectives: in male-dominated societies boys learn to see heterosexual activity as a confirmation of masculinity (and certainly know that boasting about their desire to perform it is the single easiest way of proclaiming their 'virility': 'whoooa!'); girls learn to value committed relationships above casual sex (or, at least, certainly discover that they ought to say so to escape being branded whatever the local vernacular for 'slag' might be, thereby also avoiding the assaultive behaviour such labelling condones: 'I prefer a good cuddle, myself').

The more humorous side to the shallowness of all this

research is that were men's promiscuous boasts, and women's prudent protestations, to be accepted as indicative of selectively evolved behaviour patterns, rather than – in line with my own more sceptical hypothesis – gender-differentiating, cultural 'identity work', a tiny minority of enormously hyperactive 'young and attractive' women would have to be obliging an army of dedicatedly randy men. As Dorothy Einon suggests in relation to her own research, in which heterosexual men reported having three or four times the number of sexual partners that women did, *the figures just don't compute*: fibbing, whether or not self-deceiving, is the best name for this statistical game, however many cultures Buss and his cohorts dedicatedly interrogate.[43] In fact, the one constant feature of changes in the pursuit of human sexual pleasure is their negative correspondence with reproductive ends.

Martin Daly and Margo Wilson, the leading US psychologists using evolutionary theory to account for homicide and male violence, have been concerned to trace the negative relation between murder and genetic closeness. This is the inverse of the new orthodoxy of 'kin selection', used by evolutionary psychologists to explain the supposedly anomolous existence of 'altruism': genes are selected for co-operative or helping behaviour towards those with shared genes. It would explain, they tell us, why husbands are far more likely to murder their wives (genetically unrelated) than their biological children, and why a child is much more likely to be murdered, or physically abused, by a step-parent than a child with two biological parents.[44] It would *not* explain, of course, why an overwhelmingly greater number of human parents willingly adopt children, and most typically display remarkable love and concern for them (despite the obvious lack of narcissistic gratification that comes from close physical similarity, and genetic input); neither would it explain why the American sample of males (from Detroit) should be twelve times more likely than the British sample to kill blood relatives, and a massive forty times more likely to kill nonrelatives. Further, it would not explain why midwives in both the USA and Britain have been reporting for several years that violence against women often *begins* when that woman is pregnant with a man's baby, the latest figures reported in the UK estimating this to be true for one third of women who are attacked.[45] If one must continue to take seriously the 'evolutionary rigour' supposedly on display in such explanations of male aggression in line with competitive reproductive fitness, then one must point out that it is precisely when pregnant to their live-in partners that 'females' cannot be impregnated by rival males. It is the time when they most fully 'obey' the so-called 'Darwinian' rules for 'kin-selection', carrying 50 per cent of the aggressor's genes.

It is the complete absence of any intellectually serious form of scientific rigour which most often accompanies psychology's postulated 'paradigm shift'. The ability to produce an evolutionary scenario for supposed universal behaviours does nothing to establish its validity (ignoring for the moment the instability of the 'universals' so often selected). As critics have noted, talk of 'natural selection' is merely an empty generalization unless it is can delineate something about the evolutionary history of a trait's development: the forces operating in particular contexts which select certain features because they enhance survival over other less adaptive ones which have disappeared. Convincing evolutionary biology must offer significant historical evidence of the utility of particular traits. Evolution occurs because there is *no* unitary or general notion of fitness in biology. There is only adaptation to local conditions. Adaptive explanations require data, and it is this which evolutionary psychologists choose to ignore, thereby 'presenting simplistic and impoverished biology rather than genuine biology', as Looren de Jong and Van Der Steen observe of the controversies generated by the work of Tooby and Cosmides on supposed universal cognitive adaptations, like their 'cheater detection' module.[46] To the chagrin of psychologists like Steven Pinker, this is also the view of one of the most famous theorists of language, Noam Chomsky, who, despite stressing an innate capacity for 'the language faculty', rejects adaptionist accounts of language development as mere 'fairy tale', one 'that probably would have shocked Darwin'.[47] Echoing Kuhn, several decades later, the British geneticist Steve Jones comes to much the same conclusion in his review of Pinker's *How the Mind Works* (1997), a tome in which Pinker explains cultural beliefs in Darwinian terms: 'If you want to find schizophrenia, go to a psychology department'.[48]

Sadly, we don't need to go there at all. Evolutionary psychology's flimsy evolutionary speculations could be dismissed altogether, were it not for the almost daily promotion they receive in one media outlet or another. Retiring to bed after writing this section, I flashed on the television only to be greeted by Wilson and Daly themselves, once again elaborating their narratives of sex and violence in *Anatomy of Desire*.[49] Unlike schizophrenia, these particular cognitive inventions are highly contagious.

Against the grain of the new dominant trend to focus on gender rather than race, evolutionary psychologists have even managed to restore 'sexual selection' for classic Darwinian ethnocentrism. Leslie Zebrowitz, for instance, reports adaptation for men to prefer 'lighter skinned women'.[50] The evolutionary explanation on offer is that light skin is seen as more attractive in women because it is a sign of fertility: women's skin is said to darken during periods of infertility, such as pregnancy, ingestion of contraceptives, and throughout infertile phases of the menstrual cycle (although no one seems to have noticed). The empirical evidence of skin preference cannot be attributed to Western standards of beauty, Zebrowitz reassures us, as it is documented cross-culturally. Really! For this argument to be convincing, one would have to believe that white racism had confined its influence to the West, and that cultural colour hierarchy, or 'pigmentocracy' – worked out with elaborate pyramidal precision by colonialists like the conquistadors of South America or the apartheid regime in South Africa – had never existed. Given the higher status accorded to lighter skinned people in most cultures over the last 400 years (after certain global episodes like slavery and colonialisms, old and new), you don't have to have read Toni Morrison's novel *The Bluest Eye* (1970) to suggest that it is not too taxing a task to offer a few abiding cultural explanations for empirical findings such as these.

We can, and it seems that we will, bat this ball around for

ever. 'New' evolutionary theorists like to distinguish themselves from 'old' social Darwinians, like Herbert Spencer, and also sociobiologists, by claiming that they eschew rigid biological determinism with their suggestion that genetic and environmental forces always interact. Quite so. However, as Tooby and Cosmides clarify, outlining the 'psychological foundations of culture': 'instead of culture manufacturing the psychology of social exchange [their characteristically market metaphor for social life] *de novo*, content-specific evolved psychologies constitute the building blocks out of which cultures themselves are manufactured'.[51] Although this move is presented as *less* biologically reductionist, it can be seen as exactly the opposite. In the first instance – and no doubt, also in the last instance – for such thinkers, culture never exists autonomously from genetic selection.

For example, faced with evidence of the widespread, punitive cultural policing of individual nonconformity to gender and sexual norms (which are said to underlie the evolved reproductive fitness of males and females), the evolutionary psychologist will instantly retort that, of course, culture itself is *already* selected for: 'Gender differences result from an interaction of evolved predispositions and the cultures created by people with these predispositions'.[52] How could cultures be selected for, those stressing the relative autonomy of culture would immediately ask, when they are so very diverse? Some societies deny all sexual expression to women outside marriage on pain of death; in others, women are almost as likely as men today to have multiple sexual partners before, during and after marriage – if they choose to marry at all (and whether or not we speak the truth to prying psychologists).[53] Insignificant detail, the evolutionary theorist will argue back: the important point is to establish that 'cultures are in some ways *constrained* by the genes of the individuals making up the culture'. Constrained? It is rather unfortunate that Douglas Kenrick and Melanie Trost, the two evolutionary theorists I have just been quoting, illustrate their argument about biological limits with the rather silly example that a culture which required '10-year-olds to fly off a 1,000-foot cliff would not survive long'.[54] Well, no; unless there was an airport on the cliff. A remark by Richard Lewontin, the Harvard geneticist and leading critic of such constraining applications of evolutionary theory, seems only too apt:

> If we have to characterize social organization and its consequences, it is that social organization does not reflect the limitations of individual biological beings but is their *negation*. . . . No individual human beings can fly by flapping his or her arms and legs. That indeed is a biological limitation. . . . [But] Individuals fly . . . they fly as a consequence of social organization.[55]

Lewontin thinks he knows the way to settle this tedious argument, and I agree with him. But before returning to the enemy within – the *biologists* who in my view deliver the *coup de grâce* to evolutionary psychologists seeking assimilation to a biology they erroneously perceive as unified – I want to consider those feminists who have been convinced by evolutionary arguments, but use them to their own ends. Another type of enemy within, but within a different camp!

The Tale of the Female Ape

Although many feminists have forcefully criticized the return to Darwin, others have joined the trend and become Darwinians themselves. It is an engaging coupling. For what they observe when they go down among the animals, survey our human ancestors or make comparisons across cultures is rather different from the more familiar formulations of their male peers, who reiterate legacies of male dominance, competition, promiscuity and violence. The number of women in biology, primatology and psychology has increased rapidly since the 1970s, as ever more women raced into further education. Accompanying the growth of feminism and women's studies, many shifted their focus from the male to the female ape. What a difference gender makes – the gender of the observer!

Not male baboons, but females, we would soon be told,

often dominate the social group, hold it together, and initiate sexual encounters. By 1982, Linda Fedigan, in *Primate Paradigms*, had summarized the new research: it offered a challenge to the traditional stereotypes of female monkeys and apes, and a demonstration of female bonding and self-sufficiency in relation to caring for offspring within a rich variety of patterns of female sexual behaviour.[56] The best known of the new female primatologists include Sarah Blaffer Hrdy, Jane Goodall, Meredith Small and Barbara Smuts. In *The Woman that Never Evolved* (1981), Hrdy describes female monkeys and apes who are in different ways independent, assertive and competitive.[57] Similarly, Small writes of many species of apes and monkeys where the female approaches the male, pushing her genitals in his face, slapping him, initiating sexual advances and clearly enjoying sexual games.[58] Both Goodall and Smuts used their primate studies to rebut the standard evolutionary argument that female apes are more selective and prudent than male apes, indicating that adult female chimpanzees typically mate successively with almost every male in their group during certain phases of the oestrus cycle, while adult male chimpanzees can be extremely selective in their choice of sexual contact.[59] Elsewhere, Smuts reports no consistent gender dimorphism in aggression across different primate species, arguing that environmental contexts affect both male and female aggression, as well as how the sexes influence each other.[60]

However, if we really want a glimpse of primate feminist utopia (replacing the male dominance/promiscuity thesis), we need to join those chimpanzee experts, like Frans de Waal or Wrangham and Peterson, observing the communities of the bonobo apes which, it is now generally agreed, are definitely dominated by coalitions between females. Among bonobos, living in resource-rich, gorilla-free areas, sexual activities are reported as more frequent and varied, including female to female genital rubbing (called the *hoka-hoka* by the Mongandu of Central Africa) and male on male sexual activities. The female bonding in these close primate relatives is seen as cemented through such 'genito-genital' rubbing which, by serving to strengthen female coalitions, decreases male violence.[61] Drawing on this research in support of her own political lesbian agenda in a recent issue of *Feminism and Psychology*, Louise Silverstein argues that psychologists should pay much closer attention to 'the importance of lesbian [*sic*] sex among our closest primate relatives', and explore 'the evolutionary implications of this same-sex behavior for decreasing male violence in human primate society'.[62] She also mentions the possibility of deep evolutionary origins of practices like clitoridectomy in male attempts to limit the establishment of female power coalitions and to ensure the continuity of their own genes by preventing females from having multiple sexual partners.

More promiscuous than the male evolutionary theorist, the feminist evolutionary biologist or anthropologist has sought out the variability in protohumans, stressing that evolution has selected for reproductive flexibility, rather than universal patterns. Surveying human diversity, these feminist theorists tend to emphasize the absence of any single evolutionary patterns in human development, suggesting evolutionary processes have favoured instead patterns of 'plasticity and behavioral variation'.[63] It is over a decade since the feminist biologist Ruth Bleier announced in 1986: 'Primatology thus serves as an example of the correction that a feminist perspective can effect in a field of knowledge . . . [it] is a lone example in the natural sciences of dramatic changes made under feminist viewpoints.'[64] However, I am more sceptical than Bleier about the progressive impact feminists have managed to make through their interventions in primatology.

Women primatologists have certainly helped to undermine the androcentric language and interpretations of many of their peers, for whom the male predator remains the pre-eminent narrative.[65] In their texts, much of the feminist-inflected focus in primatology appears more concerned about the dangers of anthropomorphism, and more self-reflexive. Women researchers have paid attention to the effects of differing social environments on the activities of male primates and, above all, collected information on female lives and behaviour. It was this research which first seriously challenged the consensus of the 1960s that the crucial transition to human evolution was via the hunter-gatherer adaptation: an account of human history memorialized in 1966 at the 'Man the Hunter' conference in Chicago, organized by Richard Lee and Irven de Vore.[66] A succession of feminist palaeontologists and anthropologists during the 1970s and 1980s added to the work of women primatologists, all challenging what Linda Fedigan labelled the misleading 'baboonization' of proto-hominids, used to insist upon evolutionary selection for male dominance and aggression. As Adrienne Zihlman documents, women scientists collected ethnographic studies from fossil hominid records, and researched foraging societies, to un-cover women's role in prehistory: often as efficient food-gatherers, sometimes as effective hunters, or in other ways engaged in subsistence, nutrition and work.[67]

Yet, three decades after the first challenges to the hunting hypothesis, Zihlman reflects that all this new research on female behaviour seems to have resulted in little change in the traditional tale of human origins in most mainstream text-books or educational documentaries, despite the critical mass of divergent data.[68] As Linda Fedigan similarly notes, 'the reception of feminist critique by practicing scientists, includ-ing women scientists, has often been less than positive'.[69] Furthermore, although offering forceful and vivid contrasts with earlier male researchers' neglect of female behaviour, the goal of restoring women to evolutionary history can itself prove problematic when used to explain human societies. It is vulnerable to some of the same traps as earlier sociobiological research. As anthropologist Susan Sperling wryly notes: 'The new female primate is dressed for success and lives in a troop that resembles the modern corporation: now everyone gets to eat power lunches on the savanna.'[70] It is my impression that the newer studies on female primates *have* influenced the mainstream agenda of evolutionary theorists, but not neces-sarily in ways which add to their theoretical or methodologi-cal sophistication.

Dawkins has no problem writing of the bonobo ape as being as genetically close to humans as any other type of ape. He merely adds, true to his unifying principle of natural selection propelled by the 'selfish' gene, that in this particular primate 'altruism at the level of the individual organism' just happens to be 'a means by which the underlying genes maximize their self-interest'.[71] Similarly, Robert Wright is happy to take on board that 'there are a few eccentric sex-reversed species' (referring to the phalaropes or 'sea horses'), but 'these ostensible exceptions to Darwinian logic comply with and bolster it'.[72] In the codes of his chosen theory, the zoologist Iver Mysterud urges all evolutionary theorists to show greater appreciation of the criticisms and the specific agendas of feminist biologists, in order to speed up the dissemination of evolutionary thinking and secure its status in the evolving 'hierarchies among scientists': 'Often, it is not an optimal long-term strategy to humiliate the "enemy" too much in the first round, if one can secure an ally in the next round by treating him or her politely/gently'.[73]

The work of one of Britain's leading evolutionary psychologists still doing animal research is typical of more recent agendas: Robin Dunbar's *Grooming, Gossip and the Evolution of Language* (1996) sets out to offer a more woman-friendly, post-feminist evolutionary account of the origins of human behaviour. Dunbar writes that early, or protohuman, females were central to the invention of language, as a form of 'gossip': 'The conventional view is that language evolved to enable males to do things like co-ordinate hunts more effectively.... I am suggesting that language evolved to allow us to gossip'; 'the pressure to evolve language may well have come through the need to form and service female alliances'.[74] Although more attentive to female behaviour, Dunbar nevertheless offers the same reductionist neglect of either the complexities of human evolution or the diversities of human behaviour. In his account, women today, as yesterday, and like females everywhere, want men for breeding; males today, as yesterday, are more aggressive than women, because of competition for females: 'The difference between the sexes reflects crucial differences in their reproductive strategies'.[75] And once again, informing us that we can forget that old 'bugaboo of genetic determinism', we are 'reassured' that evolutionary theorists no longer ignore what they call cultural 'rules'. They no longer need to: 'Learning is *just* another example of a Darwinian process: it is differential survival of traits (behavioural rules in this case) as a result of selection.' So much, apparently, for the objections of those who stress the significance of culture, whose 'problem', we are told, 'is largely one of misinformation – sometimes exacerbated by a refusal to listen'.[76]

I think not. This is no refusal to listen, but obstinate attention to certain new twists in the curtailing of culture. What we have here is a biological absolutism more incompatible than ever with any serious recognition of the dynamics of culture, and its role in the formation of human existence. Such scientific grandiosity is always blind to its own ideological imbrication, even when, as in Dunbar, it parrots the most fatuous, market-driven homilies: 'The other key lesson of the Darwinian approach is that in real life nothing comes for free'; 'left to their own devices, people will be moderate and tolerant', but their behaviour in groups 'has sullied the history of our species since time immemorial'.[77] Perhaps one could put them in fortune cookies, along with Steven Pinker's similar sub-Darwinian sack of clichés: '*Gratitude* calibrates the desire to reciprocate according to the costs and benefits of the original act' (as every worker who contributes to their boss's profit will know); 'The love of kin comes naturally; the love of non-kin does not' (as children who are sexually abused – between 75 and 80 per cent of them by their biological fathers – might mutter). Love of kin 'is the fundamental fact of the social world, steering everything from how we grow up to the rise and fall of empires and religions' (who needs history, economics, sociology?).[78] Enough! No more! This is helping no one.

When Donna Haraway presented her comprehensive history of primatology, in *Primate Visions*, paying attention to recent feminist work on female primates, it was almost universally panned by primatologists – including some self-defining feminists such as Meredith Small.[79] What would prove so controversial in Haraway's overview was not any lack of interest in the findings of primatologists, which tell us a great deal about both primate behaviour and those who study them. Her critics objected, first of all, to the attention she paid to the particular discourses, goals and assumptions which researchers bring to their study of the material world, making all scientific knowledge itself a product of that *interaction* between observers and their objects of study. They objected, even more strongly, to Haraway's questioning of the notion shared by most primatologists (whether focusing on male dominance or female bonding or anything else) that their studies provide us with knowledge about the growth and change in human societies and cultural formations, let alone a blueprint for them. Her views, however, are in agreement with those of some of the most eminent researchers in biology itself, reacting in equal horror to both the misuse of Darwin and the new 'gene talk' which some in their discipline condone or even flaunt.

Theoretical Pluralists: The Enemy Within

Although an increasingly influential group of biologists, psychologists and other social scientists have been explaining the hottest topics of the day – from mate preference and 'detection of cheaters' to violence and rape – according to the adaptations of our ancestral genes, others have been moving in a different direction. There is so much more to biology than the current prominence of evolutionary theory might suggest that it is hard to know where to begin. I have been intimating that Darwin himself should not be held responsible for all the simplifications now advanced in his name. The palaeontologist Niles Eldredge, for example, writes of the 'reinvention' of Darwin, while the leading British neurobiologist Steven Rose similarly tries to 'rescue Darwin' from his 'over-solicitous friends'.[80] Meanwhile, Gould reflects on what a very strange time it is 'to be a fundamentalist about adaptation and natural selection – when each major subdiscipline of evolutionary biology has been discovering other mechanisms as adjuncts to selection's centrality'.[81] So, before proceeding further, perhaps we need to remind ourselves that Darwin's basic insight is as uncontentious as it is remarkable – except to religious fundamentalists!

All living things have descended over many millions of years from the very simplest living matter, diversifying, flourishing and dying out, through a variety of means, only some of which have to do with genes: mutation, selection, accident and contingency. The lineage defined as *Homo sapiens* emerged in the Pleistocene age, a mere hundred thousand years ago. We all ought to be able to agree on this: whether or not we favour the orthodox Darwinian view of 'phyletic gradualism', the very slow and steady appearance of new species via 'the accumulation of innumerable slight variations' over thousands of years, favoured by Dawkins; or 'punctuated equilibrium', the sudden emergence of dramatic change following catastrophic natural events (like the Cambrian explosion, a short period between 535 and 530 million years ago, when nearly all multi-cellular animals first appear in fossil records), surrounded by huge spans of millions of years with little change at all in many fossil species – the theory favoured by Eldredge and Gould.[82] It is clear, however, that to accept the principle of extended stability or stasis as the standard situation for successful and widespread species (with between five and ten million years of equilibrium in many invertebrate species) is to mute somewhat the favoured apocalyptic sting, not to mention the short-term monetarist rhetoric, in the neo-Darwinian tale. In Britain, after the excesses of the first brood of eugenicist Darwinians hoping to improve the human race had faded into ignominy, the second generation, like J. B. S. Haldane or Julian Huxley in the 1940s, emphasized the significance of random variations and historical contingency as forces in evolution, alongside natural selection.[83] Today, the startling new enthusiasm for the idea that our gene histories determine our cultural futures occurs *despite*, not *because of*, new genetic knowledge. As another enemy of the new Darwinians, the Harvard geneticist Richard Lewontin, puzzles: 'the technical literature of evolutionary genetics has emphasized more and more the random and historically contingent nature of genetic change over time'.[84]

Dawkins sees the 'sophisticated academic left', in sinister alliance with the fundamentalist right, as sharing 'a joint opposition to the theory of evolution'. But I have yet to meet any one who had any serious quarrel with it, however 'sophisticated' their theory of truth, as always mediated through language, and its differing discourses. The conflict is not with Darwin, but with Dawkins's, and others', 'dumbing down' of

Darwin; ironically, the 'condescending and patronizing' practice he believes he has dedicated his life to combating.[85] As
many molecular biologists have noted, genes (and the gradual,
small changes which can lead them to 'mutate', or change)
are neither the *only*, and far from the *necessary*, driving forces
of evolutionary history. In Steven Rose's pithy summary of
those he calls the 'ultra-Darwinians': 'the individual gene is
not the only level at which selection occurs'; 'natural selection is not the only force driving evolutionary change'; 'organisms are not indefinitely flexible to change'; 'organisms
are not mere passive responders to selective forces but active
players in their own destiny'.[86] As discussed further in the
next section, there is no unifying principle which drives
either genetic or social change. On the one hand, tweaking a
rat's whiskers causes changes in gene expression in the sen-
sory cortex.[87] On the other, quite staggering changes in the
nature of the world have been propelled with very few, if
any, ties to genetic change. This should be immediately obvious from the fact that as humans we share 99 per cent of our
genes with primate apes. But with or without the primophilia
which might seduce us back to the bonobo at play, we would
have to agree that there is no parallel in their society to the
changes which have occurred within human culture.

Thus Stephen Jay Gould, the ogre of new evolutionary
theorists, remains close to the spirit of Darwin, despite his
erudition on the *incommensurabilities* between world history
and natural evolution: 'In an unmeasurable blink of a geologi-
cal eyelash, human cultural change has transformed the surface of our planet as no event of natural evolution could ever
accomplish at Darwinian scales of myriad generations.'[88] Human culture can always be passed on immediately to one's
heirs (biological or otherwise) in speedy and direct Lamarck-
ian fashion, while genetic evolution must move along the
inordinately slower, indirect pathways of Darwinian random
mutation, natural selection, or contingency. The central point,
made repeatedly by the critics of contemporary Darwinians
reversing the reel to explain why we are the way we are, is
that changes in genetic structure, which may survive as adaptations to particular environments, are precisely what Darwin

saw them to be: 'local adaptations'. The adaptations that may enable an organism to survive in one situation are not optimal in any general way, they will differ from those that promote survival in another. Genes which were not selected for may survive because they happen to reside alongside genes which were optimal for adaptation, or simply as by-products or co-options of features which survived as contributing to reproductive fitness. Gould and Lewontin have called these fortuitous features which emerge and flourish, though they may not themselves have contributed to genetic fitness, 'exaptations' or 'spandrels'.

Illustrating the non-adaptationist account of human mental functioning, Gould, Lewontin, Robert Brandon and many other scientific researchers have often commented that the complexity of the human brain and its extraordinary endowment, for example, was not selected for in order to enable humans to read and write (skills which emerged many centuries after the appearance of those bigger brains).[89] Rather, these skills emerged as by-products of the potential of those already evolved brains. Indeed, historical evidence supporting genuine adaptive explanations is lacking for all higher mental processes, which is what makes their postulation by evolutionary psychologists so vacuous and facile.[90] Against the fundamentalist or ultra-Darwinians, such Darwinian pluralists as Gould, Lewontin and Rose argue that what millions of years of genetic change has selected for in human species is not any single set of 'natural' rules for development ('sexual' or otherwise); rather, it has brought about the far more impressive, open and flexible trend towards ever greater complexity, ever greater adaptability: 'if biology is indeed destiny', Rose concludes, 'then that destiny is constrained freedom'.[91] Inside biology, there is a multiplicity of explanatory levels, although many within the field have constantly to battle against the publicly favoured followers of genetic foundationalism in order to point this out.

Gene Talk versus Social Change

'Thanks for the genes, Mom', young gay Americans declare on their T-shirts, or simply *'Xq28'*, the supposed location of the 'gay gene' in men.[92] *'Gene Police! You – Out of the Pool!'*, other Americans jest, in warning buttons on their lapels.[93] They are all tuned in to the new quasi-religious rhetoric coming from molecular biologists today working on the 'human genome project' (its birthplace and epicentre in the USA), seeking to map or sequence all the genetic material in the twenty-four different chromosomes to be found in human organisms. 'The Genetic Gods', as evolutionary biologist John Avise refers to genes, 'mastermind our lives . . . even our fears and aspirations'.[94] Robert Sinsheimer, one of the two biologists largely responsible for initiating the project in the mid-1980s, declares: 'For the first time in all time, a living creature understands its origin and can undertake to design its future'.[95] Another advocate for the genome project, Walter Gilbert, expounds his 'vision' of the 'Holy Grail', while fellow Nobel Prize scientist, and first director of the US government's genome project, James Watson, declares his dedication to the 'glorious goal'.[96] (It was Watson's and Francis Crick's discovery of the double-helix structure of DNA in 1953 – with the unsung assistance of Rosalind Franklin – which laid the groundwork for the rising supremacy of molecular biology in the sciences, disturbing the erstwhile dominance of physics and its massive funding for military research.) With hubristic certainty, these champions of our DNA believe that genes alone reveal 'what it is to be human', holding the key to our future – the ultimate solution to all our problems, individual and social alike.[97]

In Britain, gene talk is just as ubiquitous. In 1996 the late Hans Eysenck declared, quite falsely: 'molecular genetics . . . has enabled us to pinpoint specific gene alleles for specific emotional reactions'.[98] Not only 'depression', but even 'a disposition to experience unpleasant life events', is inherited, his methodological clone Michael Eysenck had already broadcast to the world in 1986.[99] One decade later, this startling claim is 'confirmed', once again with widespread media uptake in the British press, as Welsh psychologist Peter McGuffin claims to have located a 'gloom gene'.[100] Nowadays, it seems, there is hardly an area of human behaviour, no matter how clearly culturally diverse and complex – from good mothering to divorce or moral turpitude – that is not thrust back onto genetic foundations. Such is the force of the current cultural hegemony of genetic anti-culturalism that few people even bother to report that those who look just a little closer at the research which generates such media publicity find it not remotely conclusive.[101] Indeed, as we shall shortly see, some biologists argue that these claims only *sound* intelligible to those who already close their eyes to the complexities of the behaviour of living things (as well as to the mobilities of language and representation).

Despite the race to promote belief in the genetic control of human destiny from the 1980s, pursued aggressively by politicans and entrepreneurs in alliance with adroit stars from molecular biology, the Human Genome Project was from the beginning attacked by fellow biologists as 'bad science'. '"No, not the human genome!"', was the response of one 'distinguished biologist' whom James Watson consulted; 'as though he were talking about syphilis', Watson laments.[102] Another influential supporter of the project, James Wyngaarden, admitted in 1990: 'If you took a vote in the biological sciences on the project, it would lose overwhelmingly'.[103] Indeed, many of the most eminent US molecular geneticists in the early 1990s, like almost all those in the Harvard University Medical School, launched a national campaign attempting to halt the project as a 'waste of resources', diverting funds from far more important areas of biological research and training into premature and pointless sequencing of DNA molecules. (While state budgeting for the genome project rose fivefold between 1988 and 1990 – and was set to rise to $3 billion over the next fifteen years – there was a large decline in funding for other projects.)[104] Meanwhile, as more wealthy nations began to join in the venture of mapping the human genome, fearing to miss out on its popular scientific and industrial momentum, similar objections were raised by biologists elsewhere. Most graphically, the French newspaper *Le Figaro* portrayed its goal as one attempting 'to list the millions of letters in an encyclopedia without having the power to interpret them, ignoring all vocabulary of syntax'.[105]

Such distrust of the project was eminently rational. All biologists now know that between 90 and 95 per cent of the base pairs of DNA, being so painstakingly sequenced and entered as part of the human genome, are what is referred to as 'introns', or 'junk DNA', with *no* known function. They do not code for anything at all. 'How are you going to identify a gene if it is interspersed with so much junk?', Watson was repeatedly asked, admitting that it 'is obviously going to be hard in some cases'.[106] Hard indeed! The genome consists of more than *three billion* nucleotide base pairs on each of the twenty-three pairs of human chromosomes, which are believed to contain a mere *100,000* genes. (Genes are ordered sequences of nucleotides which actively encode for or send messages that have a specific functional outcome.) As the expert on Huntingdon's disease, Nancy Wexler explains, when looking for genetic mutations, 'What we are searching for is comparable to a fraction of an inch on the circumference of the globe!'[107]

But problems do not end there. For the 'gene' sequences which operate to encode outcomes do not form any single or discrete set, unlike the theoretical entities assumed in models of genetic transmission, referred to as genes 'for' some particular outcome. Thus, even when 'gene' sequences have been tracked down, this does not tell us anything like as much as we might hope, because they are in constant and shifting interaction with their cellular environment such that the same DNA messages have multiple functions within a single context, and have different meanings in different contexts. Genetic activity is not constant, but modified by the presence or absence of other genes in the genome, by the cellular environment, and by a multitude of external circumstances, from temperature or exposure to different metals to viral infection and the presence or absence of all manner of other social and physical environmental features. Thus the same behavioural outcome can result from quite different gene sequences. For example, as Steven Rose reports, the gene mutation creating high levels of cholesterol in the blood can result from quite divergent mutations in different people.[108] There are clearly a multitude of uncertainties in seeking the genetic origins of human behaviour.

Even if we could agree on how to identify behaviour phenotypically (itself profoundly contentious for many of the complex manifestations now thought in need of genetic explanation), the molecular underpinnings are inevitably forbiddingly convoluted. Moreover, despite genome rhetoric, 'the' composite human genome, when it eventually is sequenced as a model of a Eurasian male, will correspond to no one, as there is genetically no hypothetical average person: every human genome is unique, with any two individuals differing by as much as three million bases.

This is why trying to understand and treat even the very rare, genetically 'simple' diseases, like haemophilia, proves hugely complicated. As Lewontin notes: 'hemophiliacs differ from people whose blood clots normally by one of 208 different DNA variations, all in the same gene'. This leads him to conclude:

> The problem of telling a coherent causal story, and of then designing a therapy based on knowledge of the DNA sequence in such a case, is that we do not know *even in principle* all of the functions of the different nucleotides in a gene, or how the specific context in which a nucleotide appears may affect the way in which the cell machinery interprets the DNA; nor do we have any but the most rudimentary understanding of how a whole functioning organism is put together from its protein bits and pieces . . . [B]ecause there is no single, standard, "normal" DNA sequence that we all share, observed sequence differences between sick and well people cannot, in themselves, reveal the genetic cause of a disorder. At the least, we would need the sequences of many sick and many well people to look for common differences between sick and well. But if many diseases are like hemophilia, common differences will not be found and we will remain mystified.[109]

Lewontin, like Ruth Hubbard, Steven Rose, Hilary Rose and many others doing biological research, point to the dangers arising from the increasing popularity of DNA testing by employers, insurers and others. When patterns of transmission are unpredictable and depend upon unknown physical, social and psychological external factors, alongside complex and unstable internal cellular features, a new category of the 'potentially' ill or disabled can threaten the life chances made available to the perfectly healthy. Indeed, there are so many flaws in the vision of the human genome as supplying the ultimate causes of human behaviour that it is hardly surprising that its critics regard it as more treacherous than useful. They are not only concerned with the astronomical cost its sequencing entails, and the low probability of it generating useful knowledge, but even more with the very high probability of its abuse and misuse. Most of all, they fear that 'gene hunters' feed an ideological climate which diverts attention away from the analysis of environmental and social problems, in a deplorable repetition of the thinking and rhet-oric behind the delusions of eugenicists in the early decades of the twentieth century: inventing genes for 'nomadism', 'shiftlessness', 'pauperism' and 'criminality' to condemn the working class, immigrants and 'non-Aryans' alike.[110]

The claims we now hear almost daily, linking genes with diseases (schizophrenia, manic depression or cancer), with social failure (unemployment, risk-taking, hyperactivity, shyness, gloom), with social and sexual deviance (alcoholism, homosexuality, even bad mothering) or with general misfortune (homelessness), are all boosted by the existence of the genome project. As Ruth Hubbard and Elijah Wald remark, each misleading claim of some new gene 'for' any specific condition is given maximum media exposure, although invariably based upon tiny samples of people, and rarely replicated:

> Like mirages, many of these genes disappear when one tries to look at them closely – the claims about manic depression and schizophrenia genes were withdrawn soon after their announcement and the gene for alcoholism has met a similar fate. However, there are so many gene stories that people are left with the impression that our genes control everything.[111]

Meanwhile, the dangers of DNA testing stem not only from the uneven outcome of genetic markers, even those which have been shown to be reliably linked with disease, but from the fact that such knowledge at present bears negligible relation to possible cures. Thus knowledge of the biochemical abnormalities in sickle cell anaemia has been known for twenty-five years, with no cure in sight; just as there is no cure for Down's syndrome, Huntington's or Tay-Sachs disease. Even some of those who are strongly in favour of the Human Genome Project, such as Nancy Wexler, confess: 'For a while we may have the worst of all possible worlds – limited or no treatments, high hopes and probably unrealistic expectations, insurance repercussions – everything to challenge our inventiveness and stamina.'[112] But it is precisely a *lack* of inventiveness and stamina which genetic boosterism has encouraged: the denial of the intrinsic uncertainties and complexities in genetic transactions; and the reduction of social problems to flimsy biological speculations elevating dreams of genetic omnipotence and normalization. Such denial and reductionism was regularly flaunted by the molecular biologist David Koshland, while editor of the globally influential *Science* magazine, when the Human Genome Project was being launched around the world at the close of the 1980s as 'a new technology to aid the poor, the infirm, and the underprivileged'.[113] These were, of course, the very people in most danger of being scorned and neglected by beliefs in a genetic underclass, those who could be dismissed as the 'losers in life's genetic lottery' (in the words of the American psychologist Robert Plomin, who – most appropriately, given the hospital's origins and controversial history – was recruited in 1998 by the Maudsley Institute of Psychiatry in London).[114] Meanwhile, Hollywood, like Aldous Huxley half a century earlier, is once again depicting the dystopian potential of this new genetic order, in such films as *Gataca*.

Inverting earlier beliefs, it is now 'nature', rather than 'nurture', which has been deemed infinitely malleable in the dreams of some molecular biologists as well as their political and commercial sponsors. This is despite the billions invested in human biotechnology over the last forty years, so far producing so little in useful treatments – with the notable exceptions of the synthesis of a bacterial protein for use in haemophilia, and the engendering of the secretion of hormones in sheep which are useful for human growth.[115] As the eminent British geneticist Steve Jones admitted in 1997, the idea of curing known inherited disease by replacing DNA is a 'piece of biological hubris': 'How the DNA in a virtually formless egg is translated into an adult body remains almost a mystery'.[116] Undaunted, the conceptual shift to aggrandize the notion of 'genetic disease', and their biological elimination, continues apace, as often as not referring to psychological states which may well be *neither* genetic, *nor* diseases.[117] The latter is likely to include the persistent, unreliable and unreplicated reports of biological markers for varieties of sexual and social deviance, mental illness and suffering – the very human predicaments rendered so ambiguous under critical conceptual scrutiny only a few decades ago.

Ironically, two contradictory trends have intensified rather than resolved old clashes between culture and science, to the detriment of useful collaboration. On the one hand, the rise of cultural studies encouraged interdisciplinary efforts to blur the demarcations between distinct disciplinary sources of knowledge, strongly supported by most (but not all) feminist scholarship. It emphasized the constitutive role of language and cultural context in different areas of scientific thought and practices – with their inbuilt normative investments. On the other hand, this exacerbated a counter-trend, sometimes taking the form of direct backlash against cultural studies and feminist critique, in which the very notion of 'culture' is vanishing from the favoured conceptual framework of the social and biological sciences – evident in a trend to replace 'social' with 'life' or 'human' sciences. As Evelyn Fox Keller argues persuasively: 'in terms that increasingly dominate contemporary discourse, "culture" has become subsumed under biology.'[118] Evolutionary psychologists, as discussed above, have helped to consummate this particular disappearing act. Declaring their interest in culture or the effects of nurture on individual development, they nevertheless assume that 'culture is part of our biology'. In the view he favours, Henry

Plotkin explains that this is so 'because the traits that *cause* culture have been selected for'.[119] More elaborately, Richard Dawkins, Daniel Dennett and Susan Blakemore refer to cultural inheritance as 'memes'. As Dawkins outlines, in strict analogy with his founding category of the 'gene', a 'meme' is 'anything that replicates itself from brain to brain, via an available means of copying. . . . The genes build the hardware. The memes are the software.'[120] Responding in dismay to such reductionist axioms, Steve Jones protests: 'Just as geneticists begin to realize how far it is between DNA and organism, their subject is being hijacked. Society is, it seems, little more than the product of genes.' [121]

For Epistemic Diversity

It is this peculiar form of ideological reductionism which enables today's genetic aficionados to believe they can replace earlier eugenicist enthusiasm for population control (via brutal government-sponsored sterilization campaigns against the 'unfit' and 'degenerate') with the more fashionable emphasis on the 'free choice' of individuals. Every person has a right to 'normal' genes: 'individuals have a right to be born with a normal, adequate hereditary environment' (as if we could all agree on what that 'normal' might be, or could remain in control of our 'choices' should we allow some expert to genetically engineer it!).[122] Never before have social problems – present and future – been so mechanically translated into illusive individual responsibilities. The extraordinary presupposition is that attempts at tackling the escalating environmental pollutants which provoke disease (and genetic mutations), or the economic and social sources of rising poverty, homelessness, unemployment, crime, violence, family breakdown and mental illness, have all failed. Intervention must begin on what is now declared their true origins: genetic predispositions.

It is this doctrine which James Watson believes we will all eventually come to accept, giving thanks to those who work to produce the 'good genetic maps that allow us to locate culprit chromosomes': 'Ignoring genes is like trying to solve a murder without finding the murderer. All we have are victims.'[123] To the contrary, as Ruth Hubbard and Elijah Wald point out, the lives of many women with breast cancer, for example, might have been saved if funding had been redirected from genetic research to decreasing the levels of radiation and environmental pollutants to which people are exposed.[124] Even the discovery of cancer-triggering oncogenes, several decades ago, has not put a cure for cancer within reach. Instead, it has revealed just how complicated are the diverse processes which might transform normal cellular genes into oncogenic genes by viral infection and other external physical or chemical agents. Ironically, this is one of the few areas of genetic research where the key scientists met continual resistance from their peers, precisely because the factors affecting oncogenesis were environmental, which meant, as David Kevles explains, that their work was seen as not 'respectable genetics'.[125]

Yet searching for oncogenes, which provide one key to the mechanisms producing cancer (however externally triggered, and hence preventable by attention to the environment), is itself far less problematic than the activities of many other gene hunters. One thinks immediately of Dean Hamer, and his team of colleagues at the National Cancer Institute in Maryland in the USA, searching for a 'gay gene' marker on the X chromosome. Yet to be replicated, and facing instant technical criticism for its neglect of the genetic makeup of the non-gay brothers of its sample of men, Hamer's research is based upon a study of forty self-declared homosexual brothers (recruited through advertisements in gay publications).[126] It ignores what is probably the largest group of men who have sex with other men, at truck stops or in public toilets, those who are heterosexually married – since this would immediately put into question who is 'gay' and who is 'straight'.[127] It also leaves out lesbian sexuality which, despite and because of the dramatic rise in the visibility of such practices since the rebirth of feminism, is hardly attributable to some massive genetic mutation.[128]

The point is that attempting to reduce culture to biology,

or biology to culture, can only impoverish us all. There is not, and never could be, any single, unified project with the capacity to encompass the different levels of explanation necessary for understanding the complexity of human affairs. It is true that some who have turned of late to totalizing Darwinian or genetic visions have done so in criticism of recent cultural theorists' dismissal of the relevance of the body, and either its evolutionary history or changing biological potential. They rightly reject the idea that exploring the meanings we attach to bodily states, and their accompanying performative enactments (or psychic investments), is all we know, and all we ever need to know, about our corporeal reality. Such absolute cultural appropriation of the lifespans of any living creature is about as foolish as imagining that they are merely machines for the replication of DNA, irrespective of time and place.

One obvious illustration is the issue of human reproduction, so central in biological versus cultural contentions, for ultra-Darwinians, feminists and cultural theorists alike. The former see only sexually dimorphic adaptations for the most efficient gene dispersal. The latter, looking through the lens of culture, know that bodies are produced in particular discourses with strong normative and symbolic meanings. Thus, women's bodies are always defined by their capacity for pregnancy, even though they are reproductively infertile for significant portions of their lives, and their potential for childbearing is something women in the industrialized world choose *not* to exercise throughout most of their lives. Clearly, the gene's-eye view for maximum reproductive advantage explains next to nothing about – indeed can only distort – the complexity and variation in women's lives and experiences: why women today continue to have fewer children; why they have them later in life; why in growing numbers they raise them independently of the biological father (whether from choice or force of circumstance); why a significant minority choose not to have children at all.

However, knowing that we are not at the mercy of our genes does not mean that we can ignore women's reproductive biology. As described in the previous chapter, the body's biological capacity for impregnation can play a crucial role in the desires and fears which govern women's lives, at least some of the time. Moreover, it is not only cultural meanings, but also physiological events, which will be affected by cultural patterns, making reproductive cycles themselves culturally contingent. Thus, as the medical anthropologists Susan Sperling and Yewoubdar Beyene point out, there is no universal biological pattern for the female reproductive cycle, and hence, not even potentially, a universal biological experience. In non-industrial societies, for example, ovulation begins on average many years later than in Western countries, menopause occurs up to a decade earlier, and frequent pregnancy and prolonged lactation work to suppress the menstrual cycle. Thus while Western women now experience approximately *thirty-five* years of ovulatory cycles, late menarche, early menopause and prolonged breastfeeding mean that in non-industrial societies the menstrual cycles experienced by women are approximately only *four* years.[129] Sperling and Beyene therefore rightly emphasize the necessity of analysing the autonomous complexity of both biology and culture in reproductive studies, if we are to gain any clear understanding of how either biological plasticity, or cultural diversity, interact to produce reproductive experience. The one does not reduce to the other.

The dream that the explanation of life, from the molecular to the social, can be explained in terms of a few overarching laws returns us to the founding metaphors of Western science, three centuries ago.[130] Today, the favoured metaphor is that of the calculating machine or computer, especially endorsed by cognitive psychologists. As Donna Haraway notes: 'communications sciences and modern biologies are constructed by a common move – the translation of the world into a problem of coding, a search for a common language in which all resistance to instrumental control disappears and all heterogeneity can be submitted to disassembly, reassembly, investment and exchange'.[131] She should know. Her own imagery of the 'feminist cyborg' is one which breaks down distinctions between organism and machine, destroying identities, categories and relationships, in the hope of building 'a montrous world without gender'.[132]

We are living in an ideological climate where it seems increasingly easy to argue that we can, and we should, control biology, through claiming that individuals have a responsibility for their own genetic outcomes (despite the reality that 'the new genetics can diagnose but not treat'.)[133] On the one side, we look backwards to the 'constraints' of our genetic heritage as the determinants of our fate; on the other, we look forwards to the 'freedoms' of infinitely malleable future, once we put our faith in the hands of the new Genetic Gods. These new gods are not, in fact, genes; but rather the molecular biologists themselves who spin stories about their ability to create genetic blueprints for 'normality'. This is the vision which is currently preferred to any which might argue for political change and collective endeavour to prevent the physical and social hazards of life being increasingly unevenly distributed – not according to genetic laws, but rather in line with socio-economic principles.

A large part of the appeal of the new genetics is thus political. But it links up with another image of science especially influential in psychology. I have called this the psychologists' 'fear of the mind'. Psychologists have always oscillated between a focus on biology (including recent accounts of cerebral coding) and a focus on the environment – because human mental life is just too complex, too hard to grasp, too threatening, and the narratives of human experience too messy for the formulation of simple, clean theory. The life of the mind is quite unlike the predictable operation of a computer, however intricate its hardware or software. In the following chapters I turn to the complexities of psychic life and the engagement of feminist theory and politics with those who attempt its elucidation.

4

Psychic Life and its Scandals

We spend our time inventing true accounts for ourselves, content like professional historians to change our versions of events under the pressure of the present . . . Or we modify the angle of vision while affecting to forget that it alone determines the field which the eye will encompass, hiding what is left that another eye will settle on.

J.-B. Pontalis, *Love of Beginnings*

Whenever I tell stories of my own childhood, my most loving partner has an incorrigible tendency to laugh. 'You always look so happy in childhood photographs', he points out, correctly; as if the child striving to look winsome is always a happy one. Complicit with his response, I usually tell tales of my early life more to entertain than to elicit sympathy. They all sound so bizarre and extreme in their elaboration of interminable family conflicts, indigenous betrayals, maternal absence and paternal indifference, that it is hard not to laugh. And it is important to add that I am recalling an affluent and stable, non-abusive, two-parent family here: a not atypically selfish, casually adulterous father; his often jealous and resentful live-in mistress and housekeeper; and my overemployed, not atypically embittered, professional working mother. The three children starting out from that household would all eventually be able to find meaningful work and loving relationships, although we would never be free from the anxieties and insecurities such unhappy families implant. But then the experiences we had were never so cruel, so very much at odds with the conventions of those around us, that we lacked the words to voice them.

Tricks of Memory

How should we scrutinize our reconstructions of childhood pleasures and pains? How, in the present, do we assess the significance – let alone the accuracy – of the images out of which we piece together our personal histories, as we sift through and reshuffle fragments of the past? This is the issue at the heart of the current crisis over memory, especially in relation to child abuse and therapeutic interventions. But it fans out to embrace a panoply of problems in people's desire to understand – and in these times, an even stronger desire *not* to understand – the always complicated background to people's suffering, and their habitual, often harmful, ways. The uncertainties of memory have been used to excoriate already familiar objects of ridicule, especially Freud, although, day-to-day, any therapist from the ever-expanding empire of healers of the self will do. The new 'memoro-politics' (as they have been called) have also encouraged academic psychologists to step outside their characteristic computational rituals to pronounce on matters less trivial than the banal correlations routinely handed out to the media. Indeed, they have even been responsible for certain new alliances between experimental psychology and psychoanalysis, however provisional, where communication remains limited. At the heart of all this commotion over memory lies the continuing fall-out from charges detonated when feminists in the 1970s began to perceive and denounce the hitherto concealed or repudiated prevalence of child sexual abuse. It was from that time that women were heard and were helped as they spoke of their own recollections of abuse – most often, incestuous abuse inside the family, with fathers or step-fathers as the perpetrators.

Mindful of the social and political dynamics at play, and especially the backlash against feminist achievements, I want to ponder here the difficulties surrounding any exploration of the psychological arena in the understanding of human affairs. Psychic life is always intrinsically problematic, as that unique and autonomous domain only knowable, even to its subjects, via the narratives and discourses available to make sense of it. Subjective concerns are not supposed to inform the theoretical work or conceptual innovation of scientists, who like to believe that they can, indeed that they must, remain quite detached from the objects which they study and the methods they employ. But for those scientific observers who are also psychologists, this is a rather extraordinary constraint. 'Psychologists', as one of its recently acclaimed cognitive heroes likes to boast, 'don't study their own minds; they study someone else's'.[1] Yet, it is self-knowledge and the understanding of individual human actions which is supposedly the object of their disciplinary pursuit. Autobiographical material might therefore be thought to provide one of the richest sources we have to understand the strange complexities of the interaction between 'internal' and 'external' realities. Indeed, rather than requiring elimination as quintessentially unreliable or biased, autobiographical reflection could prove all the richer precisely for being, at any one time, so easily called into question, and in constant need of rethinking.

Like all aspects of experience, memory depends upon wider cultural understandings, which themselves shift over time: 'Life is lived forward but it is understood backwards', to use Kierkegaard's much cited aphorism.[2] Our own most cherished conceits, stubborn evasions or persistent illusions are all fashioned by a growing stock of cultural narratives, as we try to make sense of the past and its connections to our lives in the present. This, it seems to me, is what we need to study, not seek to evade. And this is why I see the appraisal of personal memories as one of the most important guides for thinking about psychological enquiry, in much the same way that such reflection inspired the most persistingly influential writer on human existence in modern times, Sigmund Freud. It was Freud's perpetual self-exploration which, for better or for worse, provided the framework for those in search of deeper psychological understanding of themselves over the subsequent hundred years; at least, those who could most freely choose and afford what they felt they needed, when seeking relief from intense personal miseries.

Meanwhile, the most culturally ubiquitous narrative available for explaining all manner of social problems and individual failures and misfortunes today focuses upon the fate of the helpless and vulnerable child within the bad or abusive family. From popular television to the ceaseless production of self-help manuals in the Western world, stories of child abuse within dysfunctional families introduce one of the central moral tales of our time. However, fundamental as this story has become, it is surrounded by professional controversy and dissent, with some leading psychologists putting their authority behind its complete irrelevance: 'There is evidence that neither sexual abuse nor other forms of childhood trauma damage the adult personality', the late and highly respected cognitive psychologist Stuart Sutherland used to proclaim, adding that any talk of 'repressed' or 'recovered' memories of abuse 'defies everything that is known about memory and trauma'.[3] Younger psychologists, with much the same message, follow in the footsteps of mentors like Eysenck and Sutherland, finding brief media prominence with publications dismissing the significance of parental influence and early family experience – as exemplified in the fanfare around Judith Harris's *The Nature Assumption* (1998).[4]

In contrast, the British Psychological Society, consulting its clinical members, has published a special report endorsing the existence and the significance of 'repressed' memories of childhood abuse: 'There are high levels of belief in the essential accuracy of recovered memories of child sexual abuse among qualified psychologists' [*sic*].[5] (This is presumably their ungrammatical way of affirming the beliefs of psychologists, rather than public belief in psychologists' personal histories of abuse.) The American Psychiatric Association has gone further, supporting a notion of the repression of whole psychological formations, or of amnesia associated with distinct 'personalities', resulting from childhood abuse; this was ratified as Multiple Personality Disorder in the *Diagnostic and Statistical Manual of Mental Disorders* (DSM-III) in 1980 and later reclassified as Dissociative Identity Disorder in DSM-1V.[6]

These battles over the significance of childhood trauma and the nature of memory are not only staged in the academy, the clinic and the media, they are also increasingly fought out in law courts and legislative bodies around the world. In the courts and in their aftermath, further difficulties arise as the framework of legal discourses is mapped onto the more precarious and provisional translations of the past into the present in clinical discourses.

Dilemmas of Science

The contemporary focus on the child is itself, to some extent, a testimony to the enormous significance of Freud for the culture and imagination of twentieth-century Western thought. It was Freud, of course, who most strongly insisted that as adults we are never as free as we would like to think from the often destructive residues of infantile fears, anxieties and longings. But this also means that we are never as rational as we would like to think, and that the line between impartial observation and the driving force of fantasy can be a blurred and broken one. Just as childhood intrudes into adulthood, fantasy fuels not only personal perceptions, but also shared constructions of reality. 'You only start seeing', as Jacqueline Rose condenses Freud's most basic message, 'when you know that your vision is troubled, fallible, off-key'.[7] However, psychoanalysis has remained at the margins of academic debates in psychology, and for some time now there has been a renewed assault by a formidable range of philosophers, historians and critics on Freud's 'fraudulence' and 'fakery', with his work destined, in Frederick Crews's recent emotive indictments, for 'history's ashcan'.[8] Interestingly, it is the continuing resonance of much of Freud's conceptual framework with the less reductive aspects of familiar cultural wisdom, itself derided in the cognitive sciences as 'folk psychology', which encourages its repeated repudiation within the academy, especially within psychology and psychiatry. Yet it is this congruence with the paradoxes of lived experience which motivated its rehabilitation within significant strands of feminist scholarship, especially in the humanities.

Much of the allure of psychoanalysis (its distinctiveness for its more sophisticated sympathizers) is its embrace of contradiction and conflict as central to human existence. Much of the scandal of psychoanalysis (for its closest and harshest critics, in mainstream psychology) is this same ingredient of contradiction and paradox. This puzzling complexity mocks psychologist's supposedly dispassionate construction of rational and orderly mechanistic models of mental functioning and their insistence upon computational methods for studying its outcomes. As Jerome Bruner, among others, frequently laments, no sooner had psychologists in the late 1950s begun to reverse their hitherto impoverished behaviouristic elimination of reference to mental states and cultural contexts than their new cognitive frameworks themselves began to rigidify. Having previously confined themselves to the diligent quantification of patterns of physical stimulus and response, the new 'cognitive revolution' briefly allowed academic psychologists the freedom to conceptualize the life of the mind, only to encourage them, all too soon, to bypass once again the culturally fluid and uniquely flexible human creative capacities for 'meaning-making'. Instead, cognitive psychology substituted new mechanistic models of universality in a language full of highly technical, strictly computational metaphors of 'information-processing'.[9] The recent addition of Darwinian perspectives further encourages the construction of grandiose conceptual frameworks for generating context-free, speculative totalizations.[10]

Meanwhile, the fact that contradiction and paradox is something psychoanalytic reflection shares with much of what we would call 'common sense' fuels the fire of its detractors, even as it encourages its supporters. As Freud noted in 1909, when writing his preface to the second edition of the single most influential psychoanalytic text, *The Interpretation of Dreams*, his work would be 'doomed to be sunk into complete silence' were its impact to depend upon 'the attitude adopted by reviewers in the scientific periodicals' (whether of his own day, or ours) rather than its usefulness to its 'educated and curious-minded readers'.[11] Interestingly, this book, with its 'incalculable influence on modern consciousness', as Laura Marcus notes, sold only 351 copies in its first six years.[12]

The rejection of its scientific credentials was in line with the positivistic principle that psychology could only assert its claims as a science once it could distance itself definitively from the open-ended ambivalences to be found in 'folk psychology' or common sense: the inconsistencies and contradictions in people's perceptions or beliefs must be eliminated from the conceptual language of science. Instead, psychologists must present simple, certain truths which can be exactly measured and quantified.

It has often been noted that it is the experimental methods themselves which have generally dictated research in psychology. Yet, as Michael Billig and other more sceptical social psychologists have illustrated in their own fields of enquiry, 'far from anything being made more orderly', social psychologists have produced 'a sprawling mass of conflicting principles and research findings'.[13] From his own discipline (anthropology), Clifford Geertz had long since analysed the scientific dilemma facing psychologists. With seductive self-restraint, he pointed out time and again that any attempt to understand the social lives of human beings – who live in history and have the capacity for language, intentions, visions, memories, hopes and passions – is unlikely to succeed if presented in terms of 'objectivized variables set in systems of closed causality'.[14] Geertz is one of the main figures pioneering recent interpretative anthropology. His inspiring memoir, covering four decades of research, elegantly illustrates how the quest for what we really want to know about people – why they do what they do – tends to escape the dexterities of method undertaken in the pursuit of precise objective formulations. The attempt to predict and control human behaviour is not one which orientates us in the direction of understanding it.

Certainly, on that heated topic of the moment, the nature and significance of memories of child abuse, we find that academic psychology has played almost no role in its contemporary prominence. Freud, however, has been held *responsible* for it; responsible, moreover, as prime mover of its historical denial *and* as the undeniable author of presumptions of its contemporary prevalence. Whether seen as shrouding it in secrecy, or flaunted as fashionable fiction, Freud is to blame both for the cultural disavowal *and* the professional ratification of child sexual abuse. How could this have happened?

Troubled Vision

Let us look at a vignette from life in a public school in Britain in the 1950s. 'Do you think I'm a pederast?', Paul Foot recalls being asked by Anthony Chenevix-Trench, his eminent housemaster at Shrewsbury public school. Chenevix-Trench, who quickly rose to claim the job of headmaster at Britain's most prestigious school, Eton, was relaxing after another of his regular beatings of adolescent boys, with leather strap on bare bottoms. Few of his younger pupils could hope to escape such humiliating chastisement for mistakes in their Greek translation, punishments joyfully delivered behind closed doors. Perhaps Chenevix-Trench was genuinely unsure of the nature of his 'perversion', exhibiting that strange but far from unfamiliar state of mind which Freud was to make central to his account of psychic life, when we both know and do not know something about ourselves, or others, at the same time: 'Do you think I'm a pederast?' 'Yes, indeed', a chorus of voices would immediately respond to the self-generated suspicions of any such exalted sadist today.

It is possible that Chenevix-Trench was genuinely unsure whether his behaviour was abusive. He apparently gained sexual pleasure not from acts of sodomy, but from causing pain on the exposed flesh of his younger pupils – and, of course, maybe it did belt into them a firmer knowledge of ancient Greek, in keeping with the proclaimed goal of the exercise. As Adam Mars-Jones comments, it is harder to be quite so 'unknowing' nowadays: 'The moment it becomes possible to consider such behaviour other than in terms of manly spontaneity, then it's all up with the innocent beating, weeping and kissing'. Mars-Jones was reviewing Christopher Hibbert's book *No Ordinary Place: Radley College and the Public School*, where he explains that in the 1950s: 'Weeping and kissing a boy after beating him would not then have been considered so sexually dubious as it would today'.[15] There's progress, most would agree. But, even today, some are not as discerning as others, and seem to remain no less confused than Chenevix-Trench himself, although we are supposedly far wiser about the nature and problem of paedophilia and child abuse. Indeed, Chenevix-Trench (to Foot's deep disgust) remains a hero; a hero, it is important to note, not for libertarian sex radicals proud to be sado-masochist, but rather for the self-righteous moralists of our time who, like his biographer Mark Peel, want to celebrate that particular teacher's battle against 'drift and complacency', and still cherish the use of the cane.[16]

Without any doubt, it is Freud's descriptive categories – in these times as much the common sense of cultural critics like Mars-Jones as it is baloney to disciplinarians like Mark Peel (and many academic psychologists) – which remove the 'innocence' from these 'manly' beatings and explain their perpetrators' defensive connection to their own behaviour. Freudian reflections point us towards the conscious disavowal of what one unconsciously knows, and the widespread unconscious denial, displacement, and a projection of a sense of one's own wrong-doing into the punitive punishment of others, especially when it allows some disguised expression of repressed sexual pleasure. It is the language of psychoanalysis which resonates with and helps inform what cultural wisdom we have about what is more popularly called the 'blindness of the seeing eye'. Freud communicated a way of thinking about how we are able to deceive ourselves and others via a principled and vigorous passion far in excess of any conscious attempt to mislead. Indeed, to be 'knowing', in Western culture, usually means to have picked up something of Freud's legacy.

Feminist Denunciations

Nevertheless, it is important to be clear that it was not psychoanalysts but feminists who brought to prominence, and demanded action against, the hidden and horrific reality of child sexual abuse in the 1970s. Contrary to the disinterested status ascribed to and claimed by scientists and (somewhat less successfully) clinicians, it took a political movement to refocus scholarly attention on the significance of narratives of child sexual abuse. Moreover, it was Freud whom many feminists blamed for keeping the prevalence of child sexual abuse buried for so long. The volatile and contradictory relations between feminism and psychoanalysis provide both a telling instance of the ambivalence of Freud's legacy, and the selective uses made of his conceptual framework. As explored further in chapter 6, it was used, most often, to underwrite existing gender hierarchies and normative regimes; only sometimes, more subversively, to suggest their inevitable fissures and fragility. Accordingly, the cultural impact of the feminist attack on psychoanalysis, in this instance for falsifying women's experience of sexual abuse, has been shadowed by a somewhat more elite feminist emphasis on the necessity of returning to Freud.

Some feminists, especially in the USA, such as Florence Rush in the 1970s, accused Freud of making the sexual abuse of children 'the best-kept secret in the world'.[17] Rush's essay was part of a profound and abiding cultural consciousness-raising around the criminal extent of child sexual abuse, which helped inspire feminist campaigning against the appalling neglect of such practices.[18] (This was several years before the commercial media and the psychoanalytic profession itself began to suggest the extent and tragic effects of child sexual abuse, after publications by Alice Miller and Jeffrey Masson the following decade.)[19] The feminist assault on Freud built upon Susan Brownmiller's historical survey of rape, *Against our Will* (1976), in which she had claimed that only with the advent of Freud had 'the male ideology of rape began to rely on the tenet that rape was something women desired'.[20] Meanwhile, in stark contrast with such denunciations, feminists such as Juliet Mitchell in Britain were appropriating Freud as essential for any understanding of the nature and psychology of sexual difference.

What was so significant about the beginnings of psychoanalysis in the 1890s was that Freud was listening very carefully, and uniquely sympathetically, to the stories of his predominantly female patients. He saw them as maligned by contemporary medical science (as in the views held by his mentor, Jean-Martin Charcot), which attributed their symptoms to hereditary degeneracy. Freud's early patients suffered from a diversity of painful physical and emotional symptoms which, insofar as they were seen as having no organic basis, were attributed to the psychical disorder of 'hysteria'.[21] The tales these women told when encouraged to elaborate upon whatever thoughts came to mind, often involving disturbingly precocious sexual encounters with adults (and especially fathers), led Freud to speculate upon, and search for evidence of, a 'seduction' theory of neurosis: the idea that sexual assaults in childhood provided the original trauma paving the way for neurosis in later life.

However, as Freud developed the foundations of psychoanalytic theory his paradigm case was, primarily, his own self-analysis – as in *The Interpretation of Dreams*. This led him to the further elaboration of unconscious mechanisms, the assumption of autonomous infantile sexuality and, in particular, the traumatic acquisition of sexual difference as mediated through the intense family drama embodying the Oedipus complex: the earliest desires, repressions and identifications connected with the first objects of love, fear and frustration – the parents. Again, it is important to notice that much of the strength and influence of psychoanalytic insight into mental suffering comes from the fact that Freud relied upon (and insisted his followers use) *self*-understanding as the route to comprehending the symptoms of others, in radical contrast with the psychiatric tradition which has always emphasized the alien or abnormal nature of mental illness. Nevertheless, it should come as no surprise that Freud's account of psychosexual development and sexual difference both reflects and reproduces the pervasive cultural phallocentrism of Western thought, encoding men's intense anxieties over the acquisition of 'masculinity'. Despite seeing women as the victims of this culture, and despite his deep sympathy for, and at times identification with, the hysterical symptoms of his female patients, Freud remained largely uncritical of the various male-dominated institutions which fuel what he described as boys' fear and repudiation of 'femininity' ('castration anxiety'), and girls' envy of the attributes of 'masculinity' ('penis envy'), in the classic Oedipal narrative.

Freud's theories thus reflect the psychological effects of the patriarchal, androcentric fantasies and logic of his time which, though now fiercely contested, still connect with the hierarchical structures and symbolisms of our own. All the same, if we are seeking individual targets to blame for the historical neglect of child sexual abuse, Freud is far from the most rational of choices. This is not only because his thoughts help us interpret the complex and muddied nature of psychic life, with its unpredictable, usually disavowed relation to interpersonal and cultural abuses of all sorts, but because most of the charges against him, in this instance, are largely inaccurate or confused.

Fantasy versus Trauma

Freud's female patients did not come to him complaining of having been sexually abused, only to have Freud deny their abusive memories. Rather, it was Freud himself who tried to convince his patients of the truth of his own 'seduction theory', and they who, he claimed, repudiated it.[22] Although patients provided highly charged accounts of incestuous experience in childhood, Freud wrote that they would emphasize that 'they have no feeling of remembering the scenes'. Ironically, in terms of the later insistence by his feminist critics that Freud deliberately chose to ignore or distort his patients' knowledge that they had been sexually abused, it was these patients' withholding of *their* belief in *his* suspicions of actual seduction which he at first took as their confirmation: 'This latter piece of behaviour seems to provide conclusive proof. Why should patients assure me so emphatically of their unbelief, if what they want to discredit is something which – from whatever motive – they themselves have invented?'[23]

Moreover, contrary to the accusations made by Rush or Masson's *Assault on Truth: Freud's Suppression of the Seduction*

Theory, Freud did not suddenly abandon his 'seduction theory' in 1897 – despite expressing his private doubts to his friend the Berlin physician Wilhelm Fliess in that year, and despite autobiographical reconstructions many years later. Nor was Freud's move towards the assertion of autonomous child-hood sexuality and fantasy life (as Masson suggests, although Rush does not) merely a cowardly attempt to gain profes-sional approval from medical colleagues. His next theoretical move, Freud himself seemed to believe, was no less unpopu-lar: 'Few of the findings of psycho-analysis have met with such universal contradiction or have aroused such an out-burst of indignation as the assertion that the sexual function starts at the beginning of life and reveals its presence by im-portant signs in childhood'.[24] In subsequent work Freud con-tinued to refer in different ways to the harmful effects of 'seduction', writing as late as 1931, in his essay 'Female Sexu-ality': 'Actual seduction, too, is common enough. . . . Where [it] intervenes it invariably disturbs the natural course of the developmental processses, and it often leaves behind exten-sive and lasting consequences'. Although, it is true, as well as suspicious, that he no longer pointed to fathers as the most likely initiators, but to 'other children' or 'someone in charge of the child'.[25]

Surveying all of Freud's writings when researching their dictionary of psychoanalysis, Laplanche and Pontalis argue that even with his evolving framework of autonomous infan-tile sexuality, Freud 'continued to assert the existence, preva-lence and pathogenic force of scenes of seduction actually experienced by children'.[26] As many others have noticed, years after he came to believe that neurotic symptoms and memo-ries of early sexual experience stemmed from psychical real-ity and unconscious fantasy, rather than from some single (or repeated) traumatic event, Freud also accepted his patients' accounts of actual seduction and abuse alongside his own emphasis on the significance of sexual *desires* in childhood. Nevertheless, one would have to agree that his interest was always in the way external events become invested with fan-tasy, rather than in the traumatic events themselves, seeing the former as the crucial issue for therapy: 'up to the present we have not succeeded in pointing to any difference in the consequences, whether phantasy or reality has had the greater share in these events', Freud wrote in 1916, referring to stories of childhood seduction involving the father.[27]

However, Freud's own conceptual ambivalence and uncertainties, as he felt he must *choose* between autonomous psychic life and external trauma, has not prevented many other analysts from suggesting that there is no essential contradiction between attributing adult symptoms to a destructive mix of the two – 'real' and fantasized events. Indeed, in distinctively psychoanalytic mode, Laplanche has argued compellingly that *all* material experiences are immediately invested with, and continuously worked and reworked through, psychic fantasy. Ironically, it is only those, like Masson, who broadcast Freud's 'betrayal' of women and children, who today feel that they still must *choose* between psychic life and trauma: reducing the complex and harmful effects of childhood cruelty and abuse simply to truths in need of validation, or their enforced suppression. Writing of Freud's analysis of the bizarre, paranoid fantasies of Daniel Paul Schreber, a man who had been physically abused by his rigidly disciplinarian father, and whose chief delusion during his psychotic breakdown was that he had to change, and was indeed changing, into a woman as a way of redeeming the world, Masson remonstrates: 'he analysed Schreber's *so-called delusions* on the basis of unconscious homosexual longings for his father, instead of on that father's sadistic physical manipulations of the young boy, and so on'.[28] So-called delusions! Masson seems seriously to believe that a father's physical sadism would have no psychic consequences, other than to create a need for the abused person to be allowed to tell his or her story, and have it believed. Thus he writes:

> I cannot think of a better therapy than exposing the inadequacies of therapy itself. Politicizing oneself by joining with other survivors in political actions is an excellent antidote to the powerlessness that psychiatry induces in its subjects. Becoming active in the struggle against psychiatry (and other forms of injustice) even in one's own mind, is a good alternative

to the helplessness that psychiatry encourages in patients. Writing up one's own story, even if only for the instruction of other friends, especially if nothing is omitted, is to offer people the other side of the official story.[29]

In fact, writing up his own story and thereby displaying his tragic delusional system was precisely what Schreber *was* doing in his *Memoirs of my Nervous Illness*, about which Freud was writing. Even if a 'survivors' group had somehow, anachronistically, presented itself to the very eminent Judge Schreber (who had been a highly respected lawyer and judge before his breakdown), one suspects that he could have made little use of it.

A century later, many psychotherapists are working hard with the memories and fantasies of patients who have been seriously abused, some of them tracing the origins of diverse mental disorders directly to traumas of early childhood, others seeing a more nuanced interaction. The former, like Judith Herman, are more likely to be committed to the restorative power of 'telling the truth' about the past, if patients are to be helped to gain a 'newly liberated capacity for imagination and fantasy'.[30] The latter are more concerned with simply listening to and helping to liberate patients from their destructive entrapment in narratives about the past, and less concerned with uncovering the 'facts' of the case. Like Lacan, they may even suggest that when the patient recalls events from the past in analysis: '[T]he stress is always placed more on the side of reconstruction than on that of reliving, in the sense we have grown used to calling *affective*. . . . What is essential is reconstruction. . . . I would say – when all is said and done, it is less a matter of remembering than of rewriting history.[31] However, no clinician, ever, is going to accuse his or her patients of telling untruths or lies about the past.

So why the fixation on the omissions of Freud? Part of the reason is simply the absorption of banalized Freudian notions into the superficial mix of the Western vernacular – we can all cite its 'scripture' to our own purposes. Indeed, with its highlighting of familial combat, infantile sexuality and congenital aggression, there is little to match it. Freud's theories are constantly taken up and adapted to the milieu in which they are used. With or without Freud, however, one thing which any society never wants to acknowledge is the regular occurrence of institutionalized forms of violence and abuse by the powerful against the vulnerable, most especially when it involves the sexual abuse of men's ideologically sanctioned power over women and children inside the family. It is certain that Freud's account of autonomous infantile sexuality helped some people, always more than ready to ignore or to rationalize away the horror of child sexual abuse, both within and without psychoanalytic institutions. I do not doubt earlier feminist accounts of the many supposedly therapeutic institutions and practitioners who have downplayed or dismissed the effects of child sexual abuse, perhaps in the name of Freud. This remains probable, despite surveys which suggest that Anna Freud, Donald Winnicott and other leading psychoanalysts of the mid-twentieth century were among the few observers who *did* write about such abuse and its destructive effects.[32] At the time, Anna Freud and those calling themselves the 'Freudians', most prominently Edward Glover, were always careful to distinguish between reality-oriented and primarily fantasy-originating images of objects. This was in contrast with Melanie Klein, and the 'Kleinians', who saw the influence of instinctually driven 'phantasy' in all perceptions of reality – leading some to accuse them of ignoring the influence of 'real events' in their patients' lives.[33] Indeed, it was empirical researchers of the time, such as Simon Weinberg in his *Incest Behavior* (1955), who, though *rejecting* Freud as unscientific, were more likely to insist that child sexual abuse was an extremely rare occurrence.[34]

Undoubtedly, it took the sea-change of resurgent feminism for therapists in general, and the population at large, to hear and begin to act upon accounts of children's sexual exploitation and abuse – mostly through adult memories of childhood sexual trauma. Probably, it took this change for women to find the words, and have the confidence, to *tell* such stories. (Although significant numbers of boys are sexually abused, the majority of 'victims' or 'survivors' that we hear about are still women, while their abusers, overwhelmingly, are men.[35])

Nonetheless, it is now often through the tools of psychoanalytic therapy that the most moving accounts of child sexual
abuse are recalled or 'recovered', as in Sylvia Fraser's *In my
Father's House*.[36]

Contrary to an earlier feminist approach in the 1970s, which
tended to dismiss the Freudian belief in the need to work
with unconscious material, feminist therapists now trying to
heal the sexually abused all emphasize the inaccessibility of
memories of early trauma. Speaking from over two decades
of work with sexually abused children at the Tavistock Clinic
in London, Judith Trowell emphasizes the regular distortion
of experience which occurs following such abuse. She understands this as a resort to unconscious defence mechanisms of
disavowal, displacement and, in particular, dissociation, leading to the overall 'dampening down' of fantasy in sexually
abused children (or adults who were once sexually abused),
as they attempt to rid themselves of unbearable memories:
'they are lifeless, flat, avoidant, and have psychogenic amnesia'.[37] Similarly, Valerie Sinason, perhaps the best-known British psychoanalytic psychotherapist currently working on child
sexual abuse, writes of the confusing mixture of fantasy and
reality found in survivors of abuse: 'Tragically, then, it is precisely those individuals who have been traumatized most who
are the most likely to include distortions in their narrative.'[38]

Remarkably, in recent rotations of the conflictual relations
between psychoanalysis and culture, when Freudians are not
being accused of ignoring child abuse, they are being accused
of inventing or exaggerating it. We are now witnessing a new
backlash against Freud, fronted by Frederick Crews (ironically in the same media outlet as Masson's denunciation a
decade earlier), to argue the reverse of the Rush/Masson thesis: 'It was Freud himself who taught both his followers and
his adversaries to take the seduction narratives seriously as
productions of his patients'.[39] Again just like Rush and Masson,
but in the opposite direction, Crews continues to excoriate
Freud for the fact that 'a number of parents and child-care
providers are serving long prison terms . . . on the basis of
therapeutically induced "memories" of child sexual abuse that
never in fact occurred. . . . [T]he tradition of Freudian theory

and practice unmistakably lies behind their tragic deception of both patients and jurors'.[40] Unmistakably? You may rest assured! Many of his compatriots are keen to amplify Crews's latest onslaught: 'Freud did to the unconscious mind with his theories what New York does to the ocean with its garbage'.[41] Freud had described children's primitive anxieties about adult sexuality (referring to the 'primal scene' of parental genital penetration) as intrinsically disturbing; no less, it seems, adults in our culture still regard his theories of childhood sexuality as intrinsically disturbing.[42] As the eminent New York analyst Kurt Eissler wearily noted shortly before his death in 1999: 'No one is interested if you write positively about Freud, but as soon as you write negatively everybody applauds'.[43]

Perhaps we should treat this continued fear and loathing of Freud as merely comic, with its attempt to eradicate his influence by whatever contradictory means provide suitably sensationalized stories; except that we are usually dealing with tragic matters. Organizations to prevent 'Crimes against Children' (with their 'Believe the Child' bumper stickers) are now confronted by the 'False Memory Syndrome Foundation' (claiming to have 10,000 families on their lists of those who have been victims of false allegations of abuse). As the two currently take their battles into the courtrooms of the USA, 'memoro-politics' is becoming one of the most passionate topics of the day.[44] Add to this conflagration the newly emerging third category of 'retractors', who come to denounce their families through therapy, only later to abjure the charges, and ever more people are being forced to start thinking very seriously indeed about the difficult topic of memory.

Models of Memory

What is memory? There have been three main sources of knowledge of human memory in over a century of scientific reflection: behavioural research on memory (from Hermann Ebbinghaus's study, tellingly, of the recall of nonsense syllables in the 1880s, to the computer modelling of memory processes in the cognitive sciences today); neurological studies of brain localization; and psychodynamic approaches (which owe something to Freud). Of these, however, it is only the psychodynamic approach which has influenced people's own stories about themselves.[45] 'Freud transformed Western consciousness more surely than the atomic bomb or the welfare state', Ian Hacking concludes from his exhaustive overview of the cultural impact of shifting notions of consciousness from the turn of the century.[46] This is because the concepts of memory derived from the first two traditions, on their own, tell us next to nothing about the specific contexts or often troubling contents of human practices of remembering. Memories present themselves through narratives that make sense in the present, modifying individual events and assigning them different meanings at different times.

Psychologists, in the footsteps of Ebbinghaus, set out to study what they saw as 'pure' memory in the laboratory, memorizing sequences (like nonsense syllables) in order to avoid 'contamination' from factors like meaning, affect, significance and context – the very essence of memory. The alternative tradition of Frederick Bartlett,[47] which had analysed memory as a social practice in the 1930s, was soon sidelined, provoking the anthropologist Mary Douglas to observe: 'psychologists are institutionally incapable of remembering that humans are social beings. As soon as they know it, they forget it'.[48] In tune with Douglas, the neuroscientists Gerald Edelman and Steven Rose have recently criticized the reductionist tendencies in their own discipline, which have sought to pin down the locations and molecular structure of memory processes in the brain. They have each illustrated that the recent findings of neuroscience rule out any mechanistic model of the brain: 'Given the diversity of the repertoires of the brain, it is extremely unlikely', Edelman writes, 'that any two selective events, even apparently identical ones, would have identical consequences . . . The mixture of events is individual and, in large measure, unpredictable'.[49] Human memory, they both agree, has an intrinsically collective and social dimension, requiring models of the brain which introduce creativity and indeterminacy: 'whilst for each of us the experience of collective memory is an individual biological and psychological one', Rose concludes, 'its existence serves purposes which transcend the individual, welding together human societies by imposing shared understandings, interpretations, ideologies'.[50]

Nevertheless, with the public clamour child sexual abuse has generated, there has been something of a rapprochement between the formerly conflicting traditions of academic psychology and psychoanalysis. The former favours mechanistic models of memory, from computers to filing cabinets; the latter, narrative construction and reconstruction, in highly charged emotional contexts.[51] Parallels between experimental research on memory and contemporary psychoanalytic perspectives are easy to make, at least superficially. Although there are disagreements between the memory researchers, they have repeatedly shown that memory is unreliable. In their overview of research, published in 1997, Daniel Schacter and his co-workers conclude: 'An enormous body of results from cognitive psychology and cognitive neuroscience demonstrate that memories are vulnerable to distortion, and that confidence and vividness do not always go hand in hand with accuracy'.[52] For example, in her well-known experiments Elizabeth Loftus and her co-workers found that it was relatively easy to use suggestion to induce 'false memory', or inaccurate recall, in both children and adults. In one study, subjects were made to believe that they had been lost in a shopping mall when young; in other studies researchers have been able to establish that the contents of reports about the same memory differ from one occasion to the next.[53] Cognitive research also suggests that experiences which are not talked about are more likely to be forgotten. In the technical language of cognitive psychology: 'memory construction is mediated by control processes which vary from one recall to the next and use different cues to probe autobiographical knowledge on different occasions of retrieval'.[54]

Loftus has used her results to argue that adults do not forget traumatic events, like sexual abuse, although they may have periods when they do not recall them.[55] But other cognitive researchers, like Lenore Terr, have suggested that memories for trauma may be 'encoded' in ways that make it harder to recall, although researchers are unclear about the mechanisms involved.[56] Psychologists agree that nothing can be recalled accurately before the first birthday, little before the second, and that poor memory from before the fourth birthday is normal.[57] However, despite the lack of verbal recall from early childhood, seen as largely due to the absence of language, some researchers, like Terr, have reported that children have ways of re-enacting their traumatic experiences.[58] Overall, it is hard to fault the general conclusion from academic psychology that: 'Some recovered memories may be essentially accurate, some may be largely inaccurate but nonetheless partially based on experiences of the individuals other than actual abuse (for example, imagined abuse, or situations involving emotional abuse), and still others wholly inaccurate'.[59]

Nevertheless, there are critical differences between the two traditions. Psychological research is interested in cognitive frameworks which are decontextualized and universal, not specific and embodied: exploring memory for discrete events, usually in unfamiliar settings, over relatively short periods of time. The pyschoanalytic notions of trauma and deferred action do not reduce to that of impressions which cannot be meaningfully encoded. As Erica Burman comments: 'Concern with providing a psychological explanation for the possibility of unconscious memories is not the same as indicating anything of the motives for its repression or the structure of the psychic apparatus involved'.[60] Neither cognitive science, nor the rapidly advancing research in neuropsychology, have anything to say about individual life histories or the particularities of language and shared cultural narratives through which they are constructed. Indeed, if psychoanalysts have hoped to gain greater scientific respectability for their theories by aligning themselves with cognitive frameworks and neuropsychology, at least some of the latter have seen the need to engage with psychotherapeutic reflection to connect with any issues of significance in the public domain. Commenting on the limitations of their cognitive discourses, Martin Conway writes: 'although they describe or foreshadow cognitive mechanisms of memory they imply little about when or why such mechanisms are used', adding, 'psychodynam-ically meaningful situations can rarely (if ever) be created and controlled in a way acceptable to an experimenter'.[61]

Even the manner in which the recovered memory debate is conceptualized remains distinct in the competing perspect-ives. For academic psychology, prediction remains the funda-mental problem. People must be clustered into types of individuals, or events into types of events, in order to make them statistically useful, for example, 'to predict who would repress and who would not'.[62] For the psychoanalyst, predic-tion is never the issue. The problem resides in the attempt to understand, not to predict, human behaviour through per-sistent attention to the open-ended stories of a lifetime of precariously maintained repressed material, attempting to make sense of desires which insert themselves into conscious-ness and manifest themselves in behaviour, only to be re-pressed, and yet resurface all over again. The issue here is thus not so much whether any event has been remembered or forgotten ('encoded', or not), but of trying to see the way in which we memorialize the past through fantasy or imagi-nation and in the patterns of behaviour we repeat.

Memory as Narrative

The reigning idea in the cognitive sciences since the 1960s, of memory as a storage and retrieval system along the lines of a filing cabinet or computer, thus seriously distorts the nature of human memory. When we recall the past, however recent or distant, we recall events. An occurrence is recalled as an event only when it becomes part of a narrative, something which moves the narrative forward, as the philosopher Paul Ricoeur exhaustively analyses in his three-volume *Time and Narrative*.[63] It is this theoretical understanding of memory, as a cultural construction in the present, which is also em-phasized by Ian Hacking, who concludes his history of the scientific study of memory by underlining the inevitable in-determinacy in people's attempts to describe their own past. Memory is always revised, retroactively. The so-called 'flashback' experience often reported by abuse survivors, for example, is no more likely to be a 'true' picture of the past than any other memory. We weave stories about the past from what we call memories, Hacking amplifies: 'They must mesh with the rest of the world and with other people's stories, at least in externals, but their role is in the creation of a life, a character, a self'; he recognizes that Freud was well aware of this aspect of memory from 'quite early in his career'.[64] However, no Freudian loyalist (being more attuned to Foucauldian scepticism), Hacking, in yet another twist to accepted censure, criticizes Freud for his *relentless truth-seeking*; this may not always have been successful (which seems likely), nor in the best interests of his patients, who may have been better off without the 'truth' (which to many might seem less likely).

Freudian accounts of memory, stressing meaning, affect and hidden significance, are clearly more in tune with notions of memory as narrative. However, recent accounts of memory also suggest something of the historical limitations of psychoanalysis: its failure to focus on the historical conjuncture framing its intricate accounts of psychic life and familial dynamics. The social operations of power (most obviously, in relation to those seeking psychotherapy, of gender hierarchy) have imposed their silences on the way we experience ourselves, as well as derelictions in the way we are heard, inside and outside psychotherapeutic encounters.

Today, a feminist-informed culture is less able or willing to conceal or ignore what are often compelling psychological and physical signs of sexual abuse. Indeed, we are more attentive nowadays to signs of sexual abuse than to *other* forms of physical and emotional neglect and abuse of children, which often raise little public concern or condemnation. Certainly, most clinicians are clearer about the realities and dangers of child sexual abuse, despite (at least in the more classically Freudian) an awareness of the potential for 'self-deception' in the reconstructions of memory. One of Britain's leading Freudian thinkers, Peter Fonagy, sums up the way in which psychoanalytic interpretation is shaped by (as well as helping to shape) the cultural wisdom of its day, as follows:

The psychoanalytic or psychotherapeutic situation is irretriev-
ably contaminated by its social context, which affects both
the patient's and the analyst's anticipation. Psychoanalytic
discourse that implicitly or explicitly denies the formative role
of the cultural context leaves important aspects of personal
biography fragmented and mystifying.[65]

So contemporary psychoanalytic theorizing, despite its
numerous schools, has for some time now been growing cautious about its constructions of memory and the past, seeing
the affective processes operating in clinical encounters as generating a mutual process of meaning construction. Fonagy
himself has recently attempted to clarify the psychoanalytic
understanding of 'memory', arguing that few psychoanalysts
nowadays assume that what they are doing is 'uncovering the
past', as it actually happened, rather than reconstructing personal memories with equal inputs from both analyst and
patient. Contrary to popular notions of 'Freudian' memories,
he asserts: 'Memories evolve within the analysis, obtaining
new understandings of the patient's personal history; the ana-
lysand's very "being" changes, conferring new meanings on
the same memories'.[66] As is common in contemporary psychoanalytic thought, he draws upon the notion of 'deferred
action', or '*Nachträglichkeit*', to explain the way in which the
past works upon the present in the therapeutic relationship.
Freud used this term repeatedly to clarify the strange nature
of psychic temporality, suggesting that earlier experiences
and memory traces can be *revised* subsequently in the light of
new experiences or the attainment of a new stage of development: 'I am working on the assumption that our psychical
mechanism has come into being by a process of stratification:
the material present in the form of memory-traces being subject from time to time to a *re-arrangement* in accordance with
fresh circumstances – to a *re-transcription*', he wrote to Fliess
in 1896.[67] A memory may thus become a trauma only well
after the event, by a process of deferred action.

Fonagy makes use of the research of the French psychoanalysts Jean Laplanche and J.-B. Pontalis, who had earlier
clarified Freud's notion of deferred action to explain: 'It is not

lived experience in general which undergoes deferred revision but, specifically, whatever has been impossible to incorporate fully into a meaningful context. The traumatic event is the epitome of such unassimilated experience'.[68] Laplanche has since expanded this notion of deferred action, which he calls 'afterwardness', to account for the workings of narrativization in general, as individuals attempt a reworking, or 'better translation', of the past in the present.[69] It is thus the experience of analysis itself, as his collaborator Pontalis explains, which bears the idea (one which Hacking also elaborates) that memory is a type of fiction: 'any story, however truthful it aims to be, is a reconstruction from the vantage-point of the *present*'.[70]

Many other prominent psychoanalysts and writers, especially those from the object-relations tradition, such as Christopher Bollas or Stephen Mitchell, now argue along remarkably similar lines, seeing psychic histories as worked out in analysis through negotiated interactions between patient and analyst.[71] Some, like Donald Spence, explicitly distinguish 'narrative truth' from 'historical truth', again arguing that particular symptoms can never be traced back to their 'actual origins' (historical truth) by means of interpretative insights (narrative truth).[72] Meanwhile the Lacanian psychoanalyst, from a somewhat different metaphysics of language, comes to essentially the same conclusion, since the 'real' is always that which eludes us: 'Let us be clear', Lacan announced, 'that we do not engage in retracing a succession of stages of development but rather in grasping how positions which are already taken up are retrospectively reorganised'.[73]

However, this new psychoanalytic consensus on the relationship between the psychological past and the present as an insistent and persisting – yet precarious and provisional – process of social negotiation, is precisely what many critics angrily reject, as we have already seen argued by Jeffrey Masson. For them it is crucial to insist upon a clear and permanent division between the 'fiction' of 'mere fantasies', and the 'truth' of 'genuine memories'.[74] No blurring between the imaginary and the real must be allowed. Thus Masson denounces Freud for dismissing women's accounts of actual abuse as 'the fantasies of hysterical women who invented stories and told lies'.[75] This extraordinary version of Freud's interactions with his early women patients is now widely believed, a journalistic cliché, as well as one endorsed by many psychologists (at least those who do not, as Stuart Sutherland did, underwrite its exact antithesis): 'Freud has now been exposed as a fraud because he did not want to change his theory to fit the evidence when he found that child sexual abuse had occurred. Freud invented the myth of the sexual child, while in fact his experiences with his patients showed the opposite had happened. Instead of revealing that adults had abused children, he led people to believe that children desired abuse'.[76]

Betrayal versus Abuse?

However fiercely reiterated, it is not hard to point out the caricature and confusion in such crude renderings of Freud and psychoanalysis. Nevertheless, and despite the contradictory denunciations from Crews and his cohorts, it is clear that psychoanalytic arguments *could* legitimately be used in the service of recent constructions of 'false memory syndrome': memories never simply reflect back external reality. The forms of 'recovery therapy' which have emerged at the close of the twentieth century, most prominently in the USA, have not been primarily psychoanalytic. (In fact, their origins have been traced to the alternative trauma theory of Freud's rival, Pierre Janet, in the 1890s.[77]) But 'false memory' exponents are, often correctly, seen as part of the cultural backlash against the influence of feminist revelations of the prevalence and significance of sexual abuse, organizing to legitimate the very low conviction rates of its perpetrators or in support of men who have been convicted. This has meant that Peter Fonagy's temporary decision to lend his psychoanalytic authority as an adviser to the False Memory Association in Britain has made his own thoughtful account of relations between subjectivity, memory and actuality appear somewhat compromised to feminists.[78]

There are good reasons to avoid taking any absolute stand on what Fonagy has likened to 'a religious war' between those defending the victims of child abuse and those defending adults who claim to be falsely accused – although we may not favour his rather bland call for a 'middle road' between two equally deserving positions.[79] More usefully, the combat over 'recovered' versus 'false' memory might help us to problematize the original binary, adding complexity and flexibility to all the terms we use for describing human experience. Valerie Sinason, a fierce defender of the sexually abused, who correctly stresses that the prevalence of unreported abuse far exceeds the existence of false accusations, nevertheless concedes that memory remains a confusing mixture of fantasy and reality. Indeed, she even agrees with the psychoanalyst Bob Hinshelwood that a 'false' memory of the past may represent a distorted account of the present evoked by the experience of an over-intrusive therapist, or by a true memory of some event that was falsified in the past, or perhaps some combination of the two.[80]

This happens, of course, because the clinical phenomenon of 'transference' is the classic way in which the effects of past encounters are relived in the present. We continue, as we began, to appropriate others all our lives, on and off the couch: either, when fortunate, in the maintenance of supportive intimate relationships with others; or, less fortunately, and much more precariously, in fantasy relationships with others. Freud also introduced the idea of 'screen memory', which is a childhood memory characterized by its clarity, yet seeming insignificance. Like other slips of the tongue or neurotic symptoms, he saw these as compromise formations, involving condensation and displacement of one memory into another one, leading him to wonder of childhood recollections: 'are there memories of which we may say they *emerge from*, or merely memories which are *related to*, our childhood?'.[81] As the feminist psychoanalyst Janice Haaken comments from the USA: 'the emotional truth of the past is never to the concrete facticity of events but is always bound up in interpretation, both in the initial experience of events and in the later elaboration and working through in memory'.[82]

All this takes us back to those subjective concerns and autobiographical reflections which scientists would like to avoid: to the study of personal histories of both consciously and unconsciously motivated remembering and forgetting; but also to cultural narratives and normative discourses, which give us – or withhold from us – words and stories which can give utterance to experience via local assumptions, discursive framings and narrative conventions. Both memory researchers and psychoanalysts can agree that memory is unreliable and incomplete. But it is only from within the latter that there is some explanation of the more complex ways in which 'forgetting' is continuously, actively, *motivated*. Nevertheless, it is only from the political concerns and discourses of a feminist framework that some men's systematic abuse of their paternalistic power comes fully into focus. However inimical to the programmed workings of a computer, or to any other mechanistic models of memory storage and recall, the notion that avoidance, self-deception and half-truths are part of everyday interactions is what most of us have long observed, whether in ourselves or of others. This awareness is no more supportive of any notion of 'false memory syndrome' than it is of the truth of any particular 'recovered memory' of abuse. (We may also be aware, however, that it is those who are in positions of power who are far more likely to get away with their own evasions and self-deceptions.) What we should be able to learn from this hubbub over memory is something of the enormity of the work to be done in making sense of the past as it is lived in the present.

Childhood memories are all too real; in adulthood, they remain the most vivid memories we are likely to have, and the only ones we never seem to lose: 'In my private dictionary', Pontalis writes, 'childhood and memory are synonymous'.[83] It was then, in our beginnings, that we were most receptive to everything, least able to classify or forget. Over-supplied with childhood memories as we are, they are nevertheless, necessarily, suffused with fantasy and given meanings which – especially when originally accompanied by silence and distress – can and will shift, through the sense that we finally come to make of them, only *afterwards*. This is all the more true when some new experience evokes past pain, or pleasure.

Therapists who are wary of accepting their patients' accounts of abuse experiences, seeing in childhood trauma the primordial route to all adult symptoms, emphasize instead a more complex action of the past on the present, the present on the past. They are concerned not to over-simplify the elaborate threads between the two, arguing that placing all emphasis on the linear power of some original trauma threatens to institutionalize patients into a sense of victimhood and powerlessness. In this climate of heightened awareness of child sexual abuse as *a* (if for some *the*) main cause of adult disorders, the dangers of over-simplification are real enough – however much the converse is also true: that the False Memory Foundation thrives on the support of those who would like to turn back what they see as feminism's exaggerations of the extent and significance of sexual abuse.

Almost fifty years after the death of Virginia Woolf, Louise de Salvo published a biography of her in which she attributed Woolf's adult miseries and mental breakdowns to the sexual abuse she experienced as a child at the hands of her older half-brothers, Gerald and George Duckworth. In her own memoir, 'Sketch of the Past', begun two years before her suicide in 1941, Woolf had written of feeling 'ashamed or afraid' when caught looking at herself in the hall mirror as a child, a feeling about her body she would retain all her life. She then immediately recounts a memory of Gerald Duckworth lifting her onto the hallstand when she was around six, and commencing to explore her body and her 'private parts': 'I remember resenting – disliking it – what is the word for so dumb and mixed a feeling?' Woolf analyses her own strong reaction as proof that shame at the touching of certain bodily parts 'must be instinctive', an instinct linking her to all 'her ancestresses' through time.[84] (Woolf had earlier written of George Duckworth's much later, and in her mind far more damaging, sexual advances on her as a teenager: although she used them as a type of running joke to entertain friends, she nevertheless saw herself as harmed by them.[85])

As though anticipating de Salvo, Woolf continues, immediately after describing the incident with Gerald, to expand on the difficulties of accounting for a person's life, which is always so 'immensely complicated': 'I do not suppose I have got at the truth. . . . In spite of all this, people write what they call 'lives' of other people; that is, they collect a number of events, and leave the person to whom it happened unknown'.[86] Thinking anachronistically for a moment, Woolf almost certainly would have rejected de Salvo's analysis. The central event of childhood for her, the one which brought it to a close, was the death of her mother when she was thirteen: 'the greatest disaster that ever happened', the most distressing aspect of which was that she could feel nothing other than 'the feeling that everything had come to an end'.[87] It certainly seems likely that the Duckworth's sexual exploitation of their half-sister contributed to the sense of danger, shame and panic around sexuality so often to be found in Woolf's writing. But I find more compelling the conclusions of Hermione Lee, her next feminist biographer, that it 'distorts the thick complexity of her family life' to isolate and emphasize only her memories of child sexual abuse.[88]

Narratives in Context

Disputes over memory and trauma have kept pace with the growth of Multiple Personality Disorder (MPD), and the separate but increasingly popular psychiatric classification of Post-Traumatic-Stress-Disorder (PTSD); as mentioned above, these entered the diagnostic manual of the American Psychiatric Association (DSM-III) in 1980. Surveying the cultural background to the extraordinary explosion of cases of MPD, primarily in the USA, Hacking notes that in the early 1970s there were only twelve cases of the disorder known in that country. However, by the mid-1980s there were over 6000, and the numbers have expanded exponentially ever since, with nine out of ten diagnosed 'multiples' being women.[89] There has been a parallel growth in the diagnosis of the more general category of PTSD: seen as connected, in particular, with the psychological effects of repressing the horrors of combat, although MPD is currently understood by those who use the label as a similar type of post-traumatic effect to the repression of childhood sexual abuse. As Allon Young points out, belief in PTSD created new career prospects and resources for psychologists and psychiatrists, especially those treating the stresses and strains of war veterans.[90] But it also meant that ex-soldiers often needed to mimic the trauma/repression model of psychological illness if they were to receive any psychological or material help.

Young and Hacking have both written of the 'looping effect' such notions of trauma and memory are likely to create on individual's self-perceptions, when war veterans could obtain treatment and a special pension only if they showed the memory losses thought characteristic of PTSD (the less they could remember about the stresses they had suffered, the more help they could get): 'The men who remembered very well the god-awful things that had happened were sometimes less able to benefit under this program, because PTSD was made to essentially involve not remembering but forgetting'.[91] Without any doubt, one point which at least is clear is that when trying to understand the complexities of psychic life we need to remain attentive to the impact of particular cultural contexts upon individual processes of memory, and the way these help to shape the fashioning and refashioning of identity.

Here is a personal vignette. Frightened of the dark, as a young child who was frequently asthmatic and insomniac, I knew that if I could manage to creep along squeaky corridors, past the bedroom of my father's mistress (the housekeeper), sidle into my parents' bedroom, past the sleeping body of my father, and crouch beside the figure of my sleeping mother, all fear and wheezing would vanish. A state of blissful serenity descended. But if, aware of my presence, my mother accidentally awakened my instantly angry father, all would be lost. I would be shouted at, returned at once, in disgrace, to agitated sleeplessness in my own room and trouble the next day. If I eventually succeeded in waking only my mother (by silently stroking her arm), we would both creep into the bathroom, where I would be given a very strong sleeping tablet, usually a Nembutal. Is this a memory of personal bliss – the fleeting moment of complete peace of mind and body beside my mother?; of abusive neglect – the stirring of paternal rage against a sick and frightened child?; of maternal carelessness – the giving of adult sleeping tablets to a child?; or what? It all depends on how I tell the tale, who is listening, and to the fact that my fantasies of safety beside my mother (accurate or not: I was later seriously poisoned by a drug – pure adrenaline – she had handed over to me in young adulthood) do seem stronger than the ubiquitous fear of my father (justified or not: my main fear seemed to be that he was somehow linked with evil spirits who lived under a huge desk that occupied the whole of the space in the annexe of my L-shaped bedroom, where a gloomy painting of a shipwreck hung – perhaps a Turner reproduction).

Jeffrey Masson may be right that there is no more important task for psychic health than being able to tell one's own story, given how much we suffer when our identity feels precarious (at least, outside the sympathetic arena of self-consciously queer performativity). But we need also to hear those stories through the tales of our time, to question them, and to draft them anew. As Pontalis observed, 'One shouldn't write *one* autobiography but ten of them or a hundred because, while we have only one life, we have innumerable ways of recounting that life (to ourselves)'.[92] There is also a politics, as well as a social space, involved in the telling of stories – especially the stories we tell not just to ourselves, but for the attention of others. By asking new questions about men's power over women and children, within and beyond the family, feminism gave rise to stories of sexual abuse, and ways to challenge and survive it. Today, some of the feminists who first wrote of child sexual abuse now lament its prolixity.

Back in the 1970s, Louise Armstrong called for a public 'speakout' on incest in the USA, attacking the 'patriarchal perogative' behind it – quickly confident that it could all be overturned.[93] Today, saturated with tales of childhood abuse and steps for recovery, she argues that the point of such speakouts is almost completely lost: 'In breaking the silence we hoped to raise hell. Instead, we have raised for the issue a certain normalcy. We hoped to raise a passion for change. Instead what we raised was discourse – and a sizable problem-management industry'.[94] On the one hand, the self-disclosure of survivors has been sensationalized and exploited by the media; on the other, it has been recuperated to reinforce the need for expert advice and support.[95] Other feminists have similarly criticized the depoliticized fate of many feminist ideas in the service of self-help discourses: 'One of the ways in which the recovery movement has been most destructive to women, and to progressive politics', as Elayne Rapping notes, 'is in the insistence on a single, very simplistic narrative pattern to explain our lives'.[96]

Feminists like Louise Armstrong or Michele Davies now accuse Freudianism and the therapy industry generally of seducing and undermining feminism as a political movement for women's liberation, diverting its goals from social criticism to personal 'growth' and 'healing', calling this the liberal takeover of a radical movement.[97] But such accusations fail to acknowledge that it was significant strands of feminism itself which revitalized psychoanalytic accounts, in their search for greater understanding of subjectivity, and the conflicts women faced in their own lives. Some feminists turned to Freud, and many women believe they have benefited from the rise of a feminist-informed therapeutic community.[98] Freudians did not, in general, turn to feminism; many psychoanalysts to this day remain explicitly hostile towards it.[99] Moreover, as we shall see in my next chapter, many feminists who are most concerned to explore the psychological dynamics of gender differences and conflicts are the ones who remain most antagonistic to Freud. There has indeed been a growth in psychological attempts to treat gender-related tensions and anxieties, but much of it, interestingly, is now concerned with the problems of boys and men. Moving on from the battles over memory and child sexual abuse, I want to tackle the whole sweep of contemporary personal, cultural and social anxieties surrounding gender, exploring what psychologists have been able to contribute, and the impact of feminism within that discipline.

5

Gender Anxieties at the Limits of Psychology

A profusion of images and fantasies, unstable and unintegrated, is more constitutive of the contemporary gendered subject than is the more stable, dichotomous world of gendered subjects of a century ago.

Janice Haaken, *Pillars of Salt*

Not Freud, but Darwin, provides the scientific credentials for the human sciences today, as we saw in chapter 3. But his supporters' faith in the intrinsic sexual polarities evolved to ensure 'reproductive success', stabilized over two million years, has not managed to prevent the escalation of gender anxieties. Neither the impassioned questioning, nor the staunch reaffirmation, of traditional gender polarities can shed much light on the continuing social disruption and, for some, disorientating change in the everyday lives of both women and men. Population surveys continue to inform us of people's apprehensions over gender issues. In Britain, Roy Porter and Sarah Dunant introduce their anthology of this *fin de siècle*, entitled *The Age of Anxiety*, by citing evidence of the prevailing social and psychological unease, even panic, over gender matters: family breakdown, working mothers, single parents – reflecting, in particular, change in women's choices and objectives; fears of crime and violence – reflecting, it would appear, men's increasing levels of destructive behaviour, both against themselves and others.[1]

In close agreement, when the training analyst Andrew Samuels carried out a survey of fourteen different psychotherapy organizations, across seven countries, he found that gender concerns were the primary political issues brought into therapy for every professional body he contacted, and across all countries – first of all, and usually overwhelmingly, gender issues for women, followed by gender issues for men.[2] In the same vein, Joan Raphael-Leff and Rosine Josef Perelman, surveying female analysts' clinical work with women throughout the twentieth century, conclude that women have remained perennially uneasy over their sense of themselves as 'feminine', whether manifest in symptoms of tension, depression, anorexia or other forms of psychological distress and damage.[3] Yet, women's gendered anxieties are today matched, if not surpassed, by evidence of men's fears around 'masculinity'. Certainly, it is men today who are most likely to commit suicide or call the Samaritans for help.[4] Some theoreticians may view 'gender' as primarily an ideologically prescriptive term, but few could seriously doubt its continued significance in shaping people's sense of self-identity, whatever its diversity and instability. In chapter 2, I argued that 'gender' is best seen as an analytic term referring to a complex set of interacting forces (biological, social and symbolic) producing multiple contrasts at the level of individual experience, which are rarely as distinct as many would like them to be. At the experiential level, as Muriel Dimen comments, gender 'is variably meaningful, a variability which generates uncertainty, invites inquiry, and offers richness'.[5] It is what psychologists have been able to contribute to that inquiry, and to the understanding and attempted amelioration of the high anxieties surrounding gender, to which I now turn.

Feminism Enters the Academy

It is no longer controversial to suggest that gender interrogations have produced some of the most dynamic debates in the social sciences and the humanities over the last twenty-five years. These have arisen both from the dramatic changes in routine gender practices, and from challenges to customary gender significations. Most significantly, they reflect the growing legitimacy and authority of feminist scholarship during those years; albeit always contested, and itself internally riven by theoretical and political disputes. Placing women at the centre of its analysis, feminist theorizing has been vigorously embroiled in all the wider battles of intellectual life in the late twentieth century, especially in literature, cultural studies, history and sociology. Beginning with methodological critiques of 'male-centred' empiricism in the 1960s (seen as marginalizing if not ruling out the particularities of women's lives in the name of a false universalism) it progressed to pursue new studies recording women's distinctive experiences (or women's 'voices'). As discussed in chapter 2, recent appropriations of post-structuralist thinking have led some feminists towards a more self-consciously, self-critical epistemology: problematizing experiential reports; pluralizing gender categories; questioning the stability of notions of identity or subjectivity; still all the while seeking to deconstruct existing normative knowledges while hoping to construct more self-reflexive, multi-faceted and liberatory alternatives.[6]

Within mainstream psychology, however, feminism has made comparatively less of an impact than elsewhere. For nearly three decades most feminist psychologists, like feminist scholars more generally, have consistently criticized positivist methodologies and claimed a special affinity between their goals and a plurality of qualitative methods.[7] Yet their critique of psychology's statistical traditions has remained marginal: 'Struggling with high critical theory, self-reflection and worries about "so what?"', as the American psychologists Michelle Fine and Corrine Bertram wrote in the British journal *Feminism and Psychology*, 'we, nevertheless, tootle along with our chi-squares, our hypotheses and our "limits on generalizability"'.[8] This is despite the remarkable shift in the numbers of women entering the discipline: 400 per cent *more* women than men studying psychology today, compared with the 50 per cent *less* women than men back in 1969.[9]

The difficulties faced by feminist psychologists hoping to reconstitute their discipline can be gauged from the fact that where it is most prominent, in the USA, the Psychology of Women section in the American Psychological Association is rated in the bottom third of interest or importance, whereas the Sex and Gender section of the equivalent American

Sociology Association is the largest and most influential division.[10] Nevertheless, in line with its distinct disciplinary concerns, sex-difference research (comparing and contrasting individual differences between women and men) increased a thousandfold once gender issues impacted upon experimental agendas from the late 1960s.[11] But, once measured, and *any* disparity recorded, the 'nature/nurture' debate continued to provide the theoretical framing for much of this expanding research field.

Still Searching for Sex Differences

Before the 1960s stereotyped sex differences were mostly either simply assumed or, when measured, assigned axiomatically to biology.[12] After that time, especially following Maccoby's and Jacklin's landmark publication in 1974, it became equally routine – although just as routinely challenged – to point out that there are more similarities than differences between the sexes, and to assign recorded psychological differences to environmental processes.[13] Ten years later, Kay Deaux, overviewing psychological research from the previous decade, was, even more firmly, concluding that sex differences were 'surprisingly small in most cases' (amounting to no more than between 1 and 5 per cent of the average variance between women and men). She also emphasized the overriding importance of social context, or 'situational factors', in determining whether sex differences would be found, including the significance of the sex of the researcher: women, for example, apparently show more 'helping behaviour' if they are being observed, but not when unobserved; women conform more to group pressure in face-to-face situations, but not in 'situations that lack surveillance'.[14] What we always need to ask, as Stephen Jay Gould insisted in his 1980s best-seller, *The Mismeasure of Man* (echoed a decade later in Carole Tavris, *The Mismeasure of Woman*), is just *who* is doing the measuring, and for *what purpose?*[15] Today, methodological leaps in data analysis allow the presentation of ever more grandiose meta-analytic treatments of existing statistical correlations. And we are reminded, yet again, that there *are* a few small sex differences in the average aptitudes and traits recorded on particular psychological measurements: these may, or may not, have some biological underpinning; they show far greater variability within than between biological sexes; and they change or, more precisely, appear to be decreasing, over time.[16]

However, if the developments in sex difference research spurred some women in psychology into heightened pursuit of them, arguing – as Alice Eagly and Carol Jacklin have done – that it is crucial for combating prevailing stereotypes and gender discriminations, many others are far more critical.[17] Even the search for sex similarities, these critics suggest, merely endorses a way of looking at the world which remains trapped in the deliberations generated by polarized gender categories.[18] Meanwhile, it would be hard not to notice that this particular research tradition, tirelessly measuring individual differences in cognitive or other psychological traits in order to offer up a few small differences, leaves psychologists with next to nothing to contribute to an understanding of the pervasive anxieties around the blurring of gender differences. A few small differences neither herald nor explain such very big anxieties. Yet, as the escalating genre of books about men and masculinities discussed below all testify, ongoing changes in gender arrangements have produced a pervasive sense of tension, suspicion and distrust in gender relations: this unease is, ironically, most obvious in recent documentation of men's fears and anxieties. Surveying men's differing psychological and social responses to changing gender relations in the late 1990s, one North American researcher reflects the views of most of his peers when he concludes: 'It's actually getting harder and harder for a young male to figure out how to *be* a man'.[19]

Although it fails to address such anxieties, and is now matched by a parallel intensification of debate questioning its validity and utility, the research output on sex differences in individual attributes shows no sign of abating. On the contrary, it proliferates. It proliferates not only because it conforms to the quantitative methodologies still dominating psychological research and favoured by funding bodies, and also because of the new injunctions to publish or perish as our academies are forced to operate by the rules of commodity production (or perhaps, I should say, publish as you perish, if you come from the newer universities in Britain), but because the media, and the world at large, are always eager for the products of sex difference research, however trivial and inconsistent. In particular, they doggedly search out any purportedly 'new' evidence which can be interpreted in support of biological sex differences.[20] The irony is that human beings are never simply at the mercy of their biology, even were there consistent evidence for significant sex differences which could be mapped on to the human genome. As suggested in chapter 3, any form of genetic reductionism flies in the face of all serious genetic theory since the 1970s, which rejects earlier assumptions that genes determine human action in any stable or straightforward way. A behavioural trait can be said to be genetic only if genes alone provide the best explanation for its origin, and this is simply not the case for *any* complex human trait. A multiplicity of other mechanisms always interact with the compound genetic codings bearing upon any single human event.[21]

Feminist Psychology and Social Constructionism

Many feminist psychologists, however, have managed to introduce a rich new theoretical literature by turning away from the mainstream preoccupation with sex difference research and the quantitative study of individual attributes which it endorses. They have focused instead on the conflicts and difficulties accompanying the acquisition of normative gender and sexual identities in girls. The dominant theoretical explanations they favour make use of learning theory and cognitive theory, but in line with a more general social construction framework which pays close attention to social context and meanings. This framework meets the challenge that Naomi Weisstein mounted in 1968, alleging that 'psychology has nothing to say about what women are really like', because it has looked for inner traits at the expense of social context.[22] Here gender attributes are not reduced to any fixed, specific set of individual abilities or traits, but nevertheless are seen as central, stable and abiding patterns of behaviour and cognitive frameworks typifying 'femininity' and reflecting women's subordinate position in society compared with men.[23]

Feminist work on the construction of gender, which most often adopts qualitative rather than quantitative methodologies, has introduced new perspectives and valuable research on a whole array of once stereotyped, trivialized or, most often, totally excluded topics (from menarche and motherhood to lesbian therapy or male violence), while also questioning the production of knowledge abstracted from its social context. As Leonore Tiefer recalled in her address to the American Women in Psychology Conference on its twentieth anniversary in 1989, there really was no research on sex and gender before the recent feminist input.[24] This new research has provided a chilling catalogue of data, almost all of it indicating psychological disadvantages which women face compared with men throughout all the phases of their lives. As Rhoda Unger and Mary Crawford summarize the findings to date: 'Boys have no difficulty becoming "men," but girls become "women" reluctantly and at a later age. Maturity does not confer status on women'.[25] Beyond the academy, at its crucial interface with the media, it is the work of Carol Gilligan, and her studies of adolescent girls in the USA that has provided the best-known qualitative research, very much in line with this conclusion. According to one commentator in the USA, 'not a week seems to go by without Gilligan being quoted in a newspaper or on television about the way girls suddenly lose confidence and hope at age twelve'.[26]

This work has been crucial in exposing how stereotypes of 'femininity' can undermine women's confidence, and dictate gendered performances which confirm rather than contest existing meanings and social practices securing men's dominance. Although we now often read reports of Western women's new confidence and multiple achievements, especially the rising expectations of younger women,[27] these are matched by a steady accumulation of continuing problems women face attempting to negotiate their apparently more open and autonomous lives. Feminist psychologists have been able to show just how problematic most women's lives remain, despite their new Western freedoms: whether facing the continuing (some studies even suggest increasing) stigma of women's body weight,[28] encountering menstrual tensions or menopausal distress,[29] dealing with men's sexual violence and surviving child abuse,[30] resisting racism,[31] confronting the conflicts and ambivalences of motherhood,[32] or simply struggling to communicate with men in contexts of unequal status and power.[33] Deploying social constructionist perspectives, these detailed and focused studies explore how gender still operates as a system of social control of women. They all reject theories of sex differences at the level of the individual, offering convincing support for their shared view that, as Mary Crawford summarizes concisely: 'gender is not an attribute of individuals but a way of making sense of transactions'.[34]

Openness to Gender Heterodoxy

These studies do have their critics, however, some of whom are feminist psychologists themselves.[35] Although providing a significant body of work on the limitations facing women as a *group* within their specific cultural contexts, some gender theorists, like me, have been troubled by the fact that in most of the feminist social constructionist studies it is always women, *as* women, who face problems and suffer from the consequences. Isolating gender, and conceiving it only as 'difference', inevitably tends to flatten out conflicts and diversity between and, especially, within women's experiences and behaviour (notwithstanding explicit mindfulness to race, ethnicity, class and sexual orientation).[36] It tends towards a form of gender absolutism, where alternative conceptual framings of women's experience find little space.

Moreover, despite attention to social context and meaning, many feminist psychologists, typified by Gilligan, allude to consistent *internal* dynamics as directing gender practices, whether through culturally reinforced predispositions or through the acquisition of shared meanings. The danger is that these constructivist accounts of gender identity may merely replace earlier biological reductionisms with new forms of cultural reductionism, whether in terms of the internalization of sex roles, the performance of social scripts, the deployment of dominant discourses, or the gender differentiating effects of mother-child relationships. Insofar as gender is seen as consistently internalized, the worn out biological/social polarity has not been transcended to embrace any richer psychological hermeneutics attempting to encompass the contingent, precarious, often contradictory, processes through which the social becomes embodied. Conceptions of the social have been expanded, but how they impinge upon subjectivity remains insufficiently elaborated.

Identities are indeed social, but they are also exceedingly complex – both psychologically and in terms of their sociocultural framing. One problem with social construction theory is that it has tended to erase the nuances of subjective conflict and ambivalence. It usually eschews any need for critical appropriation of psychoanalytic insights which, drawing on clinical data and detailed biographical observation, may open our eyes to the contradictory and disruptive *particularities* of psychic life in relation to culture and history. Whereas social construction theories (however interpreted) lead us to expect the successful moulding of gender identities and behaviour, psychoanalytic reflections point us towards the continual *failure* of psychic life fully to reflect consciously learned norms. For example, it is pertinent to recall that sex researchers from the time of the Kinsey report on male sexuality (1949) have suggested that 'the largest single category of homosexual men are heterosexually married'.[37] Only through some understanding of the frequent failure of the inner world to reflect cultural norms does it become easier to see why it should be men who, although the favoured and most powerful sex, and despite the continual and ubiquitous policing of any 'effeminate' deviance, should so far outnumber women in seeking gender reassignment operations.

In view of contemporary gender anxieties, it seems to me that psychoanalytic accounts are indispensable for just this insight that sexual identity (and its normative ties with heterosexual desire) is only ever a precarious achievement, and in danger of subversion from within as well as from without. As we will see in the next chapter, some well-known gender theorists now practising as psychoanalysts in the USA, such as Muriel Dimen, use their case studies to illustrate the perennial ambiguities of supposed gender contrasts and differences: 'Sometimes these contrasts remain distinct, at other times they intersect, and at still other times they fuse and exchange identities'.[38] But this openness to the central yet always fraught place of sexual difference in the grammar of the unconscious, which can often be found within psychoanalytic discourses, still comes mostly from those – like Nancy Chodorow, Jessica Benjamin, Jane Flax or Dimen herself – situated outside academic psychology.[39]

Identities, of whatever sort, are also generated in social contexts which are nowadays always dynamic and shifting, involving a plurality of signifying practices and competing cultural narratives. A second problem with social construction frameworks, especially as interpreted by psychologists, is their tendency to limit the diversity of cultural meanings which gender encodes, as well as the performative potentialities and instabilities of even the most established social relations. Thus, seemingly at odds with psychological generalizations that 'girls become "women" reluctantly', some sociologists studying adolescents have been reporting how girls today, unlike boys in their own peer group, 'speak with a palpable sense of agency, confidence, determination and hope about their future lives, even if their plans may be considered less realistic in a wider context of women's work more generally'.[40] Meanwhile, male managers, while still in fact monopolizing power and influence, feel 'besieged' on all sides, as Michael Roper reports, by economic changes and new competition from younger women, as well as other men.[41]

Gender certainly remains a central principle of social organization. But it operates at multiple and shifting levels, no longer as homogeneous or exclusive as it once was in privileging straight (white) men. Psychologists studying how gender shapes identities and perceptions need to explore the very specific ways in which it functions, paying close attention to the effects of cultural ruptures detected by sociological or historical frameworks: these may be generated by shifts in employment patterns, changes in family structures and the visibility of non-normative sexual subcultures, the emergence of ethnic or national struggles, or reorganizations within educational and other cultural, religious and political bodies. Shifts in gender relations also trigger a variety of social movements engaging explicitly with gender politics and the competing ideologies and cultural perceptions they generate. Some are dedicated to embracing change – like feminism, lesbian and gay struggles, or anti-sexist men's politics; others to arresting it – like men's rights advocates and religious or ethnic fundamentalists. These new subcultural belongings, with their radical or conservative rhetorics, crucially shape gendered self-perceptions and collective aspirations, providing their own distinct narratives of life events generating widely differing forms of collective actions and individual experience.

It is thus only by travelling between disciplines, and drawing upon diverse theoretical traditions, that I think we can begin to put together an adequate framework for understanding gender issues. Of course, we are all *positioned* as either male or female, and much of the time most of us may habitually enact gender behaviour more or less appropriate to the cultures to which we belong. Yet, if we choose to look for the *unexpected*, the counter-intuitive, there is also evidence in most life histories to suggest that the supposedly psychological foundations of gender enactments fluctuate over time. This suggests the importance of collecting 'thick' data, which is rich enough to expose the fragility, contradiction and context-bound resistance or compliance within gendered experiences and performance. It is only from such data that we can learn that women's presumed sensitivity and concern is far from ubiquitous; just as men faced with the inevitability of caring for others (as single fathers, healthy partners of ailing loved ones, and so on) may reveal hitherto underused capacities for compassion, nurturing or sexual responsibility.[42]

The Predicament of Men

One way to illustrate these theoretical arguments on the limits of psychology's role in explaining – or intervening in – contemporary gender problems, is by looking specifically at what many people now see as a, if not *the*, burning issue of our time: the presumed 'crisis' of masculinity in the Western world. How should we respond to the explosion of discourse on men's anxieties, and anxieties about men? We should respond, I will suggest, by remaining attentive, above all, to the contradictions and silences in the literature.

Seemingly completely at odds with the findings usually presented in feminist psychology texts, which have seen women as the disadvantaged sex, the new 'masculinity' literature uncannily mirrors them, in both methodology and outcome. It focuses upon men's own experiences, generates evidence of men's gender-specific suffering and has given birth to a new field of enquiry, 'Men's Studies'.[43] We are told today that boys are failing in school, and from a very early age.[44] Adolescent males are more miserable than adolescent girls. Moving onwards in life, men today have far higher incidences of suicide, alcoholism, drug addiction, serious accidents, cardiovascular disease, and significantly lower life expectancies than women.[45] As the twentieth century draws to its close, men are presented as the threatened sex (at least in this literature), even as they remain, everywhere, the threatening sex.

The evidence for the increasing intellectual, emotional and physical impoverishment of 'men' is indeed startling for those used to reading about the converse and continuing disadvantages of 'women', as the sex still most distanced from economic, cultural and political power. The puzzle is that *both* sides of this apparent contradiction are easily verified. This peculiarity is hard to grasp if you start from psychologists' preferred methodological habit of sampling individual performances and hunting down gender contrasts. More curiously, perhaps, the reality of the first set of problems around 'masculinity' are everywhere tied in with the persisting truth of women's secondary social status and identity. It is because 'manhood' still has a *symbolic* weight denied to 'womanhood' that men's apparent failings loom so large, both to men themselves and to those around them. This is why literature on masculinity keeps circling the problem, with few credible exits in sight.

The most commonplace but crucial source of the ostensible contradiction is that men, like women, are not a homogeneous group. Indeed, it is *only* in their ubiquitously cited and definitively enforced demarcation from 'women' that the deep and pervasive divisions between men can be ignored. The perpetuation and tenacity of men's power in day-to-day gender relations are easily established. Compared with women, in all parts of the world, men still have overwhelmingly greater access to cultural prestige, political authority, corporate power and individual wealth – whatever the costs, confusions and insecurities of individual men. But of course, it is only particular groups of men in any society who will occupy positions of public power and influence. Yet this is precisely what secures rather than undermines the hierarchical structuring of conceptions of gender through relations of dominance: the symbolic equation of 'masculinity' with power and 'femininity' with powerlessness. Despite forceful feminist critique, despite all the documented upheavals or 'crisis tendencies' in men's lives (as women gain greater independence and control over their own), the forces securing 'men' in power have been dented, but not, as yet, substantially dismantled.[46] The meanings and fantasies accompanying the equation of men and power are thus largely undisturbed. What has been seriously disrupted, however, is the taken-for-granted legitimation of this hierarchy as natural and inevitable. Today that legitimation is as fiercely questioned by some as it is forcefully defended by others.

And men do suffer. Pain was never the exclusive prerogative of women, whatever the distinctive role of some men's violence and sexual coercion in promoting it. Men's suffering is most easily accounted for when they are furthest removed from the status and authority which 'masculinity' presumptively confers. When we look more closely at the evidence offered for the 'crisis' in masculinity today, we can decipher a picture in which *all* the most significant differences on display are differences between men themselves, rather than contrasts between men and women. Thus, as all official statistics in Britain indicate, it is *particular* groups of men, especially unemployed, unskilled and unmarried men, who have far higher mortality and illness rates compared with other groups of men.[47] Class, ethnicity and 'race', not gender, are the major predictors of educational failure, unemployment and crime. Unemployment is the common condition of the overwhelming majority of men who commit violent offences, while boys in caring, non-violent households in non-violent neighbourhoods, are hardly more likely to be violent than girls from similar backgrounds.[48]

However, rather than addressing the appallingly destructive consequences of inequalities between men – which do indeed have a serious gender dimension as boys and men anxiously compare themselves and compete *with each other* – we are far more likely to read largely spurious reports of contrasts between men and women. 'Are Boys in Terminal Decline?', the British broadsheet the *Independent* asked in 1994, a question echoed by other serious newspapers, radio and television programmes ever since. Most suggest, for instance, that the 'Clever Girls', and the attention girls receive from feminist inclined teachers, create the problem for the 'Lost Boys'. As one representative and supposedly 'in-depth' reflection on 'The Problem of Co-Education' spelt out: 'Success for girls may now be being matched by failure for boys'. Similar alarmist rhetoric about boys has been appearing in most advanced industrial societies throughout the 1990s.[49]

Yet, these comparisons obscure a reality where most boys are neither 'failing' nor 'lost'. They are doing better than ever at school, and even better again as they move from school to university, or into their careers.[50] As the report by Madeleine Arnot and her co-workers on *Educational Reforms and Gender Equality in Schools* indicates, while overall success at the British intermediate (GCSE) educational level is a little higher for girls than for boys, boys slightly outperform girls in final 'A-level' school examinations.[51] The point is, it is only when gender contrasts can be presented in ways which question the traditional assumption that men *should* be the dominant sex that any media attention is focused upon them. There is nothing at all new in the educational failure of working class and certain ethnic minority boys, whose alienation in school has always accompanied the assertion of a rebellious, anti-learning 'masculine' bravado. As Michèle Cohen notes: 'The question that needs to be asked, then, is not "Why are boys now underachieving?", but rather that of why boy's underachievement has now become an object of concern'.[52] What is new, now that girls overall are not falling behind boys in quite the way they used to, is the attempt to blame girls, or feminist teachers, for the problem.[53] What is not so new is the diversion of attention away from the key problem: the moulding of masculinities.

Nevertheless, it is not only distortion, spurious gender comparisons or even the acute failures or distress of particular groups of boys and men that is currently feeding talk of 'crisis' in masculinity today. The ineluctable rise of men's studies and the accompanying glut of books on masculinity reveal a situation in academic and professional literature in which men and the audiences they are addressing clearly view their own 'masculinity' as an issue newly fraught with personal doubts, social anxieties and conceptual fragmentations. Echoing aspects of feminist thinking, 'masculinity' is seen here not only as damaging to others, especially women, but damaging to men themselves. As Roger Horrocks declares in his proto-typical text, *Masculinity in Crisis* (1994), men are 'haunted by feelings of emptiness, impotence and rage'.[54]

Male psychologists researching gender issues have endorsed the idea of a pervasive 'crisis of masculinity' and proceeded to offer their own explanations and remedies. An overview of most of the recent work done on the psychology of masculinity in the USA is provided in Ronald Levant's and William Pollack's weighty compendium *A New Psychology of Men* (1995). Psychologists here argue that gender relations have shifted rapidly in recent decades, but that male role expectations are slower to change, producing dysfunctional behaviour in men. Bewildered and confused, they tell us, men are unable to take any pride in being a man. As they see it, men urgently require more sensitive understanding of their emotional conflicts, and new skills to tackle them.[55]

The theoretical underpinning of this particular analysis of men's problems is elaborated most fully by the North American psychologist Joseph Pleck in his modified role theory perspective, the 'gender role strain' or 'conflict' approach. Here, it is not men's biology which creates the crisis of masculinity, nor even their psychology, but rather prescribed gender role expectations which are seen as restrictive, contradictory and confusing – promoting dysfunctional behaviour.[56] To create better lives for men, it follows, these prescriptions can and must be changed. It is because men are unable to express their emotions that many men are driven to destructive behaviours: 'certain male problems (such as aggression and violence, homophobia, misogyny, detached fathering and neglect of health) are unfortunate but predictable results of the male socialization process'.[57] Some contributors to this collection mix in reductive psychodynamic assumptions from a simplified 'object relations' theory: men as boys are forced to 'disidentify' from mothers too soon, creating lasting trauma.

Projects for Reforming Masculinity

The rapidly expanding psychological research on masculinity, much of it pursued by men, does provide useful surveys of contemporary men's lives: from fathering to health problems and increasing levels of self- and other directed violence. However, there are serious objections to an analysis of men's predicaments in terms of prescribed and conflicting gender roles, which I will quickly summarize here, as I (and others) have done many times before. The object of analysis – male role expectations – is systematically ambiguous. Pleck, for example, and most of his fellow researchers, say they reject the notion of internalized male sex role 'identity', stressing instead the low self-esteem produced by failure to fulfil shifting male role expectations, alongside the negative consequences and dysfunctional behaviour resulting from over-conformity to them. But as we read these texts, we soon learn

of men's 'nearly universal' inability to express emotions, leading to their over-reliance on aggression and failure to maintain intimacy with others. Since the notion of 'gender role
identity' has been used in social psychology to refer to the
acquisition of a stable set of gender-specific characteristics,[58]
the dysfunctional behaviours men are thought to share in
these accounts seem *inseparable* from the apparently rejected
notion of internalized sex role *identities*.

Also, we do not find in these studies any convincing
account of what it is that keeps compelling men to over-
conform to male role expectations, or others to rebel against
them. This surely needs some thoughtful explanation when it
is men themselves (rather than women) who are seen as the
losers here. Finally, there is a distinctive form of liberalism
behind the analysis and the solutions offered by Levant and
Pollack. Many men have yet to see the light, they suggest, but
self-transformation is on the agenda once men are educated
to see the concrete dangers of traditional male roles. However, since these authors believe that the light dawned during
the mid-1970s, when feminist scholars criticized 'our traditional, phallocentric, gender-biased psychology', after which
'the edifice of traditional masculinity collapsed', one is simply
left to wonder what has been holding things up? And why
should it be now, rather than at the close of the 1970s (in the
heyday of feminist critique, and the first publications by Pleck
and others on the dangers of the male sex role) that things are
going to change, with a bit of help from the sympathetic
psychologist?

What has been holding things up, some might suggest, is
that the symbolic power, or 'phallic fantasies', of masculinity
neither arise from, nor reduce to, any specific set of social
'expectations' or individual behaviour patterns. Rather, 'gender' encapsulates *shifting* relations of difference between men
and women, but differences *always already* structured through
the assumed dominance of masculinity over femininity. 'Masculinity' is an abstraction, condensing notions of power and
authority: it is that which makes it always so precarious, rather
than the individual foibles of frail and damaged men. It is also
precarious, in many psychoanalytic readings, because no child,

either male or female, emerges from the conflictual psycho-dynamics and emotional investments of family life without a certain measure of unconscious agitation and ambiguity over sexual difference and identity. 'Masculinity' is by definition opposed to 'femininity', these are relational concepts which derive their meaning from their difference from each other. This is why 'masculinity' is always at war with 'femininity', feeding gender battles and the continuing climate of misogyny (perhaps of increasing misogyny, if we consider the escalation of reported crimes of violence against women, internation-ally, over the last few decades). It is thus a mistake to think we can eliminate men's anxieties simply by reforming 'mas-culinity'. It is the complex edifice of polarized gender hier-archy, at the structural, interpersonal and psychic level, which have all to be undermined, before attempted *shifts* in the meanings adhering to appropriate gender roles or identities have any secure context or foundation.

Meanwhile, as Pleck and others take pains to establish, deploying a multitude of empirical data and diverse 'mascu-linity scales' and ratings, conspicuous displays of so-called 'feminine' skills may be just the sort of 'modernization' of men's behaviour which will increase their power as individual men (over both women and other men). Indeed, Robert Weiss's study of eight-five successful American businessmen (all upper middle class, white and identified as heterosexual), published in 1990, suggests the importance of men being able to transform their former masculine competitiveness into 'more or less affectionate alliances' with others, although the self-disclosure of feelings is carefully monitored.[59] Other men are not so fortunate. 'Gentleness' as a skill is unlikely to be much of an asset to unemployed men – or women – who live by their wits. (There are only so many ways to rob a bank – unless, of course, you own it, or work as a commodity trader.) It is only their blindness to social issues, particularly those of class, which allows Pleck and his co-researchers to believe that the 'endorsement of masculinity ideology' is itself the decisive causal factor in explaining its existing correlation with 'problem behaviors' in young men.[60]

The limitations of this personal re-skilling of men as a way of overturning men's 'traditional, phallocentric psychology' should be evident from the fact that 'machismo' derives from, and has become synonymous with, the behaviour of subordinated (originally Latino) men – working-class and ethnic minority. 'I want to be deep and not just macho', a popular cartoon depicting Victor Mature mocked the 'new man' politics of the late 1970s, reminding us of earlier attempts at gender reconstruction in the 1950s. It could serve as a précis of much recent research on masculinity in social psychology. Once we note the hybrid nature of masculinity and its internal hierarchies, traversed by class and race, we find that men have remained the dominant sex by constantly refashioning masculinity. Indeed, as Andrew Ross notes: 'the reason why patriarchy remains so powerful is due less to its entrenched traditions than to its versatile capacity to shape-change and morph the contours of masculinity to fit with shifts in the social climate; in this it shares with capitalism a modernizing hunger to seize the present and dictate the future'.[61]

Although aware of its historically specific and changing forms, and the very uneven distribution of power available to different groups of men in line with class, 'race' and other social hierarchies, Ross chooses to speak of 'patriarchy' to describe the continuing dominance of men as a sex, worldwide.[62] He shares this preference with the Australian sociologist Bob Connell, who never loses sight of what he calls the 'patriarchal dividend', nor of the possible limitations of any project to reform masculinity, suggesting that it may only 'help modernize patriarchy rather than abolish it'.[63] In his book *Masculinities* (1995), Connell studies life histories collected from contrasting groups of Australian men to illustrate the ways in which the tensions and ambiguity *within* conventional gender practices are never far from the surface, either psychologically or socially: whether he is exploring the contradictions of the compliant and passive labour that goes into acquiring the strong and active male body capable of succeeding in sport, the homosocial bonds consolidated through queer baiting, or the anxieties of those men who have embraced feminism.

Yet these inherent instabilities, which fracture even while

they maintain gender arrangements, do not automatically promote resistance through a process of enlightened self-interest. On the contrary, as Connell illustrates, except for those who consciously embrace a feminist ideology, such tensions often produce no more than attempts to shore up a personal sense of gender dominance, by whatever means possible. The 'backlash' politics of moral conservatives, whether campaigning against women's reproductive rights, punitively stigmatizing single mothers, supporting harsh cutbacks in welfare provision and the elimination of equal opportunity legislation (while fighting to preserve and strengthen paternal rights) is only the most organized side of this.[64] And while it is true that men's traditional place in the workplace and the home is now being constantly challenged and remade, we still see a continuing refusal (especially of men at the top levels of political and corporate life) to support social policies which recognize and could assist the smoother working of transformed gender relations. In Britain, for example, an emphasis on the introduction of tougher teaching styles, focused on boys' interests, alongside the hiring of successful male mentors to act as role models, have largely replaced earlier anti-sexist attempts to introduce issues of gender equality and to change existing gender cultures at school. Whether in the classroom or in the new prisons built for adolescent offenders, concern about failures or wrongdoing by 'boys' has led less to the questioning of dominant versions of 'masculinity' than to attempts to shore them up. As Lynn Raphael Reed writes of the new bellicose language and imagery of masculinity in Britain: 'We are asked to join the government "crusade", to use "tough love", send in "hit squads", "name and shame", have "zero tolerance of failure" and silence the "doubts of cynics and the corrosion of the perpetual sceptics".'[65]

Whether taking the form of social alarm over men's individual failings or personal shame over feelings of weakness and inadequacy, neither the anxieties surrounding masculinity nor the differing solutions for tackling them, are especially new. Indeed, anxiety and insecurity have *always* accompanied men's assertions of virility, as Michael Kimmel's trawl through two centuries of writing about 'Manhood in America' reveals, in line with similar overviews by historians in Britain.[66] But, as most feminists and their male sympathizers know only too well, any suggestion that men should simply abandon their quest for 'manhood', even now, has few followers. This is because the most ancient and easiest way of indulging, and at least partially assuaging, men's chronic fears of failure over whether they are 'man enough' has always been the expression of hostility towards women. Women have long been blamed for men's problems: they are the original threat, the fountain of all the forces of feminization. Confined to the separate sphere of the home, women emasculate their sons; allowed into the workplace, they threaten men's authority; today, in the public sphere, they undermine men's preserve with assertions of equality. The knowledge that it never was women who were responsible for men's dread of effeminacy, but men themselves in their collective attempt to affirm mastery over those they must definitively exclude to preserve the category of manhood, hardly offers any release for men's deep fear or resentment which, characteristically of phobic reaction, massively overestimates the power of what is feared.

Researchers into men and masculinity who have been most concerned to find new practical directions for men in Britain, usually because they deal with the most damaging, and damaged, young men, all argue that you cannot separate out the problems of masculinity from the problems of society.[67] Despite some conflicting tendencies and increasing diversity in men's lives, they paint a picture in which most men today are less secure in both their jobs and their families, and are likely to remain so, with unemployed men having the least secure emotional ties with either partners or children.[68] The general prescription they offer is not only state-sponsored social investment in job creation, but genuine public encouragement in government policies, schools and youth work, for boys and men to become more involved in both domestic life and caring work.[69] Of course, they recognize that the market-driven priorities of most Western governments at present have the opposite effect, encouraging longer hours at work, in an ever more competitive milieu. But this only makes the challenging of conventional gender cultures, and the revaluing of much that is understood and precariously enacted in the presumptively feminine domain, all the more urgent.

Deconstructing Gender

Social policies aimed at creating material opportunities for disadvantaged men would help alleviate some of the more destructive patterns of failure, violence and high-risk behaviour tied in with inequalities and differences between men. But without undermining the wider ramifications of gender as a cultural system, men will continue to displace their fears about themselves into contempt for women, and to express antipathy towards other men more excluded and subordinated than their own peers. We will never begin to understand what is at stake here, either for men or for women, without attention to projects which some would like to dismiss as the 'merely' cultural. For men to be able to accept their own multiple and conflicted identities, they need to be able to question and complicate the notion of 'masculinity' itself – all the meanings currently attached to sexual difference and gender identity which cluster around men as the dominant/active/powerful sex.

The writing on 'masculinity' most explicitly committed to the project of exposing the coercively constructed nature of sexual difference and gender binaries comes from texts influenced by deconstructive and Foucauldian scholarship. Their theorizing of 'gender' in terms of the discourses which position it in language eschews all universalizing or essentializing categories. Here 'masculinity', like its subordinated term 'femininity' (the two existing only in hierarchically imposed opposition to each other), can only ever be an anxiously claimed identity, one tied to linguistic and materialist practices that are never fixed or secure. Gender, at least in Western iconography, has for at least two centuries been conjoined with discourses of sexual desire which (as discussed in chapter 2) are construed in terms of heterosexual normativity positioning 'masculine' and 'feminine' desire as ineluctably 'active' and 'passive' encounter, respectively.[70]

Illustrating the analysis of 'masculinity' as a powerful, regulatory fiction – always haunted by what it attempts to exclude – the cultural theorist Homi Bhabha begins his evocative essay 'Are You a Man or a Mouse?' with the claim that: 'To speak of masculinity in general, sui generis, must be avoided at all costs'. As a discourse of 'self-generation', he continues, we need not so much to deny or disavow 'masculinity', as to 'draw attention to its prosthetic reality', to show how its claims to superiority are always grounded in contradiction, conflict and anxiety. Speaking personally, he adds: 'My own masculinity is strangely separated from me, turning into my shadow, the place of my filiation and my fading. My attempt to conceptualize its conditionality becomes a place to question it'.[71] Bhabha also highlights how discourses of dominant 'masculinity' intertwine not only with discourses of heterosexuality, but also with those of nationality and race.

Much along these lines, Robert Reid-Pharr ruefully surveyed the success of the Million Man March in Washington in 1995, reflecting on how the image of an 'all-powerful masculinity was [being] offered as the solution to, and compensation for' the stark curtailments of resources and opportunities currently affecting so many in the USA.[72] Mirroring Daniel Moynihan's scapegoating of black women a generation earlier, the dangers of such attempts at therapeutic reaffirmation of masculinity should be obvious: diverting attention from the pernicious racism that still, perhaps increasingly, dominates life in the USA, and damages black men in particular. Reid-Pharr concludes his analysis, wanting to replace such traditional patriarchal exhortations with his own alternative yearnings for 'a public dialogue and a civic life that celebrates multiplicity, that prizes ambiguity, and thereby recognizes the play of identity and difference that makes possible community as well as change'.[73]

Subjectivity and Change

Calling for the expansion of 'civic life' and 'community' to include and celebrate the lives of all people, however, takes us well beyond the theorizing of 'masculinity' simply as a discursive formation. The latter tends to have only the most tenuous grasp on gender relations and routines within the social institutions and organizations serving to maintain (or occasionally fracture) gender hierarchies. As we saw in chapter 2, 'gender' as an analytical category does indeed provide a set of discourses and available symbols, but it operates at multiple levels which require knowledge of diverse social structures and normative frameworks for the enacting of subjective identities, within which the singular details of particular life histories unfold. As some male gender theorists strongly committed to gender justice have argued for some time now, it is broader social forces, and political campaigns encouraging sexual and social equality, which provide the necessary background for the success of any programme for the individual reform of self-destructive and oppressive forms of masculinity.[74]

One such campaign came from collectively organized gay subcultures, especially after the impact of HIV/AIDS on politicized gay men in Western societies. It is these men who have probably done most to connect recent theoretical debates on the precarious nature of 'masculinity' with a sexual politics which works to undermine and challenge traditional masculinity. They analysed and fought the tenacious fear of gay men's sexuality (seen as symbolizing the 'receptive' or 'passive' male bodily encounters), while promoting attitudes of sexual responsibility and care ('safer sex') in men's sexual practices, so alien to many other men's carelessness, if not coercion, in sexual exchanges, whether with women or with men. They campaigned for increased public support for people living with HIV, while also exemplifying men's enduring and selfless potential to love, nurture and sustain the sick and the dying. Finally, and perhaps most inspiring of all, some gay men developed a vernacular for expressing and sharing their own terrifying fears and grief, confused impotence and rage, aching pain and continuing capacity for pleasure and love, in ways which are both cathartic and empowering for themselves and, especially, for others, in the extraordinary literature, poetry and artworks relating to AIDS.[75] There are clearly many different ways of attempting to reform or refashion 'masculinity' in a manner less oppressive to women and, indeed, to many men themselves. However, it is only when men no longer occupy the elite levels of social power that 'masculinity' will finally shed its traditional symbolic trappings. Until then 'masculinity' will continue – as it always has – to haunt most men with fears of impotence and failure, even as it motivates some of them to threaten and seek to control women.

As discussed above, it was feminist psychologists who began the work of investigating the cultural dynamics of gender as they impact upon the lives of women, moving well beyond the individualistic frameworks of traditional psychology. Their point of departure was to address the role of normative notions of 'femininity' and gender hierarchy in the lifelines of girls and women, while paying somewhat less attention to the ambiguities and contextual changes in women's experiences and behaviours (and even less to the conflicts and contradictions in the lives of men). This would encourage other psychologists, often men in sympathy with feminism and sometimes feminist psychologists themselves, to address the increasing evidence of boys' and men's suffering and anxieties, illustrating the high costs of gender conformity, at least for some men. However, any single focus on gender identity can also mislead. Perceptions like that of 'masculinity in crisis', I have argued, conveniently obliterate a constellation in which almost every other social difference is of greater significance than gender *alone* in throwing light upon the situation of those particular groups of men who are suffering most today.

However utopian or pessimistic any feminist goal of dismantling the foundations of men's privileged place in the gender system, those of us who wish to know how gender operates will need to see its multiple and conflictual layers and meanings: its location at the social and symbolic level may well be at odds with its frequently anxious negotiation at the individual or interpersonal level. Few approaches have had more to say on this than that of psychoanalysis: the movement which, like feminism itself, was as defining an influence on people's perceptions of their own lives (both waking and sleeping) as on public and political discourse throughout the twentieth century.

6

Cautionary Tales:
Between Freud and
Feminism

I always find it uncanny when I can't understand someone in
terms of myself.

Sigmund Freud, *letter to Martha Bernays*

'In the face of claims of its widely announced demise, psychoanalysis has never been more recognized in British intellectual life', the editorial of one of Britain's journals of cultural
theory announced provocatively in the mid-1990s.[1] Ironically,
it is feminist scholarship which has inspired much of the
writing on which this judgement is based – ironic because,
only a few decades earlier, feminists had singled out Freud as
their cardinal enemy, especially in the USA. As Juliet Mitchell
recalls, 'there were calendars produced by the women's movement with dartboards over the head of Freud and a bull's eye
dart through his eye'.[2]

Enthusiasm for psychoanalysis, shadowed by bitter denunciation, has engrossed feminist thought from the time of the
inception of these two key movements of modernity, over a
century ago. Mari Jo Buhle's recent overview of the complex
entanglement of the two formations is particularly illuminat-
ing.[3] The feminist and free-lover Emma Goldman sat enthusiastically in the audience when Freud first took psychoanalysis
to America in 1909, speedily affirming its affinity with feminism and declaring Freud, whom she understood as attacking
hypocrisy and being in favour of women's sexual emancipa-
tion, 'a giant among pygmies'.[4] But her contemporary Charlotte Perkins Gilman rejected the growing women's interest

in the new politics of selfhood – sexuality and maternity – wishing to refocus their attention on material conditions and employment. Such ambivalence has always been mutual, each side taking its turn to cherish or deride the other.[5] Many powerful women could be found in the ranks of psychoanalysis, one of the earliest professions to welcome women, some of whom would very quickly make lasting theoretical innovations and provide its dominant figures – especially during and after the 1920s. Yet their male mentors, from Freud to Lacan, seemed to delight in teasing women who pursued equality with men, an equality they believed feminists would never manage to achieve.

In contrast to feminist scholarship, academic psychology has maintained a more durable disdain for its nearest rival, psychoanalysis, and thus remained outside the lasting encounter between feminism and psychoanalysis. To the lifelong chagrin of most psychologists, especially the best known, like Hans Eysenck in Britain, Freud's legacy has proved indestructible throughout the twentieth century. Eysenck would die still wondering how Freud had managed to hoodwink the popular imagination with his theory of the lasting significance of familial childhood experience for adult desires and discontents: 'recent genetic research', he wrote shortly before his death, 'has shown that environmental factors linked to the family have little influence on personality'.[6] His own strict methodological regimes, tirelessly measuring people's responses to the questionnaires which produce conclusions like this (with their dubious relationship to actual 'genetic research'), have had comparatively less cultural impact, despite the growing phalanx of psychologists currently waging war on the significance of early childhood experience in the family.[7]

As discussed in the previous chapter, psychology's disciplinary project has been predominantly one of measuring and theorizing individual differences in behaviour. Its optimistic emphasis on the development of technologies for behavioural or cognitive change popularized the idea that social problems are amenable to individual solution through the acquisition of skills and enlightenment. Thus it has been psychology's task, as Derrida (glossing Foucault) has commented, to *mask* in the modern world 'a certain truth of madness . . . a certain truth of unreason'.[8] The opposite is true of psychoanalysis. At least, in its classical form, it promises not solutions to social conflicts but a heightened awareness of their tragic inevitability. Far gloomier in social outlook, far more cautious in its expectations of change, its sombre vision has been one reason for its more contentious place in cultural debate.

Opening Skirmishes

Traditionally, psychoanalysis has preferred to flaunt, rather than to disavow, the conservative side of its reflections on the links between subjectivity and the 'maladies' of modernity. Its pessimism of the intellect produces its own paralyses for those who wish to transform the relations it describes (and helps reinscribe) between sexed identity and gender hierarchy. But it is the inescapable significance of these links which continually recharges the dialogue between feminism and psychoanalysis, fuelled by their shared belief in the subjective and cultural centrality of ideas of sexual difference. This is the terrain, perhaps unfortunately, on which we encounter the battles between the two, and which I cover here. I say 'unfortunately', because it is in this area that psychoanalysis often moves farthest from what some of us see as its central strength: its potentially subversive account of psychological development, with its theories of subjectivity as always unstable and conflicting, diverse and disorderly. Instability is surely what we should expect when Freud saw subjectivity (or character) as formed through identifications with those we have loved and hated; in the beginning, those we loved as a child.

Yet the narratives grounding psychoanalytic theories of sexual difference have looked far from subversive to many feminists. Surveying the fractious relations between psychoanalysis and feminism, the British cultural critic Rachel Bowlby concluded: 'The one constant seems to be that neither side ever lets go: even when apart . . . they [are] always somewhere . . . on each other's mind'.[9] When not damning Freud and his followers for inciting men to label women's search for independence a symptom of neurosis (as Betty Friedan and Germaine Greer have done), or cursing him for condoning – if not encouraging – men's sexual aggression and making child sexual abuse 'the best kept secret in the world' (as Susan Brownmiller and Florence Rush have accused), feminists were turning to his texts for theoretical inspiration.

Why? Why should there be this dogged return to a legacy so troubled and so troubling? 'What *is* the attraction to psychoanalysis?', as Juliet Mitchell asked again, (apparently perplexed, as she surveyed the packed hall of expectant feminists who had turned up in 1994 to celebrate the twentieth anniversary of her book *Psychoanalysis and Feminism*. Her own answer, the one which first motivated her writing, was a belief in the '*political* need' for psychoanalysis: it alone could explain the global tenacity of male domination, or patriarchy, and the difficulties feminists encountered in their political struggles for equality, with its account of the unconscious construction of sexual difference. Yet, as Mitchell and other feminists would hasten to add, the deeper attraction of psychoanalysis was that while, on the one hand, it seemed to explain why it was that sexual difference should appear to be such an immutable and absolute difference (more entrenched than any other social division), it could equally be used to challenge any proclaimed certainties, any normative theorizing, about what it means to be a 'woman' or a 'man'.[10] Its enlightening presumption of the inevitable tensions, uncertainties and ambivalences at the heart of sexual difference and gender identity – which linger on, long after we outgrow the polymorphous, bisexual pleasures of infancy – was what made it possible, many feminists have felt, to wed psychoanalysis to feminism, however embittered the coupling might sometimes become: 'The radical potential in their marriage', as Jane Gallop wrote in 1982, 'is not a mystical fusion obliterating all difference and conflict, but a provocative contact which opens each to what is not encompassed by the limits of its identity'.[11]

Looked at more closely, however, this is still puzzling. For if what we are supposed to take from psychoanalysis is the inevitability of instability and complexity in the area of sexuality and sexual difference, challenging their naturalistic reduction to reproductive or gender norms, why has Freud's legacy so often been appropriated by those most dedicated to conservative moralizing about sexual difference, and women's place in the world, at least since the 1930s? It is not just Freud himself who moved towards incoherence when trying to solve dilemmas around sexual difference: repeatedly observing the worthlessness of equating 'masculinity' with 'activity' and 'femininity' with 'passivity', while immediately proceeding to reinstate the 'great antithesis' between 'masculinity' and 'femininity' as the 'bedrock' of the human psyche, *in just those terms*.[12]

Freud portrayed 'femininity' as it is culturally represented, and thus to some degree psychically stabilized; that is, through a defensive logic grounded in men's anxieties about their own 'masculinity'. From early childhood onwards, as Norman Mailer once summed things up for his sex: 'Being a man is the continuing battle of one's life'.[13] Given, of course, 'one' is a man. For a woman, especially a feminist, the battle is somewhat different: to escape from both cultural and psychic investments in notions of 'castrated' or passive womanhood, which bolster fictions of 'phallic' masculinity. And it is here that psychoanalytic reflections have often proved less than useful in suggesting any routes for escape; indeed, not infrequently, they have treated any such attempt with derision.

Yet, it is true that against both biological and behaviouristic explanations of more straightforward pathways to gender identity, only psychoanalytic discourses seem to explain the continual *failure* of individual psychic realities consistently to reflect the apparent certainties of social realities, exposing the inevitable incommensurability of the two. They also warn us of the unpredictable, often dangerous force of men's investment in the phallic lack projected onto female bodies: man has it *only* insofar as woman lacks it. Freud, sadly, did not invent the idea of the phallus as a symbol of power and desire in language and consciousness (although he did not put it quite like that). Nor did he invent the dread and repudiation of 'femininity' in his patients and in himself. That is why feminists like me live with the paradox of wanting to assert psychoanalytic arguments, while also wanting to challenge them, aware that the convergence between unconscious fantasy and cultural understandings of sexual difference are always threatened and precarious. However, the rub is that feminist deployment of psychoanalytic discourses often ties itself in slipknots, securing rather than loosening the bonds which confine women in phallic fictions of sexual difference. We frequently find just such questioning of gender certainties immediately subdued by assertion of the 'absolute' nature of sexual difference in human subjectivity and social relations. Indeed, it is this grounding of sexual difference as the single overriding difference, side-lining all other psychic complexities and other social divisions (most obviously, of class and race) which has drawn most feminists to psychoanalysis in the first place.

Imagining the Void

For all their disagreements, this is what unites the two main trajectories of psychoanalytic feminism: Lacanianism and object-relations theory. The irony is that neither Lacan and his interpreters (analysing the alienated and illusory dynamics of subjectivity) nor the object-relations school (stressing the significance of pre-Oedipal attachment), were originally primarily concerned with questions of sexual difference at all. The Lacanian tradition, particularly in Britain and the USA, has been far more influential in theoretical debate and cultural analysis than in therapeutic practice. Indeed, Lacan (and his direct heir and amanuensis, Jacques-Alain Miller) systematically posed their own 'scientific', putatively logico-mathematical, abstractions against clinicians 'impure', humanistic discourses.[14] And strange as it may seem in this new golden age of capitalist global supremacy, it was in the attempt to build a bridge to Marxism that feminists first sought to incorporate the ideas of Lacan, most notably Juliet Mitchell. For here the social order (seen as capitalist patriarchy) comes to constitute the individual through the acquisition of language – allowing no real boundary between the self and society, between the private or personal and the public or political.

However, the popularity of Lacan in feminist theory since the late 1970s has proved the most acutely paradoxical of all of feminism's flirtations with psychoanalysis. Although he was publicly scornful of social strategies for undermining or transforming existing structures of sexual difference as 'culturalist' deviation (insofar as they were treating phallic primacy as a secondary formation), Lacan has nevertheless appeared to many feminists to offer the only way to rescue Freud from *biologistic* phallocentrism – albeit at the price of acknowledging the intransigence of linguistic phallocentrism. He was uniquely influential in the late 1970s and early 1980s in inspiring now prominent feminist theoreticians, especially those engaged in literary and film studies, to hunt down the ubiquitous presence of phallic discourses and imagery, observing how they function as a fundamental area of oppression, internalized by women. However, it was a pursuit which others would sometimes come to see as ultimately self-defeating for feminist attempts to overturn phallocentrism, since for Lacan, 'strictly speaking, there can be no symbolization of the female *sexe*; the female *sexe* has the character of an absence, a void, a hole'.[15]

The theorizing of Lacanian feminists who did revolt against Lacan's uniquely fatalistic phallicism, while staying within his theoretical framework, was to prove just as controversial. From the outrageous antics of Antoinette Fouque and her followers (who attempted to hijack the French 'Women's Movement' by obtaining an exclusive legal patent to use the term – a practice they continue to this day), to Luce Irigaray and Hélène Cixous, they have sought to subvert phallic law by affirming and expressing its 'unknowable', 'ineffable', 'excessive', defiantly 'feminine' Other. With a parallel, but somewhat distinct rhetoric and goal, Julia Kristeva would attempt to analyse the pre-Oedipal semiotic space of mother-infant communication. In the process, each encouraged attacks on the limitations of so-called 'equal-rights' feminism (a term which would come to include, and thereby excise, 'socialist feminism') – when not, like the formidable Fouque herself, attempting to bury it as a betrayal of women, having learned from Lacan 'not to yield to the feminist illusion'.[16] We still suffer the fall-out from the particularly tedious and largely misleading polarization between 'equality' and 'difference' thrown up by this brand of French feminism, in timely harmony with North American 'cultural feminism'. More generally, and despite its very real strengths in encouraging greater awareness of the significant role of language and representation in the oppression of women, it seems to me that many of the feminist pirouettes on the Lacanian stage have served more to exhaust than invigorate radical theorizing – especially when they aim to taunt, while actually deferring to, the spirit of their master.

The point is this: if feminists believe Lacan, there are no intelligible strategies for overthrowing gender hierarchy. His theorizing is monolithic and ahistorical: 'no sexual revolution will shift these lines of division', the true Lacanian acolyte Eugénie Lemoine-Luccioni insists.[17] In Lacanian space we are devoid of any autonomy, constituted through a language coextensive with sexual difference in the phallic order of the Symbolic. Here, the 'phallus' refers neither to a real organ, nor to an imaginary object invested with power, but rather to *the* transcendental signifier (signifier of 'power and the advent of desire'), which is unaffected by shifts in social practices and relations across time, place and milieu, not to mention the idiosyncrasies of personal biography within which bodily encounters become so powerfully invested with meaning.[18] Despite a multitude of teasingly asserted (and immediately rejected) speculations on the signifying chain linking the phallus to the veiled or fetishized male bodily organ, the penis, all that we ever learn for certain about this 'master signifier' and its privileged role is its functioning as the paternal metaphor which (following the structuralist methodology of Claude Lévi-Strauss) receives its place in the symbolic order in the 'name-of-the-Father'. The phallus is the power which, supposedly across all cultural domains and from the dawn of history, has identified the Father with the figure of the law, and hence conferred on men (and only men) the right to exchange women, operating as the third term which comes between mother and child: 'the phallus forbids the child the satisfaction of his or her own desire, which is the desire to be the exclusive desire of the mother'.[19] The phallus, as a condition of discourse, constitutes women in terms of lack, and men in terms of the threat of lack, as the latter collectively struggle to identify with the *illusion* of the father's imaginary potency.

'Woman' is constituted in terms of lack, Lacan asserts, yet there is something which she experiences beyond lack: a feminine *jouissance* or sexual satisfaction unique to her, *outside* symbolization and intelligibility. It is this which has inspired Hélène Cixous and Luce Irigaray to embark upon their quest to inscribe the feminine by attempting to express the female 'imaginary' in texts characterized by playful excess, disruption, grammatical and syntactic subversion and other ambiguous games within the 'masculine' symbolic order. Irigaray has been perhaps the most influential: her search for an alternative to the 'One sex' economy of phallogocentrism has delighted her admirers with its enigmatic, poetic and allusive images of women's sexuality and the 'maternal' imaginary (the left-over or excess residue of maternal desire), seen as defying the limits of the 'paternal' Symbolic.[20] However, it is a strange search which, insofar as it accepts the Lacanian Symbolic, must embrace both contradiction and incoherence in representing the supposedly unrepresentable. It has mystified other feminists seeking more political coherence and direction, or wary of its apparent celebration of women's traditional coding in terms of motherhood. As the male Lacanian Slavoj Žižek declared recently (in criticism of some of his female rivals), the kernel that attempts to resist phallic authority (which we can, if we wish, call the 'feminine') is not a positive one: 'it can be defined only in terms of a certain impossibility, a deadlock, in purely negative ways'.[21] More significantly, critics like Catherine Clément have questioned the belief that preserving women's positions as outsiders to the 'masculine' symbolic could significantly change, rather than help consolidate, a social system which marginalizes women.[22]

In my opinion, the Lacanian trajectory does construct dead-lock for feminism: the wish to overthrow phallocentrism (here seen as generated in the realm of the Imaginary) is necessarily reclaimed and thwarted by the timeless Symbolic. We see the impasse, for example, in the tensions within the work of one influential North American philosopher who, while actively engaged in both important feminist critique and politics, nevertheless pushes us into a tailspin by holding onto Lacan's Symbolic order. In *Beyond Accommodation* Drucilla Cornell draws on Irigaray's notion of mimesis (imitating, affirming, performing 'the feminine') to declare it 'our only strategy' for subverting phallocentric culture: '*mimesis*', she writes, 'tells us how to re-evolve with the definition of the feminine'.[23] As she has more recently asserted, feminists 'must' fight the erasure of 'the feminine'. But the only way to do this, she warns women, is to 'make yourselves truly unreadable in terms of gender categories . . . the more unreadable you become, the better'. She admits that this is a long and arduous process, offering the caution, for good measure, that you never 'know for sure when you're doing it and when you're not!'[24] Symptomatic of trying to make one's feminism compatible with Lacan, this imperative to fight erasure through erasure is a difficult decree. And if the way to struggle against the erasure of the feminine is to attack the readability of the feminine, how then can you have a politics? For politics surely must be *communicable*, and unreadability alone is, to put it mildly, quite a disadvantage.

Feminism has always had to live with a central paradox: that of wanting to hold on to the category of 'woman', to attack the linguistic and wider social denigration of the 'feminine', while also wanting to deconstruct and critique these notions. But, the question is, are women quite so trapped within the prison house of phallogocentrism as French feminism has suggested? 'In what manner of double-speak must feminism proceed', Judith Butler asks of Lacanian psychoanalysis and some of its feminist formulations, 'when it is understood as the unrepresentable in its paradoxical effort to represent itself?' More significantly, she continues: 'Is this structure of feminine repudiation not *reinforced* by the very theory which claims that the structure is somehow prior to any given social organization, and as such resists social transformation?'[25] As Juliet Flower MacCannell has commented, 'by and large, the most elaborated counter-theories of language from feminism still play off the Lacanian insights, rather than seeking alternative theories'.[26] Some feminists who defend the Lacanian symbolic, such as Jacqueline Rose, like to point out that it cannot be seen as fixed because it is always 'the site of its own failing' (that is, its rupture by the unknowable 'real'), yet this hardly advances matters when the structure remains exactly the same: the lack remains the phallic lack, it is always the same failure within the same space which is being highlighted.[27]

As I see it, we must take issue with the philosophical premises of Lacanian psychoanalysis, without denying the social fact of phallic privilege in language and representation and hence the difficulty of affirming the 'feminine'. We can dispute Lacan's two basic principles: first, that non-psychotic subjectivity is constructed solely in and through language; second, that the 'phallus' as paternal metaphor and symbol of male power is coextensive with the emergence of language – that it has a transcendental primacy, rather than a historically constructed one. We can accept the *historical* primacy given to the 'phallus' as symbol of male power in language (and the related notion of the fantasy of 'castration' imposing a narcissistic 'wound' on the female body even as it orchestrates fear around the male body), while at the same time questioning – rather than insistently reproducing – its singular primacy in the Symbolic. Indeed the Saussurean linguistics Lacan draws upon gives no signifier any absolute privilege outside particular discourses: 'Unlike the phallus a signifier [in Saussurean linguistics] has no value in and of itself. No signifier can be privileged over any other signifier'.[28] Lacan's law, that there can be no representation except through the phallus and the acceptance of castration, is thus internal to his own theory, *not* any rule of access to language.

Moving decisively away from Lacan, the French psychoanalyst Jean Laplanche rejects the thesis that there is no extra discursive basis to psychic reality, arguing, in a way that makes a lot of sense to me, that the unconscious is *not* structured as a language, but rather consists of a disordered and conflictual array of enigmatic sexual messages derived from the verbal, non-verbal and behavioural investments which the child receives from the parents in the process of care.[29] As John Fletcher has recently elaborated, Laplanche posits a primordial *passivity* for both sexes in relation to sexuality, a sexuality which arises out of the penetrations and fantasies of the other (this time with a little 'o') who excites the infant in the process of its gestures of parental care.[30] There can be no phallic binarism in the unconscious, Laplanche has always argued, since there is no negation and opposites can coincide without contradiction there. For Laplanche, the Oedipus complex and castration anxiety are neither primordial nor universal, but rather secondary and contingent ways available to the ego for elaborating and binding the anxieties accompanying the intrusive sexual excitations (or routine 'seductions') of infancy: 'The phallic stage fetishising of penis and clitoris serve defensively to extinguish those dangerous libidinal openings to the other in both sexes'.[31] The central point here, as Philippe Van Haute neatly summarizes, is that 'the unconscious is essentially individual: your enigmatic signifiers are not mine'.[32] In contrast, in Lacan, the marginalization of issues other than sexual difference, and the reduction of that difference to phallic difference, stabilizes rather than contests the culturally established repudiation of women's (or men's) bodily experience, interactions and pleasures outside phallic imagery.

Oedipal Dramas and the Crisis of Paternal Authority

Lacanianism has exacerbated classic Freudianism's refusal to engage seriously with, or to criticize, the various male-dominated institutions of our culture which fuel 'castration anxiety' and the Oedipal narrative, creating the boy's fear and repudiation of a 'femininity' always already equated with subordination in favour of a 'masculinity' always already equated with power and authority. With the Lacanian gaze focused firmly beyond the individual, tracking down further support for its philosophical analysis of desire-as-lack, there is little interest in the particulars of specific conflicting desires, or the possible diversity of subject positions, meanings and experiences (now or in the future) corresponding to the inevitable dissonance between tangible mothers and fathers in individual life histories in comparison with the powerful, wordly Father and archaic engulfing Mother of patriarchal (Oedipal) myth. It is this which, as David Macey comments, produces such 'a curiously asexual (and affectless) psychoanalysis', when what we need for the understanding of concrete subjectivity is 'a very specific analysis of conflicting desires and power'.[33]

In reality, as others have now spelt out, the Oedipal drama is one with at least *five* rather than three protagonists (however unevenly weighted the parts): the child with its real-life mother and father, alongside the Imaginary Father and the Imaginary Mother, to which the actual mother, actual father, or, rather, actual third term (ie the husband, or other intimate adult companion of the mother, who may well be a woman), never fully corresponds. Moreover, as those who have reflected upon the cultural basis of Oedipal theory sometimes suggest, it is possible to use Freud's notion of *Nachträglichkeit* ('deferred action' or 'retrodetermination') to argue that the polarizing representation of father/phallus/masculinity as all-powerful does not arise all of a piece in the Oedipal experiences of late infancy, to inscribe phallic order and authority irrevocably as the sole means of distributing sexual positions.[34] Rather, awareness of male domination seeps into experience and reinscribes it, again and again, reordering the experiences of childhood. Possible disruptions of the Oedipal narrative are only negated when the tale is fixed for all time in the Symbolic.

During the 1980s Anglo-American feminists who wanted to move on from the theoretical limitations and intensifying political squabbles of the preceding decade's feminism that privileged notions of 'oppression' understood in terms of direct 'experience' often turned to French psychoanalytic feminism. Today, those feminists who are producing the most

interesting analyses, especially in the area of sexuality, are the
ones who are no longer taking Lacan as their point of departure, if they ever did. These theorists accept that it is psychical and social relations, not anatomies, which give the body
its meanings, and that these meanings are mediated through
existing phallocentric images and discourses. But they do
not believe they are fully constituted by them. The anthropologist Gayle Rubin, who was one of the first to introduce
Lacan's ideas to the USA in her classic essay 'The Traffic in
Women' (1974), always argued against universalizing the Lévi-
Straussian notion of kinship with which Lacan established
the fixity of his Symbolic order. Today she strengthens this
critique of Lacanian 'grandiosity' in presuming to advance *the*
theory of sexual difference:

> I didn't want to get stuck in the Lacanian trap. It seemed to
> me, with all due respect to those very skilled at evading or
> manipulating the snares, that Lacan's work came with a dan-
> gerous tendency to create a kind of deep pit from which it
> would be hard to escape. . . . I was concerned with the totalizing
> tendencies in Lacan, and the non-social qualities of the sym-
> bolic. . . . One of the nifty things about psychoanalytic
> approaches is that they explain both change and intractabil-
> ity. But there is something about the particular intractability
> of what is called the symbolic that I don't understand. . . .
> There is something intrinsically problematic about any notion
> that somehow language itself or the capacity for acquiring it
> requires sexual differentiation as primary differentiation.[35]

Similarly, Teresa de Lauretis has for some time criticized
feminist theorizing of subjectivity which adopts a conceptual
framework of 'universal sexual opposition', rather than seeing the subject as constituted 'across languages and cultural
representation; a subject engendered in the experience of race
and class, as well as sexual relations; a subject, therefore, not
unified but rather multiple, and not so much divided as con-
tradicted'.[36] (In 1994, however, de Lauretis did return, rather
unsuccessfully in my view, to a critical reworking of the
Lacanian symbolic, attempting to develop a formal model of
'perverse desire' in her book *The Practice of Love*.)[37] More

hesitantly, Judith Butler criticizes the static Lacanian foundation for the subject's entry into language, suggesting that we should consider 'the conditions and limits of representation and representability as open to significant rearticulations and transformations under the pressure of social practices of various kinds'.[38] Even Elizabeth Grosz, once a foremost feminist exponent of Lacan, suggests that perhaps 'now is the time to rethink' the value of a discourse of desire which fails to 'account for, to explain, or to acknowledge the existence of an active and explicitly female desire, and, more particularly, the active and sexual female desire for other women that defines lesbianism'.[39]

This is certainly an advance on the earlier influential but constraining conclusions of British Lacanian feminists like Juliet Mitchell and Jacqueline Rose who seemed to feel, at least in the early 1980s, that for feminists to make the attempt to understand Lacan's exposition (no small enterprise, admittedly) of how 'the status of the phallus in human sexuality enjoins on the woman a definition in which she is simultaneously symptom and myth' was to go about as far as you could go.[40] Since then, without abandoning Lacan, both have moved closer to Klein and a richer engagement with clinical issues, while Rose has herself highlighted the impasse in debates between feminists who defend, and those who contest, the Lacanian phallocentric account of feminine sexuality. She still sees no way beyond it, however. [41] The irony is that two decades before Lacan elaborated his notion of the phallus in the late 1950s, he was already aware of the historically specific nature of the patriarchal family generating the development of Freud's classic Oedipal formation. As Mikkel Borch-Jacobsen argued in 1994, commenting upon Lacan's article 'Family Complexes in the Formation of the Individual' (1938), the Lacan of the 1930s was anxiously lamenting the threat to paternal power and authority posed by modern conceptions of marriage as a partnership of equals. He described modern family forms as fostering the 'social decline of the paternal imago' and 'a narcissistic debasement of the idealization of the father' resulting in a general crisis of identification.[42]

Despite Lacan's critical disclosure of the place of sexual

difference in the structure of language, and of the significance of language in the formation of subjectivity and intelligibility, his account of the Symbolic can be seen as characteristic of many moves in psychoanalytic theorizing which attempt to shore up the inevitability of patriarchal authority as a fundamental structure of human desire. It thereby becomes as much a necessity in modern (or future) societies, as in traditionally patriarchal ones. Peter Dews points to parallels here between the worries of the young Lacan of the 1930s and the contemporary fears of Max Horkheimer and the early Frankfurt School over the weakening of men's autonomy through declining paternal authority.[43]

The point to note is the extent to which fears over the shake-up of the gender order, characteristic of modernity, have served as the central motor of conservatism in psychoanalytic theorizing. Even Dews, a critical theorist of the left, chides Borch-Jacobsen for what he sees as his 'insouciant' conclusion that it is time to stop treating the Oedipus complex as a *'problem'*, and to accept the changes which have occurred in our societies, which are now: *'defined* by a general crisis of symbolic identifications – "deficiency of the paternal function", "foreclosure of the name of the father", perpetual questioning of the symbolic "law" and "pact", confusion of lineage and general competition of generations, battle of the sexes, and loss of family landmarks'.[44] Meanwhile, the idea that *only* the father, paternal imago or phallic signifier can interrupt the infant's early fusion with the mother, and hence rescue the individual from degenerative fixation at the level of infantile narcissistic omnipotence (and potential lawless thuggery) remains, with only a few significant exceptions, a key conservative trope of the psychoanalytic imagination, often even in its ostensibly most radical forms. Žižek testifies to its undiminished prevalence when, reminiscent of both Horkheimer and the early Lacan, he comments: 'These Foucauldian practices of inventing new strategies, new identities [for undermining sexual difference], are ways of playing the late capitalist game of subjectivity', a game which produces 'multiple identities, non-identity and cynical distance'. Phallocentrism, Žižek declares, 'is not the enemy today'. (Not whose enemy?, one might well ask.) Rather it is the decline of this 'patriarchal-identitarian' dynamic which is the weapon of late capitalism for undermining resistance to it.[45] What is more, such belief in the threat presumptively posed by the weakening of paternal authority and the phallic construction of sexual difference is by no means restricted to Lacanian psychoanalysis, nor to the male psychoanalytic voice. Quite the contrary, as we shall see.

The First Bond and its Consequences

However, before returning to this issue, it is important to acknowledge that feminist object-relations theory set out precisely to reject any such emphasis on the importance of paternal authority and the Oedipal moment. It drew upon Melanie Klein and, in particular, the writings of the Independents of the British School of Psychoanalysis, Donald Winnicott, Ronald Fairbairn, Michael Balint and Harry Guntrip, to focus almost entirely on the mother-child relationship. In total contrast to Lacanian perspectives, their theorizing is about drawing attention to actual mothers and fathers (but mainly to mothers and mothering) and their place within prevailing structures and social relations of male dominance. But here, at least for quite a while, we encountered a mirror image of Lacanian reductionism: rather than ignoring the historic social and cultural production of gender categories, the psychic is collapsed back into the social relations of gender, with little space for any more complex exchange between the two. Feminist object-relations theory has played down the significance of symbolic phallocentrism, castration anxiety and penis envy, refocusing upon pre-Oedipal attachments or mother-infant bonding.

Here female experience is bound up with mother-daughter ties, as in Nancy Chodorow's now classic text *The Reproduction of Mothering* (1978), with its somewhat idealized account of the mutual identification between mother and daughter in contrast with the other-directed love between mother and son. It is the fact that it is *women* who mother that secures the 'femininity' of girls in the form of nurturing and expressive capacities, which differ markedly from what becomes the emphasis on autonomy and firm boundaries of boys, although accompanying a less secure sense of 'masculinity'. For each sex there is a direct continuity between the self and the social environment, with neither the anguish and loss, on the one hand, nor the threat of annihilation and engulfment, on the other, seeming to play such a significant part in the experience of the child around the necessity for separation from the mother. This type of feminist object-relations theory is therefore at odds with most other psychoanalytic writing on the psychic life of the child. Furthermore, it loses its grip on what seemed to be the strength of classic pychoanalytic accounts of sexual difference: their stress on the unstable nature of sexed identity, and its uncomfortable failure to conform to social expectations.

The tight circuit of social determinism in this particular feminist account of the polarizing effects of the institution of mothering thus fixes identity all too smoothly along normative gender lines, through a narrative which dismisses the language of lack and absence around which Lacanian feminism rotates. It is from this perspective, for example, that Ethel Person writes: 'Most theorists now believe that the developmental lines of gender precede those of sexuality, a complete reversal of Freud's original formulation'. Rejecting Freud's 'patriarchal bias', Person argues that her fellow New York analysts seem to agree that 'we must look to the early identifications with the idealized mother-ego ideal in order to understand the greater portion of the feminine personality organization'.[46] We now face a different dilemma. Many saw a tragic truth, reflecting Freud's perception of the inevitable frustrations of the human condition, in the stoical cynicism of Lacan's account of the necessary illusions of love and the romantic heterosexual bond ('For what is love other than banging one's head against a wall, since there is no sexual relation?'[47]) In contrast, there is a blueprint for personal salvation (and a corresponding attribution of failure) in the writing of object-relations theorists who, like Otto Kernberg and Ethel Person, remain firm believers in the consummation of human happiness through 'mature' heterosexual bonding. In this respect they are reminiscent of mainstream psychology's faith in the pathways to individual fulfilment.

Here, for instance, is Person writing lyrically on the sharing of each other's subjective reality in love: '[Love] denies the barriers separating us, offering hope for a concordance of two souls. . . . The experience of love can make time stop. . . . [It] may confer a sense of inner rightness, peace and richness. . . . [It is] a mode of transcendence . . . a religion for two'. Above all, it is a family affair: 'a stable deep object relation with a person of the opposite sex'.[48] From this perspective, through Klein and Balint to Kernberg and Person, the reinforcement of familial conservatism and heterosexual normativity continues, in a way largely absent from Freud and certainly from Lacan. As the most clinically and theoretically powerful tradition of psychoanalysis in Britain, Klein's successors have been passionately criticized by psychotherapists campaigning against what they see as the institutionalized homophobia of their profession: the largely unacknowledged exclusion of gays and lesbians from analytic training and the pathologizing of homosexual desire. The cause of their anger can be found in the pejorative views of Hanna Segal, describing homosexuality as both an attack on the parental couple and a repudiation of reality: 'The child has to accept the reality of the parents as a couple, and the couple as a creative relationship because that is what produces the baby. . . . Any deviation from sexuality of that kind is an internal attack on the parents as a couple, and in that sense is not really a complete healthy development'.[49] Balint had earlier decreed: 'without normal intercourse, there is no real contentment'.[50] Such thoughts feed the scare-mongering of Charles Socarides, a psychoanalyst from the USA, whose message that homosexuality 'operates against the cohesive elements in society' is currently traversing the globe. He adds for good measure, 'the forces allied against heterosexuality are formidable and unrelenting'.[51]

Retrenchment versus Renewal?

The challenge to such conservative deployment of psychoanalysis, which draws on Freud's own early essays on the
origins of sexuality (with their focus on actual sexual bodies
and their infinite capacity for sensual pleasure), has disappeared from many of the later appropriations of it. Whether
abandoning the study of bodily pleasures to explore the symbolic reign of the fraudulent phallus or, distancing itself from
polymorphous perversity for conventional narratives of the
gender-differentiating effects of maternal attachments, the
potential challenge of the infinite waywardness of infantile
sexuality persisting to undermine, or at least trouble, the acquisition of sexual and gender normativity is cast aside even
within many feminist versions of psychoanalysis, in both clinical and theoretical settings. This leaves them poorly equipped
to confront the conservative appropriations of psychoanalysis
which press it into the service of reactionary dogma. Such
normative appropriations of psychoanalysis flow inevitably
from any model of sexuality which focuses exclusively upon
the workings of an ineluctably heterosexual nuclear family –
whether this is reduced to a relation with the paternal Symbolic, or seen as a vehicle for the retrieval in sexual maturity
of the cross-sexed 'object relations' of childhood.

The irony is, of course, that Freud himself suggested that
'libidinal attachments to persons of the same sex play no less
a part as factors in normal mental life . . . than do similar
attachments to the opposite sex.'[52] It was he who laid the
seeds for challenging the pathologization of what we now call
'transgressive' sexualities, and he who knew that we have
reasons to problematize (but in a way he always failed to
develop) the normative assumptions of heterosexuality. As
case histories often reveal, a heterosexual may have a fully
narcissistic relation to someone of the 'opposite sex'. Yet, it is
in Freud's name, not despite it, that the widely read and
routinely cited Janine Chasseguet-Smirgel draws her far-
cically reductive links between the psychic and the social:
'reality resides', she writes, 'in the differences of sex and

generation' and, it would seem, in little else. For her, there are no other issues, no other narratives, on which we need to draw to explain either individual or global 'reality', however particular the historical context. National and international conflict, nuclear weapons, war and genocide, all become gruesome effects of failure to accept sexual difference, as we have been warned, repeatedly, by psychoanalysts throughout the twentieth century. It is a failure usually seen, in line with Chasseguet-Smirgel, as 'fed by too lax an attitude on the part of the parents, especially [of course] the mother'. And we learn, from the same source: 'The Nazi regime, the S.S. and Hitler himself, lacked the paternal dimension'.[53] Here, nonheterosexual activity becomes a synonym for murder and genocide. Today's moral right and conservative left are listening, and endlessly reiterating the message of the dangers of 'fatherlessness'.

It is also by appealing to Freud's authority that many analysts recycle the linguistic equation 'acceptance of female bodies' with 'acceptance of castration'. This literature still often alludes to a woman's (usually a lesbian's) 'disavowal of castration into adulthood' that must lead her to 'distort [her] relationship with reality'.[54] Such analytic disavowal of the fantasmatic nature of female 'castration' continues the coercive mappings of 'reality' in terms of phallic monism, often (as in Eglé Laufer or Chasseguet-Smirgel) while also, oddly, claiming to reject it.[55] Outside Oedipal theory and cultural phallicism, beyond psychoanalytic conservatism, women are not castrated. The reality is, of course, that a woman cannot be castrated – unlike a man.

The populist dissemination of psychoanalytic accounts of sexual difference can produce even stranger narratives in, for example, supposedly feminist-friendly psychotherapeutic texts by men addressing the 'crisis' of masculinity. One such, apparently following in the footsteps of object-relations perspectives, *Why Men Hate Women*, by the British men's therapist Adam Jukes, is not atypical. In the beginning was Mother. And the troubled bond with Her leads inevitably to male domination and male sexual aggression. For Jukes, male dominance does not derive from language, culture or institu-

confusion and terror, others have suggested more flexible psy-choanalytic tales, where the acceptance of gender identity does not reduce to a single psychic mapping or moment. 'Man is not only phallic', the analyst Monique Schneider comments, 'I even think that he could not be tolerated as penetrating if he were not enveloping at the same time'. Significantly, however, she adds: 'Generally, psychoanalysis doesn't want to know anything about this enveloping power because it reactivates a sort of deep feminine and maternal identification'.[59] Along these lines, Dana Breen closes her in-troduction to a reappraisal of psychoanalytic readings, *The Gender Conundrum*, with the suggestion that 'psychobisexu-ality is increasingly understood to be fundamental not just for sexuality but for psychic integration and structuring more generally'.[60] Most importantly, she stresses that we must rec-ognize the role of feminine identification in male sexuality and masculine development. But I am still not satisfied with this formulation. First, many of the readings in her collection do *not* reflect such a consensus at all; second, we are not getting to the heart of the problem. This is not so much the need to embrace 'psychobisexuality', as to find – indeed, to help to create – *a new object of knowledge*: one which can move beyond the restrictive polarization of gendered identi-ties reflected, but also rationalized, within Oedipal theory.

This new kind of knowledge would recognize – in a way classical Freudianism never could – the existence of adult female bodies as other than deformities of, or receptacles for, male bodies and the making of babies, tied in with practices of maternalism. It would be able to see the links currently existing between experiences of sexual difference, and their history of embeddedness in notions of oppositional hetero-sexuality and familial responsibilities, without collapsing the one into the other. Our relation to a sense of sexual differ-ence, as our most personal sense of identity, operates at both conscious and unconscious levels – often at odds with itself. It is one which is suffused with, but does not reduce to, all the wider linguistic, structural, interpersonal and familial rami-fications of gender conceptions and practices. There needs to be theoretical scope for the operation of diversity, at both the psychic and the cultural level, where rigid gender contrasts no longer rule.

Some feminist psychoanalysts, many of them in New York, for example Jessica Benjamin, Muriel Dimen, Virginia Goldner and Adrienne Harris (who in 1996 helped found the journal *Gender and Psychoanalysis*), are now determined to move decisively beyond some of the older barriers which keep reinscribing traditional gender ideology. Benjamin, for example, draws upon the infancy research of Daniel Stern and Elsa First to argue that it is possible for the child (unlike the more typical French or British psychoanalyst) to encompass a doubleness or tension in psychic life whereby the unconscious fantasy of maternal omnipotence can and does exist alongside the capacity for pre-Oedipal intersubjectivity between mother and child. She also discusses the potential for 'post-Oedipal' constellations, when the cross-gender identifications of early life survive to surmount the rigidity of the 'positive' Oedipal (or same-sex) identification.[61] Similarly, Goldner and Dimen both point out that the powerful, polarizing gender identifications made by the child are always confusing, and in danger of collapsing under the weight of their own contradictions. This means, as Goldner spells out as a goal for analytic treatment: 'the ability to tolerate the ambiguity and instability of gender categories is more appropriate than the goal of 'achieving' a single, pure, sex-appropriate view of oneself'.[62] The acceptance of gender ambiguity and instability is here the goal for mental health.

However, these are all theorists who have abandoned the belief in the Holy Trinity: the view that it is only via the intervention of the 'father', and the acceptance of sexual difference, that the infant can free itself 'from the helpless subjection to the omnipotent mother and enter the reality of the wider world'.[63] They do not accept, as Juliet Mitchell sternly tried to remind them in an exchange a few years ago, that: 'Sexuality is the process that enables one to find the gendered other as different from oneself so that she or he can be used as other for the purpose of engendering'.[64] They reject the idea that sexual sameness or difference is the sole marker of identity, and argue for a more flexible interaction between identificatory and object love: rejecting the Oedipal dictum that where one identifies one cannot desire; what one desires, one must disown in oneself. Benjamin, for example, suggests that gender dimorphism itself represents only one side of gendered positions, the other side being the polymorphism of the psyche.[65]

We may not be able, and certainly not yet, to abandon gender as a central analytic category, or to ignore its symbolically charged meanings as the child moves between identification with and desire for those it loves and fears. But this does not mean that we can only ever position ourselves within an *oppositional* gender *hierarchy*: notions of sexual difference are not the only markers of identity and difference, despite their power in the continuing patriarchal symbolism of global male dominance. Our identities and sexualities are still formed within the shadow of (hetero/sexual) phallic constructions, but there exists no eternal writ that they must always be so formed (whatever personal and social panic this currently induces, especially in men). The spectre which haunts the majestic phallus is its reduction to the ranks of the mutable penis. Theorists like Kaja Silverman argue that it is possible to see historical moments when 'the equation of the male organ with the phallus [can] no longer be sustained'. Seeing such moments, she suggests in *Male Subjectivity at the Margins*, paves the way for 'a collective loss of belief in the whole of the dominant fiction'.[66]

It suggests, perhaps, not so much the way as the possibility. From within phallocentric culture it is far from easy to hold a vision of transcending the hierarchical binary of sexual difference, to acknowledge the integrity of the female body or the fluctuating subtleties of the male body. My view is that feminism still needs psychoanalysis, as it provides the fullest account we have of the complex and contradictory nature of subjectivities formed through desire and identification. But feminist reappraisals could also suggest the possibility of moving beyond the single binary opposition its patriarchal narrative of sexual difference describes and fortifies, with its phallic logic and conservative family romance: 'Sameness, like difference is a (motivated) fantasy not a natural fact – a construction, and, like all constructions of its time, provisional'.[67] This would entail exploring the force *and* the instabilities of those constructions preserving male dominance in family life and sexual regulation, as they intrude into psychic experience and shape the normative Oedipal narrative of child development. It would also direct our attention to the multiplicity of adult pleasures and desires. Were the instabilities and complexities of erotic life more central to psychoanalytic reflection, it might be easier to see how often, and how inevitably (and usually without succumbing to psychotic delusion), subjective experience implodes those binaries inscribing sexual difference. Pursuing such a course would mean that the feminist cycles of embracing or denouncing psychoanalysis could be broken, since, as Adam Phillips suggests: 'It is not so much the future of psychoanalysis that anyone should worry about, but rather the finding of languages for what matters most to us; for what we suffer from or for, for how and why we take our pleasures'.[68]

Most psychoanalytic theorizing, even when feminist, has still to liberate itself from the bedrock of sexual difference. It may, or may not, take longer to liberate actual women and men from the ambivalence, the confusion and the pain of living out the effects of cultural myths which generate antagonism of the sexes. In my final chapter, I return to the diverse aspirations and achievements of different formations of feminism as they draw very different conclusions about the situation of women at the end of the millennium. It is the ever-deepening divisions between women themselves which encourages what can be seen as the stand-off within feminism today between 'culture' and 'politics': between those who privilege cultural analysis and its deconstructions of subjectivity, on the one hand, in volatile conflict with those committed to women's political activism, or the production of knowledge in the service of such activism, on the other.

7

Only Contradictions on Offer: Feminism at the Millennium

> Feminism tries to empower women so that they can create the lives they want, but it also, and simultaneously, puts their very desires into question, for it asks whether there are wants women have not yet begun, or dared, to imagine.
>
> Muriel Dimen, *Contemporary Psychoanalysis*

It is hardly news to suggest that there is a contradiction at the heart of feminism. And in these times of rapid changes in gender practices and meta-narrative mistrust, most of its thoughtful exponents know better than to think we might eliminate it. Feminism, Joan Scott pronounces, has 'only para-doxes to offer'.[1] Most have seen the dilemmas of feminism to be a result of the confusions generated between competing objectives. The first is its struggle to improve the lives and status of the majority of women, especially where they have appeared most vulnerable when classified as a sex – whether in their sexual, reproductive, working or social lives. It is campaigning for gender justice or equality that feminism presents itself in its decisively activist mode, most reminis-cent of the 1970s. The second objective is to reinvent the meanings of womanhood, to imagine the feminine in ways which radically subvert existing symbolic binaries of sex, gen-der and sexuality. This is the declared stance of a 'nineties' feminist post-structuralism (confusingly also often labelled 'post-modern'). However, operating from within the sym-bolic frame from which it aims to liberate itself, it is less obvious how feminism should launch itself into acts or accomplishments outside 'the phallacy of masculine meaning'. Moreover, this tension – sometimes described as one between reformist and revolutionary goals – is heightened by recurring friction between personal and collective struggle. Where once Women's Liberationists hoped for harmony between their own search for empowerment and the needs of women in general, no such illusion is now possible.

A resolution of the conflicts within feminism may not be either possible or desirable. But there surely are ways of embracing tension and contradiction in reviewing gender politics which can, even now, give richer meanings to our personal lives, and encourage collective endeavours towards more desirable futures. For reasons I try to draw together in this closing chapter, it seems unlikely that we can ever repackage feminism in a neat or orderly fashion. But attempting to summarize the very extensive changes in the situation of women and men, three decades after the resurgence of feminism, can help us decide whether there remain aspects of feminism which can still inspire a confrontational politics and culture, even in these times of widespread political quietude in the overdeveloped world. They would have to be feminist tendencies able to ally themselves with other progressive forces against the disparate sources of social inequality, cultural invalidation and personal misery.

Snapshots of Gender

The differing faces of feminism in the media, the academy and politics reflect competing aspects of women's lives today. Depending on our framing, we find two deeply contrasting images: one is gloomy; the other cheerful. Since the 1980s, at a time of mounting economic instability worldwide, there has been a huge expansion in low-waged, insecure jobs in Britain and the USA – the two countries with which I am most familiar. This has occurred alongside continuing attacks on welfare benefits, including the specific targeting of state assistance for single mothers and the disabled, as part of the spread of the low-tax, free-market tenets of economic

neo-liberalism, which has accompanied global economic restructuring. The rolling back of social welfare has in turn incited a renewed emphasis on the importance of traditional
family life and, in particular, fathers' rights and responsibilities. Women, overall more engaged in the work of childcare
and nurturing, suffer specifically, or disproportionately, from
welfare cutbacks and paternalistic rhetorics, and many remain
at the harshest end of deepening inequalities worldwide, in
low-paid, low-status jobs. Those who have researched the effects of the last two decades of change on women in Britain
and North America, for example, report that while many
women have made considerable progress since the 1980s, the
lives of certain other women, especially single parents and the
elderly (with a majority of women in both groups) were getting worse and worse.[2] Moreover, receding expectations of
social provision serve to undermine precisely those goals for
which the women's movement in the 1970s fought so vigorously, leading to a turning away from militant protest and the
disparaging of collective action. Thus, organized resistance to
changes in government spending dramatically decreased over
this period. Sylvia Bashevkin writes of the 'triple whammy'
effect on many women in Britain, the USA and Canada: 'Work
pressures, cuts to government spending, and the advocacy
crunch – taken together – meant many women faced low pay,
no job security, less of a government safety net on which to
rely when they were old, sick or unemployed, and fewer opportunities to protest'.[3] Those facing the harshest extremes of
poverty were also less and less likely to be white, as racial
disadvantage deepened in times of increasing inequality.

In the USA, political assaults on anything coded as feminist
scholarship grew more vicious, as in Harold Bloom's denunciation of the 'rabblement' of 'inchoate would-be Parisians'.[4]
The soldiers of the conservative 'culture wars' now march out
beyond their US birthplace and have acquired some unlikely
followers along their way. At the same time, when absorbed
into mainstream political agendas, feminist discourses have
often been twisted to accommodate more traditional moral
crusades waged in the name of women's and children's intrinsic need for 'protection' from predatory male sexuality (al-

though certain forms of radical feminist analysis – most obviously that of Catharine MacKinnon – bears some responsibility for this appropriation).[5]

Back to basics, in the UK, women's pay as a percentage of men's has remained relatively stable, with women's average earnings still at least a third less than men's (women working part-time average only 58 per cent of men's hourly earnings; full-timers' hourly average has risen to 80 per cent of men's, but their weekly wage remains over a third less, due to men's longer hours, overtime and additional benefits).[6] Indeed, women's lower wages relative to men persists throughout the world, and where women's share has risen (from around 62 per cent to 72 per cent in the USA since the 1970s) it is mainly attributable to the decline in men's wages.[7] Meanwhile, housework and childcare are still primarily seen as women's responsibility in the overwhelming majority of households – including dual-income families.[8] A more demanding workplace makes it harder than ever to harmonize jobs and outside commitments, especially for mothers.[9] Thus, research consistently indicates that women have far less leisure time than men, and many feel guilty about neglecting their children's needs due to the demands of their jobs.[10] Even in the poorest families living on benefit, men still have pocket money for themselves, while women do not, according to a recent report from the Policy Studies Unit in Britain.[11] Men's violence against women and sexual abuse remain endemic. Indeed, the reporting of rape, child sexual abuse and serious violence against women has been increasing since the mid-1980s, yet conviction rates have been decreasing; meanwhile, funding for rape-counselling, women's refuges and the rehousing of battered women and their children has shrunk in both Britain and North America.[12] Some might well wonder, some *do* wonder, has feminism been on a hiding to nothing?

Yet, tilt the frame just a little, and the picture that comes into focus is much more optimistic. Welfare reform, new policies for single mothers and an emphasis on paternal responsibilities are characteristically couched in the language of autonomy and responsibility which was at the heart of

seventies feminist rhetoric. Indeed, as others have noticed –
and the mourning for Princess Diana in Britain encapsulated
– the espousal of a new type of 'feminized', personalized or
therapeutic rhetoric abounds today on radio, television and in
a plethora of self-help books, borrowing the feminist consciousness-raising discourses of disclosure and shared pain.
More-over, the choices open to women have increased remarkably in the closing decades of the twentieth century,
mostly undermining former patriarchal presumptions: many
women now delay motherhood; more cohabit and marry later;
more divorce and separate; more remain childless; more raise
children on their own.[13] This has been made possible primarily by what has been called the 'feminization' of the economy.
Full-time jobs in many manufacturing industries have been
disappearing, as jobs in the service sector keep expanding.
Clerical jobs still account for the largest group of women
workers in developed countries, but women have also made
rapid progress within most professional and managerial jobs,
especially as doctors, lawyers, accountants and business administrators – even if rarely reaching the top levels.[14] Indeed,
rather than flaunting any observable or intrinsic 'difference'
from men, childless young professional women are working
longer hours, and earning slightly more (104 per cent) of
equivalent men's earnings. They are, as Suzanne Franks' study
reveals, 'the most desirable workers of all'.[15]

Meanwhile, the domain of women's lives, once near-
invisible, has moved closer to the forefront of international
politics, in dialogue which has become more blind to 'class',
and more equivocal about 'race'. 50,000 people (mostly
women) attended the United Nations Fourth World Conference on Women in 1995 in Beijing, and the associated Non-
Governmental Organization (NGO) Forum held nearby. The
consequent Beijing Declaration and Platform for Action, built
upon twenty years of planning, debates and action, is an impressive statement urging the promotion of women's interests worldwide.[16] Assessing its impact on government actions
internationally a few years later, Charlotte Bunch concluded
from her Center for Global Leadership at Rutgers University:
'The energy, the activity of Beijing, has not gone away'.[17] As

two other early women's liberation activists from the USA insist, the world really has changed:

> It's hard now to evoke the sea of misogyny in which more than one generation of women struggled before the women's movement. . . . One general claim feels solid: gross and unapologetic prejudice against women is no longer an unremarked-upon given of everyday life. In the long years before second-wave feminism, women and girls were unquestionably belittled. . . . Humiliation seemed fitting and pride made one faintly ridiculous. The prevailing assumption of the inferiority of women was the starting point from which one planned one's moves and shaped one's life – whether acquiescent or angry. The very difficulty of describing this prefeminist atmosphere today is a measure of how dramatically things have changed.[18]

What are we to make of these radically contrasting configurations? How we respond – whether we see litttle progress, or believe feminism has got what it wanted and should perhaps retire gracefully – will clearly depend upon the type of feminism we espouse. As we have seen, there have always been, and will always be, differing versions of what feminism is about, with the 'new' or latest trajectories invariably keen to mark their distance from the 'old'. We must 'stop looking at all our problems through men's eyes and discussing them in men's phraseology', a self-defined 'new feminist' writes: 'At last we have done with the boring business of measuring everything that women want, or that is offered them, by men's standards'. This particular advocate of a 'difference-based' feminism was determined to distance her vision and goals from, in her words, 'old feminist' campaigns for equal pay and open access to men's jobs, or for labour market reforms which could not answer the needs of unwaged women. However, she was *not* picking up on any post-structuralist theorizing of phallogocentrism, and women's nomadic, multifarious but ineluctable 'otherness' (the bedrock of those young women now 'Doing Feminism, Being Feminist' in the 1990s, some of whom call themselves 'the third wave').[19] Rather, Eleanor Rathbone – for it was she – represented the 'new' feminist vision of the early twentieth century, against the 'old' feminism of the previous decades in the last *fin de siècle*. Her distance from our own 'new' feminism of the 1990s, which also likes to distinguish itself from an 'old equal-rights feminism', of the 1970s, is easily detectable in her very next comment on the occasion of that particular address. Only 'state intervention' and 'welfare reforms', she continued, could end women's economic dependence through the 'endowment of motherhood', thereby freeing women from men's control.[20] How her 'old statist rhetoric' betrays her!

The Subject of Dependency

Women's economic dependence and welfare reforms are topics currently on everyone's minds, but generating primarily only thoughts of purging most of those receiving any benefits. Today in Britain, as in the USA, the political usage of the term 'dependency' has been refashioned through repeated discursive shifts. Via successive Atlantic crossings, the very notion of 'economic dependency' is becoming synonymous with 'welfare beneficiary', prefigured in the words of the American Democrat Daniel Moynihan in the 1970s: 'the issue of welfare is the issue of dependency'. Tracing this genealogical transformation, Nancy Fraser and Linda Gordon note its conjunction with a flourishing, deceptively feminist-sounding, self-help literature on autonomy which, by mystifying the link between the psychological and the political, inflates 'welfare dependency' into a personality syndrome, testifying to inadequacy.[21] This is why single mothers can be demonized if they *don't* work, even while married women with young children can be demonized if they *do*. Shifting a mother from 'dependence' on the state to reliance on a man for economic support, in this troubling slippage, supposedly removes her from the pathologies of 'dependence'. The truth is otherwise.

The continuing offensive against welfare provides, perhaps, the single most general threat to Western women's interests at present – at least for those many women who are not wealthy, and who still take the major responsibility for caring work in the home. As feminists in the 1970s made so clear, and sought so hard to transform, women are most vulnerable to the very worst pathologies of 'dependence' when they are most at the mercy of husbands or male partners, especially during and after pregnancy and childbirth. Indeed, midwives in Britain have recently been asked to look for signs of abuse in just such women, following alarming reports from midwives in the USA examining the bruised bodies of pregnant women, and those who have recently become mothers.[22] Similar antitheses exist in relation to needy children. Carolyn Steedman has written eloquently of how the expansion of welfare in the late 1940s gave a particular confidence to working-class children like herself:

> I think I would be a different person now if orange juice and milk and dinners at school hadn't told me, in a covert way, that I had a right to exist, was worth something . . . its central benefit being that, unlike my mother, the state asked for nothing in return. Psychic structures are shaped by these huge historical labels: "charity", "philanthropy", "state intervention".[23]

Liz Heron echoes these sentiments, although, like Steedman herself, she was well aware of the limitations of such services: it was their paternalistic, undemocratic delivery which made them vulnerable to subsequent attack. Introducing her anthology of autobiographical writings by girls growing up in Britain in the 1950s, Heron writes: 'Along with the orange juice and the cod-liver oil, the malt supplement and the free school milk, we may also have absorbed a certain sense of our own worth and the sense of a future that would get better and better, as if history were on our side'.[24] Not any more! The shedding of public responsibility for the welfare of poorer women threatens to devastate the lives of millions of children, as it has done already in the USA since the 1980s.[25]

Increasingly in Britain, as in the USA, the new myth of 'dependency culture' is used to condemn those receiving any form of state service, marking them out as vulnerable to 'welfare dependency'. Yet, as Mary McIntosh reports, despite the hassles and indignities they now face, surveys of single mothers have shown that a majority would still prefer dependence on the state to their experience of dependence on a man.[26] However, that option is disappearing. In alliance with Reagan and the American Right, there was no doubting Margaret Thatcher's determination to overturn all traces of the post-war Keynesian economic orthodoxy with its support for spending on welfare – while upholding and abetting spending on warfare. What is somewhat less clear is the extent to which the Blair government, like Clinton's 'New' Democratic Party, is simply a continuation of the same pro-scarcity neo-liberal policies undermining the public realm, while encouraging market forces into every institutional domain.

To date, Blair's self-declared respect for his Tory predecessors, his unlimited admiration for Clinton (despite the latter's capitulation to dismantling welfare), his government's tireless discourse of fiscal 'prudence' and obeisance towards the dynamism of unfettered market forces, his comprehensive ardour for Britain's 'special relationship' with the USA, have all impeded the production of any distinct or convincing alternative vision to the one he inherited. The legacy of neo-liberalism leaves the UK, in marked contrast to the rest of the EU, tailing the USA in its soaring inequality, with poverty in the USA estimated at twice that of any other advanced European nation, despite having the highest per capita income. (Sweden, with the longest tradition of social democratic organizations, still has the lowest incidence of poverty and inequality.[27])

Searching for a 'third way' between the interventionist market constraints of welfare states and the turbulence of neo-liberalism, Blair – like Clinton – has moved towards what has been labelled the 'new paternalism'.[28] This 'third way' fully endorses the earlier neo-liberal 'modernizing' crusade on restraining public spending, while insisting that market economics must reign supreme. Its characteristic 'new paternalism' (better seen as a 'new managerialism', in that women are as likely as men to implement its objectives) aims to tackle the escalating poverty, inequality, crime and social disintegration through closer supervision of the poor, rectifying what is seen as their personal inadequacies or fecklessness.

Demanding an end to the 'poverty of ambition', social deprivation and welfare are to be reduced and managed through welfare-to-work regimes, with strong encouragement of private sector backing for training and resources in the public sector: these range from the teaching of parenting skills or job application techniques to finance and pension management.[29] However, there is little evidence that 'workfare' serves as a springboard to real jobs, at least if we look at its implementation in New York over a period of several years: initial studies of the programme's success revealed that only 29 per cent of workfare participants who were forced off the welfare rolls were able to find even casual work.[30] Meanwhile, although in acute tension with its aim of creating the fullest possible employment of poor and needy people (many of whom are women caring for children or other dependants), recent attempts to roll back welfare have also strongly promoted traditional nuclear family ideology and paternal responsibilities.

Family Values

In stark contrast with the repeated avowal of the 'pathologies' of 'welfare dependency' is the steadfast disavowal of knowledge of the actual casualties when women and children are most financially dependent on familial male authority. Such denial has been strenuously cultivated by the growing strength of 'family values' campaigners since the 1980s. 'Profamily' movements first arose in the 1970s as part of an explicit New Right backlash against feminism and sexual liberation, soon to be underwritten by Reagan and Thatcher. Two decades later, however, this neo-conservative rhetoric seems ubiquitous across the political spectrum. 'Strengthening the family has to be a number-one social priority', Tony Blair announced at the Labour Party Conference in Britain in 1995, embracing the double-dealing Communitarian Agenda of the American sociologist Amitai Etzioni, and echoing the sentiments of that other fading patriarch, Bill Clinton. (A married man, of course, can hardly be *more* sexually conservative than to solicit blow jobs from his young employees!) This new family rhetoric, so powerfully promoted in the USA is, we should note, no longer explicitly anti-feminist, but hovers somewhere between post-feminist and anti-feminist agendas.

Meanwhile, the knowledge that the traditional heterosexual marriage can create a living hell of cruelty, neglect and abuse is beaten back by what the American sociologist Judith Stacey calls the 'virtual social science' of distorted data about the dangers of 'fatherless', 'divorced' or 'lone-parent' families being constantly disseminated by the media.[31] This encourages the continuing denial of lesbian and gay rights (as in campaigns to restrict custody and adoption rights to married heterosexuals) and obstructs official recognition of same-sex relationships. Furthermore, it dismisses the often invaluable role of friendships, community resources and wider structures of social support, which may be all that many individuals have to rely upon to keep them sane when most dependent on the family, for example those for whom childhood is, at the very best, a time of gritting the teeth and enduring. Most biographical narratives, clinical literature or serious self-reflection can swiftly trounce the supposedly caring values of pro-family warriors: yet such is the symbolic geography of that place we call 'home', they continue to flourish.[32] A survey by the British charity National Chidren's Home Action in the late 1990s indicated that the main anxiety of 80 per cent of the children in their study was violence in the home (closely followed by bullying at school), figures which provoked the cultural critic Judith Williamson to mourn that despite all the talk about 'concern' for children, 'in material fact, we barely care for them at all'.[33]

Even the evils of paternal incest and domestic violence (recently once again deemed epidemic in US society by no less an authority than the conservative American Medical Association[34]) are discarded for the evils of fatherlessness in the tendentious social scientific discourses of David Popenoe or David Blakenhorn in such books as *Rebuilding the Nest* and *Fatherless America: Confronting our most Urgent Social Problem*. Mysteriously, these pathologies of abuse which feminists identified as part of the warp and weave of traditional, male-dominated family patterns have been rethreaded to appear as *themselves* the product of family breakdown. Thus, when he lists the all-encompassing personal and social harms of 'fatherlessness', Blakenhorn moves on from citing 'crime' and 'adolescent pregnancy' to include 'child sexual abuse [and] domestic violence against women'.[35] We are clearly not meant to unravel the twisted appropriation of what were initially neglected feminist concerns, now placed in the service of a traditional patriarchal orthodoxy.

Sweeping Anti-statism

Again looking anxiously at trends across the Atlantic, one can observe that the once explicit, but now more often disguised or denied, anti-feminist and anti-gay sentiments expressed in family values crusades match a sweeping anti-statist rhetoric – increasingly as prevalent on the left as the right. I was dismayingly alerted to further political reversals which may lie ahead for antiquated socialist feminists such as myself, by the recent thoughts about the state expressed by that once enduringly hopeful and combative feminist radical (and long-standing friend of mine), Barbara Ehrenreich. In her 'Confessions of a Recovering Statist', she publicly renounces *any* hopes for progressive social reforms in the USA, whether around childcare or parental leave (or environmental reform). 'For the time being', she declares, 'we're not going to get anywhere with a progressive agenda consisting of . . . government initiatives. *Believe me, I have tried'.*[36] She certainly has.

Ehrenreich contrasts the situation in the USA with the kinds of universal state provision she assumes is taken for granted in Western Europe. In the USA, Ehrenreich argues that there is now no combating the right's anti-state propaganda: that is, after two decades of radical conservative pressure, and after Clinton's welfare 'reform' which removed federal responsibility for assisting children in poverty, while at the same time authorizing millions of dollars to be spent not on sex education, contraception or to prevent violence against women, but rather on a puritanical morality which consigns single mothers to courses in 'abstinence education'

(Clinton's way of having sex, perhaps!). Other feminist political scientists, based in the USA, such as Zillah Eisenstein
and Anna Marie Smith, also express their increasing suspicions of the costs of what they call the 'insider strategy' or
'feminizing the mainstream'. They believe that feminist support for Clinton facilitated his successful presentation of 'feminine' and 'feminist' signifiers, making women's votes decisive
in his re-election in 1996 (with the largest gender gap in the
history of US presidential voting), but ultimately helping to
neutralize opposition to his welfare cuts.[37] Even some of the
most sophisticated theoretical works, like Wendy Brown's
States of Injury, while skilfully exposing both the logic of
victimhood and the theoretical incoherence in feminist
rhetorics like that of Catharine MacKinnon, which demand
state protection from 'pornographic' imagery, retain a near
exclusive focus on 'the state as a negative domain for democratic political transformation', stressing the 'perils' attending
all feminist appeals to it for gender justice.[38] Without wanting to deny the oppressive role of the modern state (not only
in its official policing and militaristic role, but also in its protection of already dominant groups via normative regimes
regulating access to welfare and social resources), it seems to
me that those seeking a better world for all women can hardly
afford to abandon struggles 'in and against' it.

Meanwhile, although terminally pessimistic about feminists having any progressive alignment with mainstream politics in the USA, Ehrenreich herself is perhaps too optimistic
about Europe. Here too, welfare 'reform' is under way. Some
feminists in Britain are watching the New Labour government with their initial rising hopes often moving towards
despairing resignation, and wondering how long Anglo-
American contrasts will hold.[39] There has been some progress,
with support for childcare for single mothers, to encourage
(or will it mean force?) them into jobs. But Blair's new Britain, as we have seen, still sanctifies the Thatcherite and old
American way, with its litany for limiting public spending. As
Mary McIntosh comments on the production of new terminology for the redefining of social needs: 'Typical of the new
lexicon is the "Benefit Integrity Project", in which thousands

of people who had previously been deemed severely disabled were deprived of their Disability Living Allowance'.[40]

Such shifts in the vernacular of needs and entitlement indicate that it is the notion of universal welfare rights (as opposed to meagre provision for the poor) which is being eliminated. This serves to undermine the whole heritage and rationale of the British welfare state: one which relied upon progressive taxation to deliver a comprehensive social insurance system giving those in need of benefit a sense of entitlement. Using the defence that the 'deserving' poor – those who are absolutely unable to work for wages or have no crumb of private resources – can only be adequately assisted by removing benefits from the more 'affluent', progressive legislation involving general entitlements to child benefits, disability, or old age pensions, are now all under threat in Britain. Increasingly more people will have increasingly less reason to support a national insurance system from which they will, in principle, be excluded, feeding the destructively anti-social, anti-government feelings now so dominant in the USA: the sense that people get nothing in return for the taxes they pay, since they must take out private insurance for everything anyway. It has also been shown that welfare programmes regularly deteriorate once they assist only the most disadvantaged, and no longer cater for more powerful, middle-class interest groups.[41] Comparing the failure of US rationing with the success of austerity measures in Britain during World War II, Harvey Levenstein concluded that the British, unlike the Americans, still had 'faith in their government'.[42] In this age of socially regulated austerity, that faith in government and the social infrastructure of the public sector is being deliberately undermined.

With incentives to work as the prime focus of welfare reform, the hardship faced by significant numbers of women looks here to stay. These are the women trapped between the Scylla of longer hours at work and the Charybdis of increasing demands from children and other needy people at home, for which they are still held, and often feel, uniquely responsible. No amount of hollow familial ideology, contradictory workfare incentives or redefining of equality as 'social inclusion' solves the problems faced by so many working women today. As Suzanne Franks concludes: 'It seems unlikely the new millennium will bring a new balance of working and sharing – more likely a society that exacerbates the all or nothing divisions. Work will mean either the all-consuming 60-hour week or the insecure temporary life. Caring and everything else will have to fit in between.'[43]

Yet pessimism is not entirely appropriate. It is false to claim that women's situation has stayed much the same, and even more misleading to suppose it has worsened. Women's growing economic independence has continued to undermine all the old structures of male domination, removing privileges which men could once take for granted at home and at work, and enhancing women's expectation – though not, perhaps, the practical choices open to them. Moreover, as Manuel Castells has exhaustively analysed, the displacement of the 'patriarchalism' which had ruled for millennia is increasingly global – notwithstanding its clashing and vicious entrenchment in certain nationalistic struggles.[44] The dilemmas of the cultural transitions in gender practices indicate that new strategies are urgently needed to solve the increasing imbalance between caring commitments, employment practices and the rest of life. Everywhere gender relations still matter, generating conflict and anxiety for both sexes. They matter for women, who are usually the most directly affected by the conflictual demands of home and work. They matter for men: for the minority who attempt to participate in the home on equal terms, often with considerable strain; for the majority who have been slower to change, and face the resentment (and increasing levels of divorce and eviction) if they cannot, or will not, sustain more egalitarian relations. Most of all, gender issues matter for children and other dependent people in the home, who bear the brunt of poverty, overstretched and guilt-ridden carers and inadequate public services. It is clear that feminist concerns cannot be separated from struggles for an alternative vision and politics to those currently in command. Childcare provision, expanding social services, state regulation of minimum wages and maximum working hours, recognition of household diversity and strong incentives for the full sharing of caring in the home, would all form part of that vision – not unlike the socialist feminist agenda of a recent now-proscribed era. Accepting its elimination, Toril Moi has commented, '"socialist feminism" is not really a meaningful term in the 1990s'; although, curiously, she does want to know 'what kind of feminist a socialist feminist could be today?': the creature is dead, but its spectre survives her.[45]

Switching to the Subject

As illustrated in chapter 1, welfare struggles were central to what is now seen as seventies 'equality' feminism: a democratizing, egalitarian and essentially modernist, reformist movement, with many utopian overtones. Back then, when 'reform or revolution' was the dominant rhetorical binary, most feminists stubbornly refused to choose, twisting and turning around it. Exchanging old binaries for new, 'equality or difference' has become *the* central conundrum within feminist thought. The latter embraces, rather confusingly, both identity and – increasingly important in academic feminism – anti-identity politics: the joys and sorrows of subjectivity *and* the question of its dismantling, each at different times harnessed to affirmations of a 'post-modernist' kind. Clashes over this conceptual divide continue to reverberate, feeding into the most futile and unhealthy of divisions within the left: that between class-based and cultural politics.

On its own, it is no secret that the theorizing of 'difference' paradigms in feminism, rightly suspicious of the chauvinisms, gaps and silences in old emancipatory rhetorics and practices of class, have tended to overshadow material differences within oppressed subject groups. Inside the Western academy, the intellectual prestige of post-structuralism and deconstruction led prominent feminist theoreticians to emphasize the discursive formations of selfhood via logics of exclusion and repudiation. Primarily concerned with ways of displacing or subverting the negation or subordination of the 'feminine' in language, or the silencing of women's voices in culture, the focus on identities, their affirmations and negations, has directed attention away from questions of redistributive justice and social restructuring, which were once central to socialist feminism – that current which is now so often excised from feminist texts, abridged into the retrospectively constructed 'equality' paradigm.

In a widely rehearsed debate on Italian feminism, for example, a minority, including Adriana Cavarero and Patrizia Romito, complain of the 'mamismo' in its mainstream movement, which has so exalted the 'maternal' that it plays into the hands of conservative forces violently hostile to change in traditional gender arrangements.[46] Such exaltation certainly has little purchase on the reason Italian women have the *lowest* birthrate in the developed world. More ironically, the tension between identitarian struggles (affirming hitherto demeaned or abjected subjectivities) and other political struggles prioritizing social equality and material need (which have often challenged or denied inherent subjective differences) have only deepened as the meanings of the 'difference' paradigm has expanded to include the multiply diverse, internally fragmented, post-colonial, anti-heterosexist, queer, 'in-between', subject positions occupied by women.[47]

It is over a decade since Juliet Mitchell argued that feminism had unwittingly eased the way for new developments in capitalism, in an article assessing the effects of the first two decades of second-wave feminism.[48] With its theorizing of the 'free play of multifarious differences', feminism has helped to construct an ideology that could disregard class and could side-line socio-economic comparisons to focus almost exclusively on the all-embracing opposition between men and women. It was easier in 1986, she noted, to get statistics on gender differences in educational achievement than on class comparisons. Twenty years ago the situation was completely the reverse.[49] Misleadingly, in my view, Mitchell attributes far too much agency to feminism in assisting capitalist market forces, rather than seeing women as ensnared within them. Her words foreshadow those of many an incorrigible old chauvinist, like Norman Mailer, announcing that feminism was so successful because it 'was perfect for the corporation', promoting women as its 'gilt-edged peons'.[50] More usefully, however, Mitchell highlighted, as others would soon also notice, the way in which feminist rhetoric and goals could be appropriated to legitimate technological, economic and legislative changes, which were not in themselves what feminists had been fighting for. Again we could look at Judith Stacey's work, in particular her study of women working for the Silicon Valley corporations, in *Brave New Families*.[51]

The crucial point, and one often displaced in the turn to theorizing subjectivities in the 1980s, is the need to pay careful attention to the relationship between feminist discourses and practices as they at times contest, and at others are more likely to serve, shifting economic and social change. Such change has often little to do with eliminating the worst forms of social injustice, in a world where women in general continue to have significantly fewer resources and less power than men. If feminists are not to hide away in a largely misleading romance of women's ineluctable 'otherness', we will need to turn outwards more often: observing the zealously embraced centrality of many women in the new managerial and professional world, even as others are pushed more securely to the margins. Attending more closely to the mutating gendered dynamics of selective advancement and deterioration can also enlighten us about the refashioning of particular, class-based practices of masculinity which keep a small group of men at the very pinnacle of corporate power, despite having now to encourage women into their ranks, and even having to acquire the more expressive, conversational skills once coded as 'feminine'.[52]

Activist Challenges

Do not misunderstand me. I am well aware of the importance of the study of identities and differences: whether to explore how they are constructed and reconstructed, or to draw attention to all those subordinated and excluded by previously uncontested universalisms. Hierarchically gendered, sexualized, racialized or hybridized productions of identity are all *material* in their injurious effects, and usually, though

not necessarily, and in differing ways, tied up with the structuring of economic disadvantage and marginalization. Furthermore, it is identity-based politics which have so often
inspired the cultures of activism which, in the best of times,
form part of, or in other ways service, class-based trade-union
and community struggles for better lives.[53] As most feminists
were once well aware, the really difficult challenge remains
that of building culture and class coalitions, where sexism,
racism and the radical complexities of other forms of exclusion or invalidation can find a place on the agenda. This is still
the only way 'to prevent white male interests from dominating class politics and middle class interests from dominating
cultural politics', as Andrew Ross concisely summarizes.[54] If
the left is ever to reconstitute itself as a popular movement, it
can only do so by embracing the greatest possible diversity of
progressive cultural alignments, while attending to the
volatilities of 'class' itself, as it is culturally produced and
experienced.

The ethnic and racialist provincialism of some earlier incar-
nations of feminism needed to be challenged by both the
insights of black and Third World feminisms, on the one
hand, and those theorists now emphasizing the intrinsic instabilities of being positioned as a 'woman', on the other:
these two tendencies, retrospectively, are often confusingly
conflated. Whether mapping the discourses or studying their
modes of normalization, recent forms of feminist theory have
usefully stressed the cultural particularities and psychic complexities of women's subjectivities (at least, when not sub-
mitting themselves to the dogged singularity of Lacan's law).
However, for feminists in the academy, it was never going to
be easy to return from the individual pleasures (or torments)
of abstract thought to the heated exchanges of collective con-
frontation and strategic coalition.

As Jane Gallop, one of the most provocative and passionate
defenders of feminist pedagogy, has mused: 'We don't seem
very able to theorize about how we speak, as feminists wanting social change, from within our positions in the academy'.[55]
More bitterly, the African Americanist Hazel Carby pointed
out in 1992 that the scholarly recognition of 'diversity and

difference', and the inclusion of black writers in the syllabus of women's studies and literature departments in the USA over the last decade, has accompanied the significant and steady *decline* in the percentage of black students reaching college. Observing how few alliances have been forged in recent times between the academy and the black working class and urban poor, Carby concludes (understandably, if somewhat harshly): 'Black cultural texts have become fictional substitutes for the lack of any sustained social and political relationships with black people in a society that retains many of its historical practices of apartheid in housing and school-ing'.[56] The problem, according to left critics of multi-culturalism, is not that it politicizes the academy (to the horror of its right-wing critics), but that it constitutes politics as *primarily* academic.

In a particularly painful debate on the links between theory and action published in 1996 in *Signs*, some of the best-known feminist activists in the USA, all of whom are in or close to the academy, maintain that they no longer read feminist theory. Rightly or wrongly, they argue that it bears little rela-tion to the empirical complexities of analysing the demands of the women in ongoing struggles to whom they are com-mitted – most often women fighting for what they see as basic 'human' rights (rather than specifically women's concerns) for health, housing, better educational or other welfare re-sources, as well as an end to poverty.[57] One problem is that the struggles these activists refer to require an overall vision of a radically egalitarian society, in considerable tension with the positioning of much recent feminist theory as anti-humanist, post-Enlightenment, and post-nation-state.

The form of feminist activism involving solidarity with women in struggle worldwide is thus one which harks back to the so-called 'equality' feminism of the 1970s. Theorizing subjectivities and differences rarely inspires engaged rapport with those who, in Temma Kaplan's words, are most 'crazy for democracy' – women leading human rights campaigns against the very worst exploitation and abuses, whether in Southern or Northern hemispheres. For where women are most actively engaged in grassroots struggles today, as Kaplan's research illustrates, is also where their leaders are blurring rather than affirming differences between groups in favour of reclaiming, on their own terms, a rhetoric of *universal* human rights: for example, that 'all human beings are entitled to safe housing and a clean environment and that sometimes only women can secure them'.[58] Patricia Williams, in *The Alchemy of Race and Rights*, argues similarly that rights rhetoric has been and remains important for black struggles, even though, and in part just because, 'rights' are historically 'unstable and shifting'.[59] On the one hand, then, it has been essential for feminists to dismantle notions of the disembodied, abstract universal, hitherto operating to exclude them in their particularity. On the other, the paradoxical empowerment of rights rhetoric is precisely that its universal ideal can *never* be fixed, once and for all, but remains an abiding source of conflict and struggle, as Etienne Balibar, among others, has forcefully argued.[60]

Disciplinary Feminism

Meanwhile, whatever the political potential of appeals to 'ambiguous universalities', the grassroots movements for social justice which women are leading today require a variety of types of scholarly servicing, some of which are increasingly absent from the most esteemed forms of feminist theorizing, as it has moved from its earlier stronghold in sociology and the social sciences into English and the humanities (producing its own somewhat embittered rejoinder).[61] Such servicing would need to encompass theories of world markets, and seek to explain why increasing globalization has gone hand in hand with the rolling back of welfare rights, even in developed capitalist countries such as Britain – although not, like Mitchell, in order to impugn feminist complicity. Without such theory, it is hard to know the possibilities and limits of effective resistance, especially when we are faced with the largely unjustified alarmism that nation-states are necessarily powerless in the face of such globalization.[62] One might note here that the market dictatorship which has encouraged the crisis of public finance, allowing the wealthy worldwide to contribute less and less to the financing of public expenditure, is still dominated by Anglo-American capital and ideological convictions. There are continuing, large differences in state expenditures on welfare, with – contrary to most globalization rhetoric – no consistent effect on growth rates.[63] Moreover, the global economy always displays strong national elements. While transnational corporations currently operate in the context of volatile world financial markets, both the production and consumption of most goods and services occurs at national levels: only 15 per cent of commodities derive from lower wage countries.[64]

Feminist studies, like cultural studies, began as a genuinely *interdisciplinary* field of knowledge. But the current pressures of the academy are such that it is almost impossible to maintain genuinely cross-disciplinary interests and knowledge, so harnessed are we to ever narrower channels of disciplinary career and publication. Attending feminist conferences seemed once to promise access to areas of knowledge far removed from one's own, but the disciplining of feminism within the academy makes that much less likely today. Indicatively, the conference *At the Millennium: Interrogating Gender* organized by *Woman: A Cultural Review*, although explicitly 'interdisciplinary' in conception and subtitle, reflected the predominance of English and cultural studies in the vanguard of academic feminism. Indeed, I was the sole speaker from the social sciences. This stimulated distinctive modes of gender interrogation which, although certainly diverse, thoughtful and creative, authorized specific but mostly narrowly conceived visions of futurity: many of them in search of the most enabling metaphors for feminists to work with. One, for example, offered the 'trickster', as post-modern shape-shifter, who can be both man and woman, hence paying no deference to single categories like that of gender or sexuality. While helping us explore the instabilities of gender, however, its champion on this occasion (Gillian Beer) was careful to caution us that her particular future-orientated, feminist figurine has little concern for others, indeed performs her/his tricks at the expense of others. Another (Elizabeth Bronfen) suggested

the 'hysteric' as futuristic feminist icon. Once we depath-
ologize her, we were told, she offers a strategy for questioning
and teasing the master's narrative, revealing its fraudulence.

These playful, transgressive emissaries of change or resistance can help us not only to address the agonies and duplicities
of subjectivities, but encourage us to attend to their potentially mutually contradictory descriptions of and investments
in reality. They cannot, however, provide the theoretical resources most useful for women hoping for a stake in the
future while positioned at the sharpest edge of struggles for
justice and survival. That requires more attention to actually
existing social relations and their discursive boundaries. One
can see the same disciplinary dominance in an American vol-
ume, published in 1997, entitled *Generations: Academic Feminists in Dialogue*; nineteen of the twenty-one contributors
come from literature departments. Distinguishing what she
sees as the 'personal' and 'political' strands of feminism from
the 'intellectual', one contributor sums up her view of the
intellectual dimension of feminism through a now prevalent
but exclusively disciplinary lens: 'Intellectual feminism is analytical; it concerns itself with "reading" the representations of
women in culture and its texts and artifacts'.[65] Academic feminism has taken a very particular route here, one which might
seem strange to the poet and short-story writer whom feminist literary scholars once studied, Grace Paley: 'Feminism
means political consciousness. It means that you see the relationship between the life of women and the political life and
power around her. From there you can take any route you
want'.[66]

But can we take any route we want as feminists within the
academy today? There is an important connection between
the last two problems I have been addressing: the academ-
ization of feminist politics and the logic of a narrow disciplin-
arity. Many feminists have worked hard to keep open a space
for interdisciplinary work in the academy (which is not the
same thing as renouncing scholarly expertise and academic
specialization). Yet, the harsh irony is that the more disciplin-
arity has been undermined by philosophical and political
critique of its founding assumptions,[67] the more competing

pressures inside the academy have forced disciplinary boundaries to tighten up in fiscally contracting times for higher education. Meanwhile, the move in academic fashions from
sociology and the social sciences to English and the humanities was itself, at least in part, a sign of the decline of left
politics after the close of the 1970s. There has been a corresponding change in the character of cultural studies, away
from the sociology and cultural history of literature – manifest in the work of Raymond Williams and some of his ex-
students, for example Terry Eagleton and Francis Mulhern,
and in Stuart Hall and Birmingham cultural studies – towards
more ahistorical and non-sociological theories of representation.[68] Whether mourning the move away from the histor-
icizing and contextualizing of culture, or castigating its
reduction to 'recycled semiotics', a number of scholars, like
Cary Nelson in the USA, have begun arguing for the
repoliticization of cultural studies, and its opening up to other
disciplinary resources: 'Recognizing how fragile and contingent both moral and historical consensus is', Nelson argues,
'only increases the need for advocacy and interpretation'.[69]
Similarly, among feminist scholars, even such a radical decon-
structionist as Barbara Johnson has admitted: 'I think it's true
that in order for certain things to happen, sites have to be
occupied blindly or out of a passion for justice'. The most
intellectually productive thing, she now concludes, is to be
both politically committed at the same time as retaining
'skepticism toward the authority of existing cultural arrangements, [and] toward the supposed "universality" or "imparti-
ality" of existing "truths" '.[70]

Cultural Imperatives

Although desiring greater cross-disciplinary communication in
feminist forums, I am not endorsing those academics now making a name for themselves through an anti-theoretical populism.
Least of all am I trying to jettison cultural analysis for what is
often falsely posed against it as 'materialist'. Any feminism still
seeking to overturn the indignities many women face (whether
gender-specific or not, though the two are unlikely to be easily

unravelled) needs to work to overcome the rifts which repeatedly arise between those advocating cultural and economic analysis as opposing priorities. For it is precisely cultural analysis of the pivotal place of sexual difference in the formation of subjectivity, combined with the coercive repetitions of gender in structuring social relations, that remains at the heart of gender politics worldwide, past and present. Whatever general rights and pragmatic distinctions need to be called upon in mobilizing support for women fighting for better lives, feminists cannot afford to retreat to reductive positions which would definitively distinguish the economic and political terrain from that which some would like to marginalize, if not jettison, as the discursive, or 'merely cultural' (as Judith Butler has described such dismissals).[71] Indeed, few intellectual efforts are less politically productive, or more symptomatic of morbidity, than the attempts of left offshoots of the culture wars in the USA (now also making their appearance in Europe) to defend the supposedly 'real' left against a phony 'cultural' left. This was most egregiously expressed in the hoaxing of *Social Text* by physicist Alan Sokal in 1996, with the assistance of two well-known feminist scholars (Barbara Epstein and Ruth Rosen), to the applause of many others (Katha Pollitt and Barbara Ehrenreich being two of the best known).[72] It also seems to have motivated the philosopher Martha Nussbaum into accepting a platform offered her by the conservative US journal the *New Republic* to pose feminists 'with eyes always on the material conditions of real women' and their 'real struggles' against the 'hip defeatism of Judith Butler', with her focus on the symbolic.[73] (Illustrative of the muddle produced by such polarizing polemic, Nussbaum offers Catharine MacKinnon's work as exemplary of a 'materialist' feminism despite her exclusive focus on forms of sexual symbolism and what many see as politically dangerous ways of eliminating it.)

Economic realities and the shifting fortunes of women worldwide are, everywhere, enmeshed within cultural understandings of sexual difference, which still, on all sides, help to promote male paranoia, misogyny, homophobia and related violence against women, gays and other subordinated or dissident men. As we saw in chapter 4, there is no other way to understand the pervasive sense that women in the West are now the 'winners', and men the 'losers', in an ongoing battle of the sexes.[74] We need to understand that it is this very terminology – the positioning of the sexes as embattled primarily with each other – which is quintessentially cultural, and which defers recognition that men, like women, are disparately affected by wider forces of economic restructuring, downsizing and increased job insecurity. Perceiving men as 'losers' obscures an array of crucial questions: which men are losing out?; according to what criteria?[75] We will never understand what is at stake here in generating defensive masculinities by posing men as inferior to the very group over whom their 'manhood' should render them superior, without attention to 'the cultural' and its material embeddedness. The burgeoning literature on men and masculinities can reveal little about the predicament and anxieties of men unless it understands the dynamics of power which have hitherto structured gendered meanings and institutional practices. The one cannot be parted from the other – at least, not until women are everywhere already seen as commensurate to men.

Feminism without Politics

Throughout this book I have conveyed a sense of the disruptions and strains caused by changing gender relations, everywhere apparent yet everywhere unresolved. Whether we notice them in the underachievement or misdeeds of boys, potential sexual hazards facing girls, the failures and uncertainties of men, the bitterness or overwork of married women, the impoverishment of lone mothers and their children, the deliberate provocations of sexual dissidents, daily fears of violence or simply in the continuing debates within and about feminism itself, gender is part of our very existence, our social being.

The proliferation of discourses about gender problems has given birth to a growth industry designed to handle some of the more manageable protests. Thus the delivery of individually packaged 'equal opportunities' is a key theme of the ever more compulsory implementation of human resource management for teaching improved social and interpersonal skills, flexibility, time-budgeting and resourcefulness: these are differently marketed across a broad social terrain from administrators to the jobless or homeless. Assessing its impact on management itself, some researchers have suggested that male managers adapt to the new discourses of gender equality by playing with their gendered identities and improving their interpersonal skills, thereby ensuring they remain in control.[76] The provision of more personal and intimate resources to assist those grappling with gender troubles comes from an expanding array of individual and group therapies, and the explosion of self-help books. They encourage the sharing of feelings, vulnerabilities and anxieties, all geared towards greater self-understanding and self-acceptance. It is noteworthy that many of these therapies and most of the self-help agendas draw upon the resources of early feminist consciousness-raising, while discarding its political analysis and collective confrontational strategies.

A feminist would hardly want to negate the dissemination of equal opportunity discourses and practices, even if suspicious of the instrumental absorption and reproduction of its message. It would be even more foolish to join the popular sport of ridiculing therapy, as though most of us are not to varying degrees in need of the personal support, greater self-awareness and emotional expressiveness it attempts to offer. Moreover, many radical therapists, like Susie Orbach and Andrew Samuels, have been using their clinical expertise to work with others offering more imaginative ways for approaching political issues – from crime and punishment to parenting and sexuality.[77] And least of all, should we expect to find perfect harmony between our public and private selves, or any easy, or even necessary, integration of feminist theoretical work with effective political practice. Nevertheless, the diffuse acceptance and commercial marketing of 'equal ops', self-help and therapeutic cultures, return us to the expedient accommodation of mainstream culture to selective aspects of feminism, even as it rejects or ridicules others, sometimes managing a strange combination of the two: 'If feminism no longer has any consistent ideology, it still prides itself on its own righteousness'.[78] Feminist rhetoric has been widely accepted (if still the butt of satire), especially insofar as it applauds a gentle type of care-based ethic, the affirmation of a benevolent 'femininity', open and sensitive to the needs and vulnerabilities of others (for example, in the media-friendly, widely promoted, work of Carol Gilligan or Jean Bethke Elshtain), but distanced from radical or threatening challenges, whether of thought or action.

The continuing dissemination of just such a 'feminist' into 'feminizing' personal ethos can offer a feminism *without* an oppositional culture or politics, one which has encouraged some feminists to replace what they now describe as their former 'hardened' language of politics, with a 'cosier' language of feelings. However, the particular structure of feeling they elaborate, although frequently attributed to the effects of pain and suffering, is one which is always seen as adjustable. Not for them, the intractable terrors of paranoia, sadism or terminal despair. 'I suppose I am more interested in average grief, inner grief, the grief most of us feel', one such newly retrained psychotherapist reflected when interviewed in 1997.[79] It is ironic that at a time when the air is full of therapeutic re-skilling, the man who provided the seedbed from which such diversified trainings have grown, is everywhere denounced for his 'fraudulence' and 'fakery'. Freud, as discussed in chapter 6, offered a far bleaker, more pessimistic vision. The cosier therapeutic version of feminism can easily slide into, or at least be used in the service of, a wider culture of blandness and denial: one which collapses the political into the personal, the collective into the individual. Such a culture can accommodate governments which pretend that they cannot change what it is *only* in their power to change, while demanding that individuals – whether parents, teachers or simply as luckless souls – *can* change what they have little hope of changing (given socially generated scarcity, deepening levels of inequality and ever-growing competitiveness). Joining those who suggest that the *political* point of studying personal life has been disappearing from a lot of feminist writing, Juliet Mitchell argues that feminism now needs to put women back into a 'transformational' political arena, to ask of the personal: '*Does it become part of the political program or does it just stay there as the personal*'.[80]

In Britain in the late 1990s, widespread publicity accompanied the appearance of a book declaring the dawn of a 'New Feminism': this time as a mainstream, majority movement in which women – from the Spice Girls to Cherie Blair and her husband's hundred new women MPs – can celebrate their own sudden power and achievements (in part thanks to Margaret Thatcher for normalizing female success). Its author, the journalist Natasha Walter, like Naomi Wolf before her, offers a form of power-feminism, applauding women's growing success, identification with their jobs and their ability to help each other. She reports on the penetration of feminist beliefs throughout society, reflected in mainstream culture and evident in the increasing support by men for women at home – if still from only a minority. Her book is useful, not only in outlining the real progress many women have made, but also in highlighting how much is still to be done. It is packed with pertinent statistics and the words of a diversity of women. Listing the multiple problems women still face, from grinding poverty, meagre childcare, dead-end jobs, inadequate public services to absence from power-elites, she wants more change to enable all women to find a place, where she hopes to see them, 'in the corridors of power'. However, her sketch of women's lives is one emptied of political theory or any specific strategies for combating the many obstacles she describes still confronting the majority of women. Instead, she appears to believe that it is feminism itself which has failed to deliver change for women, and this is because it 'gradually became primarily associated with sexual politics and culture'.[81]

But quite how 'feminism' will manage to deliver, once it remedies its ways and adopts 'a new, less embattled ideal', remains mysterious. Walter's analysis promotes no particular collective political formations or affiliations. We are simply told: 'We must understand that feminism can give us these things now, if we really want them'. Fingers crossed! Although pleasantly symptomatic of many women's goodwill towards a 'feminism' they feel free to fashion, it lacks the very thing it hopes to promote: political seriousness.[82] Introducing her follow-up collection a year later, again offering us 'feminism for a new generation', Walter is even more confident that feminism is 'on the move', evident in women's strong desire for a more equal society. The fact that our society is actually becoming ever more *unequal*, and her authors often committed to a wholly individualistic ethic (one of them offers an exemplary tale of her heroine, Jade Beaumont, who believes that 'People should deal with their own problems; you shouldn't get yourself into situations you can't handle and then slop all over everybody else') does not give her pause for thought about the significance of the political ravine between personal declarations in favour of a fairer world, and its attainment. It should.[83]

Political Futures

The last *fin de siècle* was seen as an optimistic era by many first-wave feminists. This time around, for all its internal conflicts and ambivalence, and despite co-option by commercial, conservative or gender-normalizing forces, feminism remains a powerful cultural presence. Walter is right about that. Despite the continuous presence of anti-feminist manoeuvres (sporadically operating with lethal effect, as in the anti-abortion movement in the USA) and the frightening extremes of some men's misogyny and violence, women will not abandon their quest for personal autonomy and equality. After all, significant numbers live in a world where they experience its actuality, at least when young and childless. But, as time goes by, they too are increasingly likely to encounter painful injustices in gender settlements.

The multifarious voices still speaking in the name of feminism offer not so much paradoxes as full-blown contradictions. The more flexible and volatile our identities, bodies and lives are conceived to be in academic discourses deconstructing genders and sexualities, the more predictably social constraints and pressures, or personal compulsions, manifest themselves in the lives of many women, and men. With individual choice and personal responsibility the mantra of the 'Third Way', feminism's own 'women's right to choose' is mocked by a culture in which lack of childcare, fear of poverty or career demands means that more women feel they have no choice at all: the social supports they hoped for are absent. Meanwhile, as one staunch feminist campaigner laments: 'the tabloids feel free to vilify one woman for not wanting as many as two babies and another for trying to have more than two'.[84] Until quite recently feminists still hoped to transform the relations between employment and family lives. Today, Blair's new Britain installs an old and punishing 'work' ethic which, despite feminist attention to the 'labours of love' from the 1960s onwards, remains incapable of questioning any of the old terms – whether that of 'labour' or 'love'. A decade ago, there was still a debate in the British and American media on the future of the nuclear family. Today the superiority of that family structure over all possible alternatives is once again everywhere trumpeted, even as its prevalence continues to decline.

In the most technologically innovatory of times, as some feminists write of women's particular affinity with the supposed freedoms of cyberspace (despite men's dominance of 90 per cent of its highways),[85] many women face a future where we are leading the most comprehensively conservative of lives: less politically engaged, less utopian in vision, less time, even, for friends and family. Writing of the unexpected decline of leisure in the USA, Juliet Schor points out that since the 1970s there has been a steady increase in the number of hours on the job put in by fully employed workers, while the same alarms about expanding working hours are sounding in the UK.[86] It is primarily women who are still somehow expected to make up for the hours lost from creating loving homes and healthy communities, simultaneously being applauded for how far they have come in gaining equality with men. Given the persisting strength of this aspect of traditional gender ideology, it is, as it always has been, the daily lives of women which most directly absorb the shocks and contradictions of these mean yet widely disparate times. What women do, when they do what is most expected of them as women, is not something best organized according to the dictates of profit or capitalist market relations. Therein lies the radical potential of feminism as an oppositional politics: one which dares to fight a culture and a political system which tries to numb us into acceptance that it can fulfil our needs and desires.

Why feminism? Because a feminism which is serious about the potential and obstacles to political change, and which knows that we are never outside either the personal or the cultural, still has something unique – if hardly 'new' – to offer. Part of that offering should be an understanding of the complexity of subjectivity, and the significance of representation, not to mention the difficulty of arguing for a socialist economics in the present climate. The special legacy of feminism lies in its striving to keep relating the personal and cultural to the economic and political, however forbidding and precarious that enterprise may be. Although academia has been the easy target of recent disparagement, feminism needs the time and resources it can still help to provide – so long as we can preserve it from the worst effects of reshaping by pseudo or actual market forces. It is more true than ever that few women have the time, even if they had the inclination (in these days when only instrumentalized self-serving is applauded), to sift through the differing versions of feminism. And this leaves a contentious minority of women to dominate the airwaves, especially those selected by commercial publishers for offering simple or sensationalized positions and prescriptions (invariably packaged as 'new' and 'subversive' on account of their discarding prior radical convictions). Part of the ongoing project of feminism should be the attempt to map out and assess which different pieces in the jigsaw of feminism get picked up, and why; it should also be asking, at any given time and place, who is selecting the fragments, and – however unintendedly – whose particular interests their delivery serves. This commands less media space, but is at the heart of the political presence of any movement.

Given the diversity of reformist, identitarian, deconstructive, activist, therapeutic and power feminisms, it is true that we can indeed take many different routes as feminists leaving the twentieth century. We need to learn from each other's journeys, and to recognize that what will engage the attention and further the interests of one group of women will not be most relevant to the needs of another. The political never simply reduces to the personal, nor to the unfettered analysis of culture, even though attention to desire, discourse and the promotion of caring and responsible sexual politics remains one of the crucial resources feminism delivers to politics. It is only by finding ways to foster effective vehicles for change that feminists can still hope to open spaces for more women to flaunt the diverse pleasures, entitlements and self-questioning to which recent feminist thinking has encouraged us to aspire (often, disconcertingly, in line with late capitalist consumerism). This means women collectively cherishing the existence of the left: whether in alliance with social democratic forces (fighting to preserve their redistributive egalitarian instincts, which will never be smoothly compatible with commercial entrepreneurialism, while opposing their traditional paternalism); with trade unions (continuing to overturn their erstwhile straight, white, male hegemony); with whatever manifestations of local or international struggles emerge to defend those at the sharpest end of market forces or regressive nationalisms, persisting racisms and xenophobia. Why feminism? Because its most radical goal, both personal and collective, has yet to be realized: a world which is a better place not just for some women, but for all women. In what I still call a socialist feminist vision, that would be a far better world for boys and men, as well.

Notes

Introduction: Why Feminism?

1 Jean Bethke Elshtain, *Public Man, Private Woman: Women in Social and Political Thought'*, Princeton, Princeton University Press, 1981, p. 216.
2 Jürgen Habermas, 'The New Obscurity and the Exhaustion of Utopian Energies', in *Observations on the Spiritual Situation of the Age*, ed. Habermas, Cambridge, Mass., MIT Press, 1984.
3 See Juliet Mitchell, 'Reflections on Twenty Years of Feminism', in *What is Feminism?*, ed. J. Mitchell and A. Oakley, Oxford, Blackwell, 1986, p. 36.
4 This published comment is from Pat Woolley, founder of Redress Press in Australia, in Jane Sullivan, 'Sisters Ink: Tales from the Revolution', *Sydney Morning Herald Magazine: Good Weekend*, 8 August 1988, p. 5; I have received several similar comments from erstwhile and current feminist publishers in Britain and the USA.
5 The majority of book buyers are said to be women, especially at the most popular end of the book market, in supermarkets. Information from Richard Knight at BookTrack, UK.
6 Adrienne Rich, 'Towards a Woman-Centered University', in *Lies, Secrets and Silences: Selected Prose, 1966–1978*, New York, W. W. Norton, 1979, p. 126 (written 1973).
7 Polly Toynbee, 'Fay Plays the Fool', *The Guardian*, 1 July 1998, p. 20.
8 See Catherine Hall, 'Feminism and Feminist History', in *White, Male and Middle Class*, Cambridge, Polity Press, 1992, p. 12; Rosalind Coward, *Our Treacherous Hearts: Why Women Let Men Get their Way*, London, Faber & Faber, 1992.
9 See Nancy Miller, 'Review Essay: Public Statements, Private Lives: Academic Memoirs for the Nineties', *Signs: Journal of Women in Cul-*

ture and Society, 1997, vol. 22, no. 4, 1997, p. 981.

10 Nicci Gerard, 'Interview: Calista Flockhart', in *The Observer Review*, 14 June 1998, p. 11.

11 Germaine Greer, 'Thirty years ago I fought for women to say yes, yes, yes. Now we've forgotten how to say no', *The Observer Review*, 19 October 1997, p. 4.

12 Andrea Dworkin, 'The Next Thousand Years', in ed. Charlotte Cole and Helen Windrath, The Female Odyssey: Visions for the 21st Century, London, Women's Press, 1999, p. 88.

13 Rosalind Coward, 'Do we Need a New Feminism?', *Women: A Cultural Review*, forthcoming; Coward, *Sacred Cows*, forthcoming.

Chapter 1   Generations of Feminism

1 Patricia Romney, Unpublished Notes Prepared for Roundtable Discussion, 'Writing about a Visionary Movement in the "Get Real" World of the '90s: The History of Women's Liberation in the United States', 10th Berkshire Women's Conference, State University of North Carolina, June 1996.

2 Margaret Strobel, in ibid.

3 Rachel Blau DuPlessis and Ann Snitow, 'A Feminist Memoir Project', in *The Feminist Memoir Project: Voices from Women's Liberation*, ed. DuPlessis and Snitow, New York, Three Rivers Press, 1998, p. 23; see also Katie King, *Theory in its Feminist Travels: Conversations in U.S. Women's Movements*, Bloomington, Indiana University Press, 1994.

4 Meredith Tax, 'For the People Hear Us Singing, "Bread and Roses! Bread and Roses"', in *Feminist Memoir Project*, ed. DuPlessis and Snitow, p. 321.

5 Michèle Barrett and Anne Phillips, 'Introduction', *Destabilizing Theory: Contemporary Feminist Debates*, ed. Barrett and Phillips, Cambridge, Polity Press, 1992, p. 2.

6 Ibid. pp. 2–4. Michèle Barrett had expressed her reservations about her own 'seventies' thinking in *Women's Oppression Today*, London, Verso, 1988, in a new preface, indicating (accurately) that recent feminist debate has problematized the notion of 'women' and 'woman', while suggesting that the notion of oppression 'looks decidedly dated today'.

7 Barrett and Phillips, *Destabilizing Theory*, pp. 5, 8, 6.

8 Judith Butler and Joan Scott, eds, *Feminists Theorize the Political*, London, Routledge, 1992.

9 Ibid., p. xiii.

10 Butler, 'Contingent Foundations', in ibid., p.17; emphases in original.

11 DuPlessis and Snitow, *Feminist Memoir Project*, p. 21.

12 Butler has at times distanced herself from the narrowness of some of the 'theory' debate within feminism, pointing out in 1993: 'It seems to me that the disagreements which exist among us as thinkers are perhaps less salient than others which now hold sway in public intellectual life'. Judith Butler, 'For a Careful Reading' in *Feminist Contentions: A Philosophical Exchange'*, ed. Seyla Benhabib et al., London, Routledge, 1995, p. 132.

13 See, for example, Linda Gordon, 'Review of *Gender and the Politics of History* by Joan Wallach Scott', *Signs* 15, Summer, 1990.

14 Joan Wallach Scott, 'Response to Gordon', *Signs* 15, Summer, 1990, p. 859. See also the measured and thoughtful account of the erasure of feminist theoretical heterogeneity in Susan Stanford Friedman, 'Making History', in *Feminism Beside Itself*, ed. Diane Elam and Robyn Weigman, London, Routledge, 1995.

15 Patricia Clough, *Feminist Thought*, Oxford, Blackwell, 1994.

16 Julia Kristeva, 'Women's Time' (1979), trans. Alice Jardine and Harry Blake, *Signs* vol. 7, no. 1, 1981, p. 33.

17 Toril Moi, *Sexual/Textual Politics, Feminist Literary Theory*, New York, Methuen, 1985, p. 13.

18 Sheila Rowbotham, *Threads through Time: Writings on History and Autobiography'*, London, Penguin, 1999, pp. 4, 2.

19 Sheila Rowbotham, *Dreams and Dilemmas*, London, Virago, p. 354; emphasis added.

20 Ibid., pp. x, 351.

21 Ibid., p. 351.

22 Sheila Rowbotham, 'How to Get Your Man: *The Female Eunuch* by Germaine Greer', in *Oz*, vol. 31, Nov.–Dec. 1970, p. 19.

23 Sally Alexander and Barbara Taylor, 'In Defence of Patriarchy', in *People's History and Socialist Theory*, ed. Raphael Samuel, London, Routledge & Kegan Paul, 1981.

24 Rowbotham, *Dreams and Dilemmas*, pp. 353, 2.

25 Sheila Rowbotham, *Woman's Consciousness, Man's World*, Harmondsworth, Penguin, 1973, pp. 34, 66.

26 Rowbotham, *Dreams and Dilemmas*, p. 83.

27 Ibid., pp. 59, 75.

28 Ibid., pp. 32–3.

29 Joan Scott, 'Experience', in *Feminists Theorize the Political*, ed. Butler and Scott.

30 Rowbotham, *Woman's Consciousness, Man's World*, p. 27.

31 Ibid., p. x. Rowbotham prefers, as she writes in 1972, the idea of 'consciousness moving' to 'consciousness raising', since 'your own perception is continually being shifted by how other women perceive what has happened to them. . . . The main difficulty, still, is that while the social composition of women's liberation remains narrow it isn't

possible to move naturally beyond certain limitations in perspective',
Rowbotham, *Dreams and Dilemmas*, p. 59.

32 Rowbotham, *Dreams and Dilemmas*, pp. 74, 208, 218.

33 Ibid., p. 83.

34 Ibid., p. 82.

35 Elizabeth Wilson, *Women and the Welfare State*, London, Tavistock, 1977; Mary McIntosh, 'The State and the Oppression of Women', in *Feminism and Materialism: Women and Modes of Production*, ed. Annette Kuhn and AnnMarie Wolpe, London, Routledge & Kegan Paul, 1978. Some later commentators, though sympathetic to the accounts of the state provided in this writing, would suggest, I think correctly, that they diminished the intrinsically male-dominated structures, practices and discourses of the many differing sectors of the state. See S. Franzway, D. Court and R. W. Connell, *Staking a Claim: Feminism, Bureaucracy and the State*, London, Paladin, 1989.

36 Michèle Barrett and Mary McIntosh, *The Anti-Social Family*, London, Verso, 1982.

37 Sheila Rowbotham, *The Past Is before Us: Feminism in Action since the 1960s*, London, Pandora, 1989.

38 As Jo Freeman argued, from her own personal experience, in her widely read and frequently anthologized 'The Tryanny of Structurelessness', *The Second Wave*, vol. 2, no. 1, 1972.

39 Muriel Dimen, 'In the Zone of Ambivalence: A Journal of Competition', in *In Feminist Nightmares: Women at Odds*, ed. Susan Weisser and Jennifer Fleishner, New York, New York University Press, 1994, p. 362.

40 Joan Nestle, 'A Fems Feminist History', in *Feminist Memoir Project*, ed. DuPlessis and Snitow, p. 345.

41 Valerie Amos, Gail Lewis, Amina Mama and Pratibha Parmar, 'Editorial: Many Voices, One Chant: Black Feminist Perspectives, *Feminist Review* 17, Autumn 1984.

42 Barbara Smith '"Feisty Characters" and "Other People's Causes"', in *Feminist Memoir Project*, ed. DuPlessis and Snitow, p. 481.

43 Vivian Gornick, 'What Feminism Means to Me', in ibid., p. 374.

44 Ellen Willis, 'My Memoir Problem', in ibid., p. 483.

45 Melissa Benn, 'Women and Democracy: Thoughts on the Last Ten Years', *Women: A Cultural Review*, vol. 4, no. 3, 1993, p. 237.

46 Rowbotham, *Threads Through Time*, p. 4.

47 Alix Kates Shulman, 'A Marriage Disagreement, or Marriage by Other Means', in *Feminist Memoir Project*, ed. DuPlessis and Snitow, p. 291.

48 Arlie Russell Hochschild, *The Second Shift*, New York, Viking, 1989; *The Time Bind: When Work Becomes Home and Home Becomes Work*, New York, Henry Holt/Metropolitan Books, 1997.

49 Lynne Segal, *Is the Future Female?: Troubled Thoughts on Contempo-*

rary Feminism, London, Virago, 1987.

50 Catharine MacKinnon, *Feminism Unmodified: Discourses on Life and Law*, London, Harvard University Press, 1987, p. 149.

51 Ann Snitow, 'Retrenchment vs. Transformation: The Politics of the Antipornography Movement', ed. K. Ellis et al., in *Caught Looking: Feminism Pornography and Censorship*, New York, Caught Looking, Inc., 1986.

52 Lisa Duggan and Nan Hunter, *Sex Wars: Sexual Dissent and Political Culture*, London, Routledge, 1995.

53 'I do not consider my work to be "postmodern"', Butler writes, in *Feminist Contentions*, ed. Benhabib et al., p. 133.

54 Hélène Cixous, 'The Laugh of the Medusa', in *New French Feminism*, ed. E. Marks and I. de Courtivron, New York, Schoken Books, 1981, p. 256.

55 Cixous, ibid.; Luce Irigaray, *This Sex which Is Not One*, Ithaca, NY, Cornell University Press, 1985, p. 32.

56 See, for example, Laura Kipnis, 'Looks Good on Paper: Marxism and Feminism in a Postmodern World', in *Ecstasy Unlimited: On Sex, Capital, Gender, and Aesthetics*, Minneapolis, University of Minnesota Press, 1993.

57 Lynne Segal, 'Whose Left? Socialism, Feminism and the Future', *New Left Review*, no. 185, Jan.–Feb. 1991.

58 For imaginative political appropriations of 'French feminism' see, for example, Drucilla Cornell, *Beyond Accommodation: Ethical Feminism, Deconstruction and the Law*, London, Routledge, 1991; Moira Gatens, *Imaginary Bodies: Ethics, Power and Corporeality*, London, Routledge, 1996.

59 Gayatri Chakravorty Spivak, 'French Feminism in an International Frame', *Yale French Studies*, vol. 62, 1981, pp. 154–84; reprinted in Spivak, *In Other Worlds*, London, Routledge, 1988; Barbara Christian, 'The Race for Theory', in *Gender and Theory: Dialogues on Feminist Criticism*, ed. Linda Kauffman, Oxford, Basil Blackwell, 1989; Deborah McDowell, 'The "Practice" of "Theory"', in *Feminism Beside Itself*, ed. Elam and Weigman.

60 See, for example, Alice Jardine, 'Men in Feminism: Odor di Uomo or Compagnons de Route?', in *Men in Feminism*, ed. Alice Jardine and Paul Smith, London, Methuen, 1987, p. 58.

61 Gayatri Chakravorty Spivak, *Outside in the Teaching Machine*, London, Routledge, 1993, p. 4.

62 See, for example, Denise Riley, *Am I That Name?: Feminism and the Subject of 'Women' in History*, London, Macmillan, 1988.

63 Donna Haraway, 'A Manifesto for Cyborgs: Science, Technology, and Socialist Feminism in the 1980s', in *Feminism/Postmodernism*, ed. L. Nicholson, London, Routledge, 1990, pp. 197, 215.

238   *Notes to pp. 32–7*

64 Ibid., p. 215.
65 Gayatri Chakravorty Spivak, 'Remembering the Limits: Difference, Identity and Practice', in *Socialism and the Limits of Liberalism*, ed. Peter Osborne, London, Verso, 1991, p. 229; emphasis in original.
66 Judith Butler, *Gender Trouble: Feminism and the Subversion of Identity*, London, Routledge, 1990, p. 33. For critiques see Amanda Anderson, 'Debatable Performances: Restaging Contentious Feminisms', *Social Text*, 54, vol. 16, no. 1, Spring, 1998; Tania Modleski, *Feminism without Women: Culture and Criticism in a "Postfeminist" Age*, London, Routledge, 1991.
67 Butler, in *Feminist Contentions*, ed. Benhabib et al., p. 131; See also Butler, *Bodies that Matter: On the Discursive Limits of Sex*, London, Routledge, 1993, p. 231; see also Peter Osborne and Lynne Segal, 'Gender as Performance: An Interview with Judith Butler', *Radical Philosophy*, 67, Summer, 1994; reprinted in *A Critical Sense: Interviews with Intellectuals*, ed. Osborne, London, Routledge, 1996.
68 See, for example, Gregor McLennan, 'Feminism, Epistemology and Postmodernism: Reflections on Current Ambivalence', *Sociology*, vol. 29, no. 3, August 1995, pp. 391–401.
69 See, for example, Nancy Fraser, 'From Redistribution to Recognition? Dilemmas of Justice in a "Post-Socialist" Age', *New Left Review*, no. 212, July–August, 1995. For a discussion and critique of Fraser, see Judith Butler, 'Merely Cultural', *Social Text*, vol. 15, nos 3–4, Fall–Winter, 1997.
70 Terry Eagleton, *The Illusions of Postmodernism*, Oxford, Blackwell, 1996, p. 22.
71 Anne Phillips, *Democracy and Difference*, Cambridge, Polity Press, 1993, p. 7.
72 See Sheila Rowbotham, *Women in Movement: Feminism and Social Action*, London, Routledge, 1992, pp. 8–15.
73 See Julie Peters and Andrea Wolper, eds, *Women's Rights Human Rights: International Feminist Perspectives*, London, Routledge, 1995.
74 See Suzanne Gibson, 'On Sex, Horror and Human Rights', *Women: A Cultural Review*, vol. 4, no. 3. Winter, 1993, Laura Flanders, 'Hard Cases and Human Rights: C. MacKinnon in the City of Freud', *The Nation*, 9–16 August 1993, pp. 174–7. For a stimulating commentary on the challenge of human rights internationalism to the recent philosophical embrace of a 'politics of difference', see Bruce Robbins, 'Sad Stories in the International Public Sphere: Richard Rorty on Culture and Human Rights', *Public Culture*, vol. 9, no. 2, Winter, 1997.
75 Rosemary Pringle and Sophie Watson, ' "Women's Interests" and the Post-Structuralist State' in *Destabilizing Theory*, ed. Barrett and Phillips, p. 65.
76 Jonathan Rée, quoted in Francis Mulhern, *The Present Lasts a Long*

Time: Essays in Cultural Politics, Cork, Cork University Press, 1998, p. 5.

Chapter 2   Gender to Queer, and Back Again

1 According to the feminist historian Joan Wallach Scott, *Gender and the Politics of History*, New York, Columbia University Press, 1988, p. 29.
2 Simone de Beauvoir, *The Second Sex* [1949], New York, Vintage Press, 1973, p. 301.
3 Ann Oakley, *Sex, Gender and Society*, London, Temple Smith, 1972, p. 170.
4 Jane Chetwynd and Oonagh Hartnett, *The Sex Role System: Psychological and Sociological Perspectives*, London, Routledge & Kegan Paul, 1978.
5 Vivian Gornick and Barbara K. Moran, 'Introduction', in *Women in Sexist Society: Studies in Power and Powerlessness*, ed. Gornick and Moran, New York, Basic Books, 1971, p. xxiv.
6 Sandra L. Bem, 'The Measurement of Psychological Androgyny', *Journal of Clinical Consulting Psychology*, vol. 42, 1974; Bem, 'Sex Role Adaptability: One Consequence of Psychological Androgyny', *Journal of Personality and Social Psychology*, vol. 31, no. 4, 1975.
7 Sandra L. Bem, 'Gender Schema Theory: A Cognitive Account of Sex Typing', *Psychological Review*, vol. 88, no. 4, 1981, pp. 354–64; Susanne Kessler and Wendy McKenna, *Gender: An Ethnomethodological Approach*, New York, Wiley, 1978.
8 Gayle Rubin, 'The Traffic in Women: Notes on the "Political Economy" of Sex', in *Towards an Anthropology of Women*, ed. R. Reiter, New York, Monthly Review Press, 1975.
9 Beauvoir, *The Second Sex*, p. 16.
10 Monique Wittig, 'The Mask of Gender', in *The Poetics of Gender*, ed. Nancy K. Miller, New York, Columbia University Press, 1986, p. 66.
11 Elaine Showalter, 'Introduction: The Rise of Gender', in *Speaking of Gender*, ed. E. Showalter, London, Routledge, 1989, p. 1.
12 Robert Stoller, *Sex and Gender*, London, Hogarth Press, 1968.
13 See Susan Coates and Kenneth Zucker, 'Gender Identity Disorder in Children', in *Clinical Assessment of Children: A Biosocial Approach*, ed. C. J. Kestenbaum and D. T. Williams, New York, New York University Press, 1988.
14 Joan Wallach Scott, 'Is Gender a Useful Category of Historical Analysis', in Scott, *Gender and Politics*.
15 Jane Flax, *Disputed Subjects: Essays on Psychoanalysis, Politics and Philosophy*, London, Routledge, 1993, p. 23.

16 R. W. Connell, *Gender and Power*, Cambridge, Polity Press, 1987.
17 Ann Snitow, 'Feminism and Motherhood: An American Reading', *Feminist Review*, no. 40, Spring, 1992, pp. 32–51.
18 Shulamith Firestone, *The Dialect of Sex: The Case for Feminist Revolution*, New York, Morrow, 1970.
19 See Sheila Rowbotham, *The Past Is before Us: Feminism in Action since the 1960s*, London, Pandora, 1989, esp. chapters 2 and 7.
20 Jane Alpert, 'Mother Right: A New Feminist Theory', *Ms.*, August 1973, pp. 52–5.
21 Adrienne Rich, *Of Women Born*, London, Virago, 1977, p. 285.
22 Adrienne Rich, 'Compulsory Heterosexuality and Lesbian Existence', *Signs*, vol. 5, no. 4, Summer, 1980.
23 Nancy Chodorow, *The Reproduction of Mothering: Psychoanalysis and the Sociology of Gender*, Berkeley, University of California Press, 1978.
24 Jane Flax, 'Theorizing Motherhood', *Women's Review of Books*, vol. 1, no. 9, 1984, p. 13.
25 Carol Gilligan, *In a Different Voice*, London, Harvard University Press, 1982; Mary Belenky et al., *Women's Ways of Knowing: The Development of Self, Voice and Mind*, New York, Basic Books, 1986.
26 Catharine MacKinnon, *Feminism Unmodified: Discourses on Life and Law*, Cambridge, Mass., Harvard University Press, 1987, p. 3.
27 Ibid., pp. 219, 61.
28 Germaine Greer, *The Whole Woman*, London, Transworld, 1999.
29 Sylvia Ann Hewlett, *A Lesser Life: The Myth of Women's Liberation in America*, New York, William Morrow, 1986.
30 Audre Lorde, 'An Open Letter to Mary Daly', in *This Bridge Called my Back: Writings by Radical Women of Color*, ed. C. Moraga and G. Anzaldúa, Watertown, Mass., Persephone Press, 1981, p. 95; Alice Walker, 'One Child of One's Own: A Meaningful Digression within the Works', in *The Writer on her Work*, ed. J. Sterburg, New York, W. W. Norton, 1980, p. 136.
31 Barbara Smith, 'Racism and Women's Studies', in *All the Women are White, All the Blacks are Men, But some of Us are Brave*, ed. G. Hull, P. B. Scott and B. Smith, New York, Feminist Press, 1982, p. 49.
32 Gloria Anzaldúa, *Borderlands/La Frontera: The New Mestiza*, San Francisco, Spinsters/Aunt Lute, 1987.
33 Valerie Amos and Pratibha Parma, 'Challenging Imperial Feminism', *Feminist Review*, no. 17, July 1984, p. 4.
34 Chandra Mohanty, 'Under Western Eyes: Feminist Scholarship and Colonial Discourses', in *Third World Women and the Politics of Feminism*, ed. C. Mohanty, A. Russo and L. Torres, Bloomington, University of Indiana Press, 1991, pp. 51–80.
35 This equation occurs in the preface of a collection in which Chandra Mohanty worries that the post-modern critique of identity can mean

the dissolution of the category of race, at the expense of a recognition of racism, while attention to differences can mean 'the generation of discourses of diversity and pluralism which are grounded in an apolitical, often individualized identity politics'. Michèlle Barrett and Anne Phillips, 'Preface and Acknowledgements', *Destabilizing Theory: Contemporary Feminist Debates*, Cambridge, Polity Press, 1992, p. viii; Chandra Talpole Mohanty, 'Feminist Encounters: Locating the Politics of Experience', in ibid., p. 75.

36 Joseph Bristow and Angela Wilson, 'Introduction', in *Activating Theory: Lesbian, Gay, Bisexual Politics*, ed. Bristow and Wilson, London, Lawrence & Wishart, 1993, p. 2.

37 Jacques Derrida, *Writing and Difference*, London, Routledge & Kegan Paul, 1978.

38 Jacques Lacan, 'God and the *Jouissance* of Woman: A Love Letter', as translated and reprinted in *Feminine Sexuality: Jacques Lacan and the Ecole Freudienne*, ed. J. Mitchell and J. Rose, London, Macmillan, 1982, pp. 137–60.

39 Jacqueline Rose, 'Femininity and its Discontents', *Sexuality in the Field of Vision*, London, Verso, 1986, p. 91.

40 Gayatri Chakravorty Spivak, 'French Feminism in an International Frame', *Yale French Studies*, vol. 62, 1981, pp. 154–84; reprinted in *In Other Worlds*, London, Routledge, 1987.

41 Mary Jacobus, 'Freud's Mnemonic: Women Screen Memories, and Feminist Nostalgia', *Michigan Quarterly Review*, vol. 26, no. 1, 1987, p. 118.

42 Drucilla Cornell, 'Rethinking the Time of Feminism', in *Feminist Contentions: A Philosophical Exchange*, ed. Seyla Benhabib et al., London, Routledge, 1995, p.147.

43 Rita Felski, 'The Doxa of Difference', *Signs*, vol. 23, no. 1, Autumn, 1997.

44 Ibid., p. 6.

45 Channel 4, 'Voices', 3 May 1984, cited in Ann Rosalind Jones, 'Julia Kristeva on Femininity: The Limits of Semiotic Politics', *Feminist Review*, no. 18, Nov. 1984, p. 56.

46 Luce Irigaray, from *Je, tu, nous*, cited in Toril Moi, *Simone de Beauvoir: The Maling of an Intellectual Woman*, Oxford, Blackwell, 1994, p. 183.

47 Lynne Segal, *Slow Motion: Changing Masculinities, Changing Men*, London, Virago, 1990, 1997. My examination of men and masculinity is grounded in this type of analysis.

48 Rosi Braidotti, with Judith Butler (interview), 'Feminism by any Other Name', *Differences*, vol. 6, nos 2–3, Summer–Fall, 1994, pp. 47, 51, 54.

49 See Linda Alcoff, 'Cultural Feminism versus Post-Structuralism: The Identity Crisis in Feminist Theory', *Signs*, vol. 13, no. 3, Spring, 1988.

50   Ann Snitow, 'A Gender Diary', in *Conflicts in Feminism*, ed. M. Hirsch and E. Fox Keller, London, Routledge, 1990, p. 19.

51   Ibid., pp. 9, 36.

52   Denise Riley, *Am I that Name?: Feminism and the Category of 'Women' in History*, London, Macmillan, 1988, p. 5.

53   As in Felski's conclusion to 'The Doxa of Difference', p. 19.

54   Gayle Rubin, 'Thinking Sex: Notes for a Radical Theory of the Politics of Sexuality', in *Pleasure and Danger: Exploring Female Sexuality*, ed. C. Vance, London, Routledge, 1984.

55   Eve Kosofsky Sedgwick, *Epistemology in the Closet*, Berkeley, University of California Press, 1991, p. 34.

56   Henry Abelove, Michèle Barale and David Halperin, *Lesbian and Gay Studies Reader*, London, Routledge, 1993, p. xv.

57   Eve Kosofsky Sedgwick, *Tendencies*, London, Routledge, 1994, p. 8.

58   Ken Plummer, 'Speaking its Name', in *Modern Homosexualities: Fragments of Lesbian and Gay Experience*, ed. Ken Plummer, London, Routledge, 1992, p. 3.

59   For example, see *Inside Out/Outside In: Lesbian Theories, Gay Theories*, ed. Diana Fuss, London, Routledge, 1992.

60   Michel Foucault, *The History of Sexuality*, vol. 1, London, Allen Lane, 1979, p. 70.

61   Judith Butler, *Gender Trouble: Feminism and the Subversion of Identity*, London, Routledge, 1990.

62   Ibid., p. 33.

63   Monique Wittig, *The Straight Mind*, London, Harvester Wheatsheaf, 1992.

64   Butler, *Gender Trouble*, p. 31.

65   Ibid., p. 136.

66   See Peter Osborne and Lynne Segal, 'Gender as Performance: An Interview with Judith Butler', *Radical Philosophy*, vol. 67, Summer, 1994; reprinted in *A Critical Sense: Interviews with Intellectuals*, ed. Osborne, London, Routledge, 1996. Butler criticizes the idea that one can voluntaristically construct and deconstruct identities via transgressive performance in her next book, *Bodies that Matter: The Discursive Limits of Sex*, London, Routledge, 1993.

67   See Segal, *Straight Sex*, chapters 2 and 6; see also *Pleasure and Danger*, ed. Vance.

68   See Ti-Grace Atkinson, *Amazon Odyssey: Collection of Writings*, New York, Links Books, 1974.

69   Cindy Patton, 'Stonewall is a State of Mind', *Z Magazine*, Nov. 1989, p. 106.

70   Quoted in Osborne and Segal, *Critical Sense*, p. 34.

71   Joan Nestle, *A Restricted Country*, Ithaca, NY, Fireband Press, 1987.

72   Baukje Prins, 'How Bodies Come to Matter: An Interview with Judith

Butler', *Signs*, vol. 23, no. 2, 1998, p. 277.

73 Michael Warner, 'Introduction', in *Fear of a Queer Planet: Queer Politics and Social Theory*, ed. Warner, Minneapolis, University of Minnesota Press, 1993, p. xxvi.

74 See Susan Bordo, *Unbearable Weight: Feminism, Western Culture and the Body*, Berkeley, University of California Press, 1993; Kathy Davis, ed., *Embodied Practices: Feminist Perspectives on the Body*, London, Sage, 1997.

75 Kate Bornstein, *Gender Outlaw: On Men, Women, and the Rest of Us*, London, Routledge, 1994, p. 118.

76 Kate Bornstein, 'Transsexual Lesbian Playwright Tells All!', in *High Risk*, ed. Amy Scholder and Ira Silverberg, London, Serpent's Tail, 1991, p. 261.

77 Anne Bolin, 'Transcending and Transgendering: Male-to-Female Trans- sexuals, Dichotomy and Diversity', in *Third Sex, Third Gender: Be- yond Sexual Dimorphism in Culture and History*, ed. Gilbert Herdt, New York, Zone Books, 1994, pp. 447–86.

78 Mari Jo Buhle, *Feminism and its Discontents: A Century of Struggle with Psychoanalysis*, Cambridge, Mass., Harvard University Press, 1988, p. 349.

79 Judith Halberstam, 'Mackdaddy, Superfly, Rapper: Gender, Race and Masculinity in the Drag King Scene', *Social Text*, 52/3, vol. 15, nos 3–4, Fall/Winter, 1997.

80 As Marjorie Garber, for instance, so skilfully depicts in her book *Vested Interests: Cross Dressing and Cultural Anxiety*, London, Routledge, 1992.

81 Segal, *Straight Sex*, chapter 5.

82 Mandy Merck, 'Figuring Out Andy Warhol', in *Pop Out: Queer Warhol*, ed. Jennifer Doyle et al., London and Durham, NC, Duke University Press, 1996, p. 234.

83 Roger Lancaster, 'Transgenderism in Latin America: Some Critical Introductory Remarks on Identities and Practices', *Sexualities*, vol. 1, no. 3, 1998, p. 263.

84 Marlon Riggs, 1992, quoted in Suzanna Walters, 'From Here to Queer: Radical Feminism, Postmodernism, and the Lesbian Menace (or, Why Can't a Woman Be More Like a Fag?)', *Signs*, vol. 21, no. 4, Summer, 1996, p. 843.

85 In Osborne and Segal, *Critical Sense*, p. 111.

86 Judith Butler, 'Afterword', *Sexualities*, vol. 1, no. 3, 1998, p. 359.

87 Lancaster, 'Transgenderism', p. 266.

88 Arthur Kroker and Marilouise Kroker, 'Introduction', *The Last Sex: Feminism and Outlaw Bodies*, ed. Kroker and Kroker, New York, St Martin's Press, 1993, p. 15. See also Halberstam, 'Mackdaddy'.

89 See Garber, *Vested Interests*, p. 98. For the fullest illustration of queer

theorists lining up on different sides of this debate, see Jay Prosser, *Second Skins: The Body Narratives of Transsexuality*, New York, Columbia University Press, 1998, pp. 6–17.

90 Prosser, *Second Skins*, p. 11.

91 Decca Aitkenhead, 'A Life More Ordinary', *The Guardian 2*, 27 August 1998, p. 3.

92 The research being quoted here, by Aitkenhead (ibid.), comes from Dick Swaab (at the Netherlands Institute for Brain Research in Amsterdam), who dissected the brains in autopsies of six transsexuals, reporting that in a tiny section of the hypothalamus no bigger than a pinhead, the BSTc, the size of the dead transsexual tissue was slightly smaller than that of an average woman and definitely smaller than that of an average man. Dick F. Swaab et al., 'Sexual Differentiation of the Human Hypothalamus: Differences according to Sex, Sexual Orientation, and Transsexuality', in *Sexual Orientation: Towards Biological Understanding*, ed. Lee Ellis and Linda Ebertz, Westport, Conn., Praeger, 1997. Were one less in tune with the ideological underpinning of all this (biology alone holds the key to all things), one would certainly wonder at the bizarre leap to a causal explanation of transsexuality from this particular correlation, especially knowing the enormous levels of oestrogen hormones consumed by transsexuals, the levels of stress in their lives, and so on. For a report on this research see Kathleen Hayden, 'Researchers Discover a Biological Basis for Transsexuality', *Time Magazine*, Vol. 146, November 1995, no. 20.

93 Alan Sinfield, *Gay and After*, London, Serpent's Tail, 1998, p. 163.

94 Adam Phillips, *On Flirtation*, London, Faber & Faber, 1994, p. 124.

95 Sukie la Croix, quoted in Jonathan Dollamore, 'Bisexuality', in *Lesbian and Gay Studies: A Critical Introduction*, ed. Andy Medhurst and Sally Munt, London, Cassell, 1997, p. 252.

96 Prosser, *Second Skins*, pp. 11–12. For another interesting analysis of the politics of transgenderism and the dilemmas of transsexuality, see Pat Califia, *Sex Changes: The Politics of Transgenderism*, San Francisco, Cleis Press, 1997.

97 Jean Baudrillard, 'Transpolitics, Transexuality, Transaesthetics', in *The Disappearance of Art and Politics*, ed. W. Stearns and W. Chaloupka, New York, St Martin's Press, 1992, pp. 20–2. (I thank Mandy Merck for drawing my attention to this particular text.)

98 Simon Watney, 'Lesbian and Gay Studies in the Age of AIDS', in *Lesbian and Gay Studies*, ed. Medhurst and Munt, p. 369.

99 Ibid., p. 381.

100 Dennis Altman, 'The Uses and Abuses of Queer Studies', in *Gay and Lesbian Perspectives IV: Studies in Australian Culture*, ed. Robert Aldrich and Garry Wotherspoon, Australian Centre for Lesbian and

Gay Research, University of Sydney, 1998, p. 17.

101   Suzanna Walters, 'From Here to Queer', p. 856.

102   Barbara Smith, quoted in Walters, ibid., p. 864.

103   Elizabeth Wilson, 'Is Transgression Transgressive', in *Activating Theory*, ed. Bristow and Wilson, p. 116; see also R. W. Connell, 'Bodies, Intellectuals and World Society', Plenary address to the British Sociological Association Annual Conference *Making Sense of the Body: Theory, Research and Practice*, Edinburgh, April 1998 (publication forthcoming).

104   Sinfield, *Gay and After*, p. 198.

105   Virginia Goldner, 'Towards a Critical Relational Theory of Gender', *Psychoanalytic Dialogues*, vol. 1, no. 3, 1991, p. 251.

106   Ibid., p. 268.

107   Butler, in Osborne and Segal, *Critical Sense*, p. 113.

108   Connell, 'Bodies'; emphasis added.

109   Muriel Dimen, 'Deconstructing Difference: Gender, Splitting, and Transitional Space, *Psychoanalytic Dialogues*, vol. 1, no. 3, 1991, p. 349.

110   Martha Nussbaum writes that the economist Amartya Sen always began his economics courses by referring to these 100 million 'missing women' in her article, 'Through the Prism of Gender: How New Scholarship about Women's Lives is Changing our Understanding of the Past – and the Present', *Times Literary Supplement*, 20 March 1998, p. 3.

111   Jacqueline Zita, *Body Talk: Philosophical Reflections on Sex and Gender*, New York, Columbia University Press, 1998, p. 108.

112   Gayle Rubin with Judith Butler, 'Sexual Traffic', *More Gender Trouble: Feminism Meets Queer Theory*, special issue of *Differences*, vol. 6, nos 2–3, 1994, p. 97.

113   This is Butler's primary theme in her essay 'Against Proper Objects', *Differences*, vol. 6, nos 2–3, 1994.

114   Rubin, 'Sexual Traffic', p. 97.

115   See Debra Haffner, 'What's Wrong With Abstinence-Only Sexuality Education Programs', *Siecus Reports*, vol. 25, no. 4, April–May 1997.

116   Suan Flinn, 'The Clinton Administration's Adolescent Pregnancy Prevention Program: Ignorance Does Not Equal Abstinence', *Siecus Report*, vol. 25, no. 4, April–May 1997, p. 18.

117   Martin Bright, 'UK Eyes Dutch Sex Lessons', *The Observer*, 21 February 1999, p. 12.

118   Reported in the excellent overview by Judith Levine, 'How we're Hurting Children by Protecting them for Sex', in Levine, *Harmful to Minors*, forthcoming.

119   Ibid.

120 Bright, 'Dutch Sex Lessons', p. 21.
121 Many of these have been scripted by women, for example, the many television dramas in the manner of Nanette Newman's *Bouquet of Barbed Wire*.
122 Kessler estimates that between 1 and 2 per cent of infants at birth could be characterized as 'intersexed', in Suzanne Kessler, *Lessons from the Intersexed*, New Brunswick, NJ, Rutgers University Press, 1998, p. 135. These include females with a large clitoris, fused labia or diminutive vaginas; males with a micropenis, unusual urethral opening; individuals with aberrant genitals, gonads or chromosomes from either sex, insofar as they can be assigned a sex.
123 Ken Plummer, 'Introduction', in *Modern Homosexualities*, ed. Plummer, pp. 14–15.
124 John Gagnon, 'Commentary on "Towards a Critical Relational Theory of Gender"', *Psychoanalytic Dialogues*, vol. 1, no. 3, 1991, p. 274.
125 Biddy Martin, 'Extraordinary Homosexuals and the Fear of Being Ordinary', *Differences*, vol. 6, nos 2–3, Summer–Fall, 1994, p. 103.

Chapter 3   Genes and Gender: The Return to Darwin

1 Robert Wright, 'Feminists Meet Mr. Darwin', *New Republic*, 28 November 1994, pp. 34–6.
2 Andrew Ross, *The Chicago Gangster Theory of Life: Nature's Debt to Society*, London, Verso, 1994, p. 15.
3 Roland Barthes, *Mythologies* [1957], London, Paladin, 1973.
4 Richard Dawkins, *Unweaving the Rainbow*, London, Penguin, 1998, p. 29.
5 Ross, *Chicago Gangster*, for one.
6 In Colin Hughes, 'The Guardian Profile, Richard Dawkins: The Man who Knows the Meaning of Life', *The Guardian: Saturday Review*, 3 October 1998, p. 6.
7 *Matters of Life and Death: Demos Quarterly*, no. 10, London, Demos Publications, 1996.
8 A latter-day Leavisite would, however, perhaps feel driven to cross sides and join forces with his old enemy, who at least retains some categorical faith in universal truths. C. P. Snow, *The Two Cultures*, [1962], reprinted Cambridge, Cambridge University Press, 1993.
9 See Daniel Kevles, *In the Name of Eugenics: Genetics and the Uses of Human Heredity*, New York, Alfred Knopf, 1985; Hilary Rose, 'Moving on from both State and Consumer Eugenics?, in *Nature at the Millennium*, ed. Noel Castree and Bruce Willis, London, Routledge, 1998.

10 Anne Fausto-Sterling, 'Sex and the Single Brain', in Fausto-Sterling, *Myths of Gender: Biological Theories about Women and Men*, rev. edn, New York, Basic Books, 1992, p. 179.

11 Charles Darwin, *The Origin of Species by Means of Natural Selection* [1859]; Harmondsworth, Penguin, 1968, p. 460.

12 Ibid., p. 435, where Darwin recapitulates the arguments of his book. See also Stephen Jay Gould, *Life's Grandeur: The Spread of Excellence from Plato to Darwin*, London, Jonathan Cape, 1996, p. 137.

13 Karl Marx, 'Introduction', *Grundrisse* [1857], trans. Martin Nicolaus, Harmondsworth, Penguin, 1973, p. 105.

14 Quoted in Steve Jones, *New York Review of Books*, 6 Nov. 1997, p. 13.

15 Darwin, *Origin of Species*, pp. 130–5.

16 Ibid., p. 136.

17 R. Dawkins and J. R. Krebs, 'Arms Races between and within Species', *Proceedings of the Royal Society of London Bulletin*, vol. 295, 1979, pp. 489–511.

18 Robert Wright, 'The Dissent of Woman: What Feminists can Learn from Darwinism', in *Matters of Life and Death: Demos Quarterly*, no. 10, 1996, p. 23, adapted from 'Feminists Meet Mr. Darwin'.

19 Ibid., p. 22.

20 Robert Wright, *The Moral Animal: Why We Are the Way We Are: The New Science of Evolutionary Psychology*, New York, Pantheon, 1994.

21 Anne Fausto-Sterling, Patricia Adair Gowaty and Marlene Zuck, 'Review Essay: Evolutionary Psychology and Darwinian Feminism', *Feminist Studies*, vol. 23, no. 2, Summer, 1997, pp. 403–17, (404).

22 E. O. Wilson, *Sociobiology: The New Synthesis*, Cambridge, Mass., Harvard University Press, 1975; Richard Dawkins, *The Selfish Gene*, Oxford, Oxford University Press, 1976, David Barash, *The Whisperings Within: Evolution and the Origins of Human Nature*, New York, Harper & Row, 1979; Donald Symons, *The Evolution of Human Sexuality*, New York, Oxford University Press, 1979.

23 Quoted in Dorothy Nelkin, 'The Social Power of Genetic Information', in *The Code of Codes: Scientific and Social Issues in the Human Genome Project*, ed. D. Kevles and L. Hood, Cambridge, Mass., Harvard University Press, 1992, p. 181.

24 Robert Trivers, 'Parent-Offspring Conflict', *American Zoologist*, no.14, 1974, p. 249.

25 Dawkins, *Selfish Gene*, pp. 153, 162; emphasis added.

26 E. O. Wilson, *On Human Nature*, Cambridge, Mass., Harvard University Press, 1978, pp. 552, 553.

27 Randy Thornhill and N. Thornhill, 'Human Rape: An Evolutionary Analysis', *Ethology and Sociobiology*, vol. 4, 1983, p. 141; see also Thornhill et al., 'The Biology of Rape', in *Rape*, ed. S. Tomaselli and R. Porter, Oxford, Blackwell, 1986.

28   Barash, *Whisperings*, p. 54.

29   Symons, *Human Sexuality*, p. 285.

30   M. Sahlins, *The Use and Abuse of Biology*, London, Tavistock, 1977;
     Ashley Montague, ed., *Sociobiology Examined*, Oxford, Oxford Uni-
     versity Press, 1980; Dialectics of Biology Group, ed., *Against Biologi-
     cal Determinism*, London, Alison & Busby, 1982; Dialectics of Biology
     Group, ed., *Towards a Liberatory Biology*, London, Alison & Busby,
     1982; Ruth Hubbard et al., eds, *Biological Woman: The Convenient
     Myth*, Boston, Shenkman, 1982; R. C. Lewontin, Steven Rose and
     Leon Kamin, eds, *Not in Our Genes*, Harmondsworth, Penguin, 1984;
     Lynda Birke and Jonathan Silverton, eds, *More than the Parts: Biology
     and Politics*, London, Pluto Press, 1984; Ruth Bleier, *Science and Gen-
     der: A Critique of Biology and its Views of Women*, Oxford, Pergamon,
     1984.

31   Ross, *Chicago Gangster*, p. 239.

32   See Rose, 'State and Consumer Eugenics?'; Daniel Kevles, 'Out of
     Eugenics: The Historical Politics of the Human Genome', in Kevles
     and Hood, *Human Genome Project*, pp. 18–36.

33   John Archer, 'Sex Differences in Social Behavior: Are the Social Role
     and Evolutionary Explanations Compatible?', *American Psychologist*,
     vol. 51, no. 9, Sept. 1996, pp. 909–17, (909, 914).

34   John Tooby and Leda Cosmides, 'The Psychological Foundations of
     Culture', in *The Adapted Mind: Evolutionary Psychology and the Gen-
     eration of Culture*, ed. Jerome Barkow, Leda Cosmides, and John Tooby,
     New York, Oxford University Pess, 1992, p. 49; David Buss, 'Evolu-
     tionary Psychology: A New Paradigm for Social Science', *Psychological
     Inquiry*, vol. 6, 1995, pp. 1–30.

35   Martin Daly and Margo Wilson, 'Homicidal Tendencies', in *Matters of
     Life and Death: Demos*, no. 10, 1996, p. 44.

36   Reported in Henry Plotkin, *Evolution in Mind: An Introduction to
     Evolutionary Psychology*, London, Penguin, 1997, p. 265.

37   Leda Cosmides, 'The Logic of Social Exchange: Has Natural Selection
     Shaped how Humans Reason?', *Cognition*, vol. 31, 1989, pp. 187–
     276; Barkow, Cosmides and Tooby, eds, *Adapted Mind*; Buss, 'Evolu-
     tionary Psychology'; Steven Pinker, *How the Mind Works*, London,
     Penguin, 1997.

38   Archer, 'Sex Differences', p. 916.

39   David Buss et al., 'Apatations, Exaptions, and Spandrels', *American
     Psychologist*, vol. 53, no. 5, 1998, pp. 533–48 (535).

40   Ibid., p. 544.

41   David Buss, *The Evolution of Desire: Strategies of Human Mating*, Lon-
     don, Harper Collins, 1994.

42   See Donald Symons and B. Ellis, 'Human Male-Female Differences in
     Sexual Desire', in *The Sociobiology of Sexual and Reproductive Strat-*

egies, ed. A. S. Rasa et al., New York, Oxford University Press, 1989, pp.131–46. For a Darwinian account of male violence, see Martin Daly and Margo Wilson, *Homicide*, New York, Aldine de Gruyter, 1988; David Buss, 'From Vigilance to Violences: Tactics of Mate Retention among American Undergraduates', *Ethology and Sociobiology*, vol. 9, 1988, pp. 291–317.

43 D. F. Einon, 'How Many Children Can One Man Have?', *Evolution and Human Behavior*, vol. 19, 1998, pp. 413–26.

44 Daly and Wilson, *Homicide*.

45 *Why Mothers Die: The Confidential Enquiry into Maternal Deaths*, London, HMSO, Nov. 1998; reported in Sarah Boseley, 'Abuse Risk Higher during Pregnancy', *The Guardian*, 24 Nov. 1998, p. 7.

46 H. Looren de Jong and W. J. Van Der Steen, 'Biological Thinking in Evolutionary Psychology: Rockbottom or Quicksand?', *Philosophical Psychology*, vol. 11, no. 2, 1998, p. 196.

47 Noam Chomsky, *Powers and Prospects: Reflections on Human Nature and the Social Order*, London, Pluto Press, 1996, p. 15.

48 Steve Jones, 'The Set Within the Skull: How the Mind Works', by Steven Pinker, *New York Review of Books*, 6 November 1997, p. 14.

49 *Anatomy of Desire: Repression*, Channel 4, 23 Nov. 1998, 10 p.m.

50 Leslie Zebrowitz, *Reading Faces: Window to the Soul*, New York, Westview Press, 1997. I am grateful to Mandy Merck for drawing my attention to this research.

51 Tooby and Cosmides, in *Adapted Mind*, p. 207.

52 Douglas Kenrick and Melanie Trost, 'The Evolutionary Perspective', in *The Psychology of Gender*, ed. A. Beall and R. Sternberg, New York, Guilford Press, 1993, p. 150.

53 William Simon, *Postmodern Sexualities*, London, Routledge, 1996; E. O. Lauman et al., *The Social Organization of Sexuality: Sexual Practices in the United States*, Chicago, University of Chicago Press, 1994.

54 Kenrick and Trost, 'Evolutionary Perspective', p. 164; emphasis added in first quotation.

55 Richard Lewontin, *Biology as Ideology: The Doctrine of DNA*, London, Penguin, 1991, p. 121.

56 Linda Fedigan, *Primate Paradigms: Sex Roles and Social Bonds*, Montreal, Eden Press, 1982.

57 Sarah Blaffer Hrdy, *The Woman that Never Evolved*, Cambridge, Mass., Harvard University Press, 1981.

58 Meredith Small, *Female Choices: The Sexual Behavior of Female Primates*, Ithaca, NY, Cornell University Press, 1993; *What's Love Got to Do with It?*, New York, Anchor Books, 1995.

59 Jane Goodall, *The Chimpanzees of Gombe: Patterns of Behavior*, Cambridge, Mass., Harvard University Press, 1986; Barbara Smuts, 'The

Evolutionary Origins of Patriarchy', *Human Nature*, vol. 6, 1995, pp. 1–32.

60 Barbara Smuts, 'Gender, Aggression and Influence', in *Primate Societies*, ed. Smuts et al., Chicago, University of Chicago Press, 1987.

61 Frans de Waal, *Good Natured: The Origins of Right and Wrong in Humans and Other Animals*, Cambridge, Mass., Harvard University Press, 1997; R. Wrangham and D. Peterson, *Demonic Males, Apes and the Origins of Human Violence*, Boston, Houghton Mifflin, 1996.

62 Louise B. Silverstein, 'New Directions for Evolutionary Psychology', *Feminism and Psychology*, vol. 8, no. 3, 1998, p. 375.

63 Quoted in Fausto-Sterling et al., 'Evolutionary Psychology', p. 412.

64 Ruth Bleier, 'Introduction', in Bleier, *Feminist Approaches to Science*, New York, Pergamon Press, 1986, p. 10.

65 Linda M. Fedigan, 'Science and the Successful Female: Why there Are so Many Women Primatologists', *American Anthropologist*, vol. 96, 1994, pp. 529–40.

66 Richard Lee and Irven de Vore, eds, *Man the Hunter*, Chicago, Aldine, 1968.

67 See Adrienne Zihlman, 'The Paleolithic Glass Ceiling', in *Women in Evolution*, ed. Lori Hager, London, Routledge, 1997, esp. pp. 100–5.

68 Zihlman, ibid.; Linda M. Fedigan, 'Is Primatology a Feminist Science?' in *Women in Evolution*, ed. Hager.

69 Fedigan, ibid., p. 67.

70 Susan Sperling, 'Baboons with Briefcases vs Langurs with Lipstick: Feminism and Functionalism in Primate Studies', in *The Gender Sexuality Reader*, ed. Roger Lancaster and Micaela di Leonardo, London, Routledge, 1997, p. 256.

71 Dawkins, *Unweaving the Rainbow*, p. 212.

72 Wright, 'Dissent of Woman', p. 19.

73 Iver Mysterud, 'Communicating Ideas about Humans and Evolutionary Theory', *Trends in Ecological Evolution*, vol. 11, Feb. 1996, p. 310.

74 Robin Dunbar, *Grooming, Gossip and the Evolution of Language*, London, Faber & Faber, 1996, pp. 79, 150.

75 Ibid., p. 184.

76 Ibid., p. 34; emphasis added.

77 Ibid., pp. 32, 143.

78 Pinker, *How the Mind Works*, pp. 404, 429. For figures on perpetrators of child sexual abuse, see Jean La Fontaine, *Child Sexual Abuse*, Cambridge, Polity Press, 1990, p. 121.

79 See Linda Fedigan, 'Is Primatology a Feminist Science?', in *Women in Human Evolution*, ed. L. Hager, London, Routledge, 1997, p. 56.

80 Niles Eldredge, *Reinventing Darwin: The Great Debate at the High Table of Evolutionary Theory*, New York, John Wiley, 1995; Steven

Rose, *Lifelines: Biology, Freedom, Determinism*, London, Penguin, 1997, p. 176.

81 Stephen Jay Gould, *New York Review of Books*, 12 June 1997, p. 35.

82 Darwin, *Origin of Species*, p. 435; N. Eldredge and Stephen Jay Gould, 'Punctuated Equilibria: An Alternative to Phylogenetic Gradualism', in *Models in Paleobiology*, ed. T. Schopf, San Francisco, Freeman, Cooper & Co., 1972.

83 J. B. S. Haldane, 'The Interaction of Nature and Nurture', *Annals of Eugenics*, no. 13, 1946, pp. 197–205; Julian Huxley, *Evolution: The Modern Synthesis*, London, George Allen & Unwin, 1942.

84 Richard Lewontin, 'Survival of the Nicest?' *New York Review of Books*, 22 Oct. 1998, p. 60.

85 Dawkins, *Unweaving the Rainbow*, pp. 20, 22.

86 Rose, *Lifelines*, p. 246.

87 Reported in Robert Plomin, *Genetics and Experience: The Interplay between Nature and Nurture: Individual Differences and Development Series*, vol. 6, London, Sage, 1994, p. 14.

88 Gould, *Life's Grandeur*, p. 220.

89 Ibid.; R. C. Lewontin, *The Doctrine of DNA: Biology as Ideology*, London, Penguin, 1993; Robert Brandon, *Adaptation and Environment*, Princeton, Princeton University Press, 1990.

90 R. C. Richardson, 'The Prospects for an Evolutionary Psychology: Human Language and Human Reasoning', *Minds and Machines*, vol. 6, 1996, pp. 541–77.

91 Rose, *Lifelines*, p. 245.

92 David Fernbach, 'Biology and Gay Identity', in *New Left Review*, no. 228, March–April 1998, p. 34.

93 Nelkin, in *Code of Codes*, ed. Kevles and Hood, p. 182.

94 John Avise, *The Genetic Gods: Evolution and Belief in Human Affairs*, Cambridge, Mass., Harvard University Press, 1998, p. vii.

95 Quoted in Kevles, *Eugenics*, p. 18.

96 Walter Gilbert, 'A Vision of the Grail', in *Code of Codes*, p. 83; ed. Kevles and Hood, James Watson, 'A Personal View of the Project', in *Code of Codes*, ed. Kevles and Hood, p. 165.

97 Ibid.

98 H. J. Eysenck, 'Emote Controls', *Times Higher Education Supplement*, 17 May 1996, p. 24.

99 Heard on Greater London Radio, interview with Emma Freud, some time in 1986.

100 See P. McGuffin and R. Katz, 'Genes, Adversity and Depression', in *Nature, Nurture and Psychology*, ed. R. Plomin and G. E. McClearn, Washington, DC, American Psychological Association, 1993.

101 See Fausto-Sterling, *Myths of Gender;* Ruth Hubbard and Elijah Wald, *Exploding the Gene Myth*, Boston, Beacon Press, 1993.

102   Watson, in *Code of Codes*, ed. Kevles and Hood, p. 167.
103   James Wyngaarden, 'Reflections', in *Code of Codes*, ed. Kevles and Hood, p. 357.
104   Ibid., pp. 300–3.
105   Quoted in Kevles, 'Out of Eugenics', p. 29.
106   Watson, in *Code of Codes* , ed. Kevles and Hood, p. 171.
107   Nancy Wexler, 'Clairvoyance and Caution: Repercussions from the Human Genome Project, in *Code of Codes*, ed. Kevles and Hood, p. 212.
108   Rose, *Lifelines*, p. 116.
109   Lewontin, *Doctrine of DNA*, p. 69; emphasis added.
110   Kevles, *Eugenics*.
111   Ruth Hubbard and Elijah Wald, *The Ecologist*, vol. 23, no. 5, Sept.–Oct. 1993; see also Hubbard and Wald, *Exploding the Gene Myth*, Boston, Beacon Press, 1993.
112   Wexler, in *Code of Codes*, ed. Kevles and Hood, p. 243.
113   Daniel Koshland, 'Sequences and Consequences of the Human Genome', *Science*, vol. 146, 1989, p. 189.
114   Robert Plomin, *The Guardian*, Feb. 1996, cited in Rose, *Lifelines*, p. 275.
115   Steve Jones, 'Biology and Bile', reviewing *The Double Helix: James Watson*' in *Prospect*, March 1997, p. 63.
116   Ibid., p. 62.
117   See Edward Yoxen, 'Constructing Genetic Disease', in *Cultural Perspectives in Biological Knowledge*, ed. Troy Duster and Karen Garett, Norwood, NJ, Ablex, 1984, pp. 41–62.
118   Evelyn Fox Keller, 'Nature, Nurture and the Human Genome Project', in *Code of Codes*, ed. Kevles and Hood, p. 297.
119   Plotkin, *Evolution in Mind*, pp. 111, 231.
120   Dawkins, *Unweaving the Rainbow*, pp. 302, 308.
121   Jones, 'Biology and Bile', p. 63.
122   Office of Technology Assessment, *Mapping Our Genes*, quoted in Evelyn Fox Keller, 'Nature, Nurture, and the Human Genome Project', in *Code of Codes*, ed. Kevles and Hood, p. 295.
123   Watson, in *Code of Codes*, ed. Kevles and Hood, p.167.
124   Hubbard and Wald, *Exploding the Gene Myth*, p. 91.
125   Daniel Kevles, 'Pursuing the Unpopular: A History of Courage, Viruses, and Cancer' in *Hidden Histories of Science*, ed. Robert Silvers, London, Granta, 1997, p. 81.
126   M. Baron, 'Genetic Linkage and Male Homosexual Orientation: Reasons to be Cautious', *British Medical Journal*, vol. 307, no. 7, 1994, pp. 337–8; A. Fausto-Sterling and E. Balaban, 'Genetics and Male Sexual Orientation', *Science*, vol. 261, 1994, p. 1257.
127   James Harrison, 'Roles, Identities and Sexual Orientation: Homo-

sexuality, Heterosexuality, and Bisexuality', in *A New Psychology of Men*, ed. Ronald Levant and William Pollack, New York, Basic Books, p. 375.

128 Dean H. Hamer et al., 'A Linkage Between DN Markers on the X Chromosome and Male Sexual Orientation', *Science*, vol. 261, no. 5119, 6 July 1993. See also Michael Bailey and Richard Pillard, 'A Genetic Study of Male Sexual Orientation', *Archives of General Psychiatry*, vol. 48, 1991, pp. 1089–96.
129 Susan Sperling and Yewoubdar Beyene, 'A Pound of Biology and a Pinch of Culture or a Pinch of Biology and a Pound of Culture?: The Necessity of Integrating Biology and Culture in Reproductive Studies', in *Women in Evolution*, ed. Hager, p. 145.
130 John Dupré, *The Disorder of Things*, Cambridge, Mass., Harvard University Press, 1993, p. 2.
131 Donna Haraway, 'A Manifesto for Cybourgs: Science, Technology and Socialist Feminism in the 1980s' in *Feminism/Postmodernism*, ed. Linda Nicholson, London, Routledge, 1990, p. 206.
132 Ibid., p. 223.
133 As Hilary Rose aptly summarizes, in *Nature at the Millennium*, ed. Castree and Willis, p. 11.

Chapter 4   Psychic Life and its Scandals

1 Steven Pinker, *How the Mind Works*, London, Penguin, 1997, p. 563.
2 Quoted in Clifford Geertz, *After the Fact: Two Countries, Four Decades, One Anthropologist*, Cambridge, Mass., Harvard University Press, 1995, p. 166.
3 Stuart Sutherland, 'Welcome to the Doll House', *Times Higher Education Supplement*, 16 May 1997, p. 29.
4 Judith Rich Harris, *The Nature Assumption: Why Children Turn Out the Way They Do*, London, Bloomsbury, 1998.
5 British Psychological Society, *Recovered Memories: The Report of the Working Party of the British Psychological Society*, Leicester, British Psychological Society, 1995, p. 29.
6 See John Morton, 'Cognitive Perspectives on Recovered Memories', in *Recovered Memories of Abuse: True or False?*, ed. Joseph Sandler and Peter Fonagy, London, Karnac Books, 1997, p. 58.
7 Jacqueline Rose, *States of Fantasy*, Oxford, Oxford University Press, 1996, p. 144.
8 Frederick Crews et al., *The Memory Wars: Freud's Legacy in Dispute*, London, Granta, 1997.
9 Jerome Bruner, *Acts of Meaning*, Cambridge, Mass., Harvard University Press, 1990.

10 Pinker, *How the Mind Works*, 1997.
11 Sigmund Freud, *Interpretation of Dreams*, Standard Edition, IV, xxv (Preface to 2nd edn, 1909), quoted in John Forrester, *Dispatches from the Freud Wars: Psychoanalysis and its Passions*, London, Harvard University Press, 1997, pp. 166–7.
12 Laura Marcus, 'Introduction: The Interpretation of Dreams', in *Sigmund Freud's The Interpretation of Dreams: New Interdisciplinary Essays*, ed. Marcus, Manchester, Manchester University Press, 1999, p. 1.
13 Michael Billig, 'The Rhetoric of Social Psychology', in *Deconstructing Psychology*, ed. I. Parker and J. Shotter, London, Routledge, 1990, p. 55.
14 Geertz, *After the Fact*, p. 127.
15 Adam Mars-Jones, commenting upon and quoting Christopher Hibbert, in review of Christopher Hibbert, *No Ordinary Place: Radley College and the Public School*, *Observer Review*, 10 August 1997, p. 18.
16 Mark Peel, *Land of Local Content: The Biography of Anthony Chevenix-Trench*, Melbourne, Melbourne University Press, 1995.
17 Florence Rush, 'The Freudian Cover-up', *Chrysalis*, no. 1, 1977, reprinted as *The Best Kept Secret: Sexual Abuse of Children*, New York, MacGraw Hill, 1980.
18 See Valerie Sinason, ed., *Memory in Dispute*, London, Karnac Books, 1998, p. 14.
19 Alice Miller, *For Your Own Good: The Roots of Violence in Child-Rearing*, London, Virago, 1987; Alice Miller, *Thou Shalt Not Be Aware: Society's Betrayal of the Child*, London, Pluto, 1986; Jeffrey M. Masson, *The Assault on Truth: Freud's Suppression of the Seduction Theory*, London, Faber & Faber, 1984.
20 Susan Brownmiller, *Against our Will*, Harmondsworth, Penguin, 1976, p. 130.
21 Some critics of Freud have disputed the absence of organic aetiology in Freud's patients; see Richard Webster, *Why Freud was Wrong: Sin, Science and Psychoanalysis*, London, HarperCollins, 1996, pp. 76–86. Others feel that we tend to overlook the prevalence of hysterical symptoms at both the personal and the cultural level; see Elaine Showalter, *Hystories: An Inquiry into a Feminist Auto Da Fe*, London, Picador, 1997.
22 For the fullest elaboration of this point see J. Schimek, 'Fact and Fantasy in the Seduction Theory: A Historical Review', *Journal of the American Psychoanalytic Association*, vol. 35, 1987, pp. 937–65.
23 Sigmund Freud, *The aetiology of hysteria* [1953], Standard Edition, 111, p. 204.
24 Sigmund Freud, *An Autobiographical Study* [1925], Standard Edition, XX, 1953, p. 33.
25 Sigmund Freud, *Female Sexuality* [1931] in Pelican Freud Library,

vol. 7; *On Sexuality*, Harmondsworth, Penguin, 1977, p. 379.

26   J. Laplanche and J. -B. Pontalis 'Scene of Seduction; Theory of Seduction', in *The Language of Psychoanalysis*, pp. 404–8.

27   Sigmund Freud, Lecture 23, in *Introductory Lectures on Psychoanalysis* [1916], Pelican Freud Library, vol. 1, Harmondsworth, Penguin, 1977, p. 418.

28   Jeffrey Masson, 'The Tyranny of Psychotherapy', in *Psychotherapy and its Discontents*, ed. W. Dryden, A. Feltham and A. Samuels, Milton Keynes, Open University Press, 1992, p. 16; emphasis added.

29   Ibid., p. 22.

30   Judith Lewis Herman, *Trauma and Recovery*, New York, Basic Books, 1992, p. 202.

31   Lacan 1988, quoted in Ruth Leys, 'Traumatic Cures: Shell Shock, Janet, and the Question of Memory' in *Tense Past: Cultural Essays in Trauma and Memory*, ed. Antze and Lambeck, London, Routledge, 1996, pp. 140–1.

32   See Ann Scott, 'Feminism and the Seductiveness of the 'Real Event', *Feminist Review*, no. 28, 1988; *Real Events Revisited: Fantasy, Memory and Psychoanalysis*, London, Virago, 1996.

33   For an overview of different psychoanalytic positions on the relation between internal and external objects, see Meir Perlow, *Understanding Mental Objects*, London, Routledge, 1995, p. 126.

34   Simon Weinberg, *Incest Behavior*, New York, Citadel Press, 1955.

35   Department of Health, *Child Protection: Messages from Research*, London, HMSO, 1995, pp. 75–7.

36   Sylvia Fraser, *In my Father's House: A Memoir of Incest and Healing*, London, Virago, 1989.

37   Judith Trowell, 'Memories of Abuse, or Abuse of Memories?: Discussion', in *Recovered Memories of Abuse*, ed. Joseph Sandler and Peter Fonagy, pp. 23–4.

38   Valerie Sinason, 'Introduction', in *Memory in Dispute*, ed. Sinason, p. 5.

39   Frederick Crews, 'The Unknown Freud', *New York Review of Books*, 18 Nov. 1993, p. 61.

40   Ibid., p. 65.

41   Quoted in Ian Hacking, *Rewriting the Soul: Multiple Personality and the Sciences of Memory*, Princeton, NJ, Princeton University Press, 1995, p. 136.

42   Sigmund Freud, 'From the History of an Infantile Neurosis' [1918], in *Case Histories II*, Pelican Freud Library, vol. 9, Harmondsworth, 1979, p. 263.

43   Quoted in Janet Malcolm, *In the Freud Archives*, London, Flamingo, 1986.

44   Hacking, *Rewriting the Soul*, pp. 8, 122.

45 Ibid., p. 205.
46 Ian Hacking, 'Memory Sciences, Memory Politics', in *Tense Past* ed. Antze and Lambeck, p. 70.
47 Frederick Bartlett, *Remembering*, London, Cambridge University Press, 1932.
48 Mary Douglas, *How Institutions Think*, London, Routledge & Kegan Paul, 1986, p. 81.
49 Gerald M. Edelman, 'Memory and the Individual Soul: Against Silly Reductionism', in *Bright Air, Brilliant Fire: On the Matter of the Mind*, New York, Basic Books, 1992, p. 69.
50 Steven Rose, *The Making of Memory: From Molecules to Mind*, London, Anchor Books, 1992, p. 56.
51 See John Morton, 'Cognitive Perspectives on Recovered Memories', in *Recovered Memories of Abuse*, ed. Sandler and Fonagy.
52 Daniel L. Schacter et al., 'The Recovered Memories Debate: A Cognitive Neuroscience Perspective', in *Recovered Memories and False Memories*, ed. Martin Conway, Oxford, Oxford University Press, 1997, p. 1.
53 E. F. Loftus and J. A. Coan, 'The Construction of Childhood Memories', in *The Child Witness in Context: Cognitive, Social and Legal Perspectives*, ed. D. Peters, New York, Kluwer, 1994; D. Poole and L. White 'Two Years Later: Effects of Question Repetition and Retention Interval on the Eyewitness Testimony of Children and Adults', *Developmental Psychology*, vol. 29, no. 5, 1993, pp. 844–53.
54 Martin Conway, 'Introduction: What Are Memories?', in *Recovered Memories*, ed. Conway, pp. 4–5.
55 E. F. Loftus, et al., 'Forgetting Sexual Trauma: What does it Mean when 38% Forget?', *Journal of Consulting and Clinical Psychology*, vol. 62, 1994, pp. 1177–81.
56 E. F. Loftus, 'The Myth of Repressed Memory', in *Recovered Memories*, ed. Conway; L. C. Terr, 'What Happens to Early Memories of Trauma? A Study of Twenty Children under Five at the Time of Documented Traumatic Events', *Journal of the American Academy of Child and Adolescent Psychiatry*, vol. 27, 1988, pp. 96–104.
57 British Psychological Society, *Recovered Memories*, p. 29.
58 Terr, 'Early Memories of Trauma'.
59 Schacter et al., in *Recovered Memories*, ed. Conway, p. 89.
60 Erica Burman, 'Children, False Memories and Disciplinary Alliances: Tensions between Developmental Psychology and Psychoanalysis', *Psychoanalysis and Contemporary Thought*, vol. 21, no. 3, Summer, 1998, p. 324.
61 Conway, in *Recovered Memories*, pp. 14–15.
62 Ibid., p. 19.
63 Paul Ricoeur, *Time and Narrative*, 3 vols, trans. Kathleen McLaughlin

and David Pellauer, Chicago, Chicago University Press, 1984–8.

64 Hacking, *Rewriting the Soul*, pp. 248, 251.
65 Peter Fonagy, 'A Psychoanalytic Understanding of Memory and Re-construction', *British Psychological Society Psychotherapeutic Section Newsletter*, no. 16, 1994, pp. 3–20.
66 Ibid., p. 10.
67 Freud, quoted in Laplanche and Pontalis, 'Deferrred Action; Deferred', in *The Language of Psychoanalysis*, p. 112.
68 Ibid., pp. 111–12.
69 Jean Laplanche, 'Psychoanalysis, Time and Translation', in *Jean Laplanche: Seduction, Translation, Drives*, ed. John Fletcher and Martin Stanton, London, Institute of Contemporary Arts, 1992, pp. 176–7.
70 J. -B. Pontalis, *Love of Beginnings*, London, Free Association Books, 1993, p. xv.
71 Christopher Bollas, *Being a Character: Psychoanalysis and Self Experi-ence*, London, Routledge, 1993, p. 78; Stephen A. Mitchell, *Hope and Dread in Psychoanalysis*, New York, Basic Books, 1993, p. 10.
72 Donald Spence, *Narrative Truth and Historical Truth: Meaning and Interpretation in Psychoanalysis*, London and New York, Norton, 1982, p. 288.
73 Jacques Lacan, Seminair 1V Session of 6 March 1957, quoted in John Forrester, *The Seduction of Psychoanalysis: Freud, Lacan and Derrida*, Cambridge, Cambridge University Press, 1990, p. 204.
74 Masson, in *Psychotherapy and its Discontents*, ed. Dryden and Feltham, p. 15.
75 Masson, *Assault on Truth*, p. 11.
76 Rosemary Rowley, 'Advancement of Women: The Third Phase', *WPA* [Women in Psychology Association] *Annual Journal*, 1997, p. 6.
77 Leys, in *Tense Past*, ed. Antze and Lambek.
78 Burman, 'Disciplinary Alliances', p. 325.
79 Peter Fonagy, 'Forward', in *Memory in Dispute*, ed. Sinason, p. xiv.
80 R. D. Hinshelwood, 'False Memory Syndrome – False Therapy Syn-drome', in *Memory in Dispute*, ed. Sinason; cited approvingly by Sinason in her introduction, ibid., p. 11.
81 Quoted in Laplanche and Pontalis, 'Screen Memory' in *The Language of Psychoanalysis*, p. 411. See also S. Freud, *Screen Memories* [....] Standard Edition, III, p. 304–22.
82 Janice Haaken, 'Sexual Abuse, Recovered Memory and Therapeutic Practice', *Social Text*, no. 40, 1994, p. 118. See also Haaken, *Pillar of Salt: Gender, Memory, and the Perils of Looking Back*, New Brunswick, Rutgers University Press, 1998.
83 Pontalis, *Love of Beginnings*, p. 79.
84 Virginia Woolf, 'A Sketch of the Past', in James McConkey, *The Anatomy of Memory: An Anthology*, Oxford, Oxford University Press.

85 See Hermione Lee, *Virginia Woolf*, London, Chatto & Windus, 1996, pp. 154–9.
86 Woolf, in *Anatomy of Memory*, p. 320.
87 Ibid., p. 328.
88 Lee, *Woolf*, p. 127.
89 Hacking, *Rewriting the Soul*, p. 69.
90 Allon Young, 'Bodily Memory and Traumatic Memory', in *Tense Past*.
91 Hacking, *Tense Past*, p. 78.
92 Pontalis, *Love of Beginnings*, p. xv.
93 Louise Armstrong, *Kiss Daddy Goodnight*, New York, Pocket Books, 1978.
94 Louise Armstrong, 'Making an Issue out of Incest', in *The Sexual Liberals and the Attack on Feminism*, ed. Dorchen Leibholdt and Janice Raymond, Oxford, Pergamon Press, 1990, p. 43.
95 See Linda Alcoff and Laura Gray, 'Survivor Discourse: Transgression or Recuperation?, *Signs*, vol. 18, no. 2, 1993.
96 Elayne Rapping, *The Culture of Recovery: Making Sense of the Self-Help Movement in Women's Lives*, Boston, Beacon Press, 1996, p. 9.
97 Louise Armstrong, *Rocking the Cradle of Sexual Politics: What Happened when Women Said Incest*, London, Women's Press, 1996; Michele Davies, *Childhood Sexual Abuse and the Construction of Identity: Healing Sylvia*, London, Taylor & Francis, 1995.
98 See, for example, Sheila Ernst and Marie Maguire, *Living with the Sphinx*, London, Women's Press, 1987.
99 For recent confirmation that such negative attitudes persist, see Kendra Gilbert and Adrian Colye, 'Reconciling the Irreconcilable?: Psychoanalytic Psychotherapists' Constructions of Feminism and Psychoanalysis', forthcoming.

Chapter 5   Gender Anxieties at the Limits of Psychology

1 Sarah Dunant and Roy Porter, eds, *The Age of Anxiety*, London, Virago, 1996, p. 2.
2 Andrew Samuels, *The Political Psyche*, London, Routledge, 1993, pp. 222–3.
3 Joan Raphael-Leff and Rosine Josef Perelman, eds, *Female Experience: Three Generations of British Women Psychoanalysts on Work with Women*, London, Routledge, 1997.
4 Trefor Lloyd and Tristan Wood, eds, *What Next for Men*, London, Working with Men, 1996.
5 Muriel Dimen, 'Deconstructing Difference: Gender, Splitting and Transitional Space', in *Psychoanalytic Dialogues*, vol. 1, no. 3, 1995, p. 349.

6   See Diane Elam and Robyn Wiegman, *Feminism beside Itself*, London, Routledge, 1995.

7   See Jill Morawski, *Practicing Feminism, Reconstructing Psychology*, Ann Arbor, University of Michigan Press, 1994; Jeanne Marecek, 'Gender, Politics and Psychology's Ways of Knowing', *American Psychologist*, vol. 50, 1995, pp. 162–3; Karen Henwood and Nick Pidgeon, 'Remaking the Link: Qualitative Research and Feminist Standpoint Theory', *Feminist Psychology*, vol. 5, no. 1, 1995, pp. 7–30; Mary Gergen and Sara Davis, ed., *Towards a New Psychology of Gender*, London, Routledge, 1997.

8   Michelle Fine and Corrine Bertram, 'Feminist Futures: A Retrospective'; *Feminism and Psychology*, vol. 5, no. 4, Nov. 1995, p. 460.

9   Graham Richards, *Putting Psychology in its Place: An Introduction from a Critical Psychology Perspective*, London, Routledge, 1995, p. 150.

10 Herbert Harari and Jean Peters, 'The Fragmentation of Psychology: Are APA Divisions Symptomatic?, *American Psychologist*, vol. 42, 1987, p. 822; Judith Stacey, 'Disloyal to the Disciplines: A Feminist Trajectory in the Borderlands', in *Feminism in the Academy*, ed. D. Stanton and A. Stewart, Ann Arbor, University of Michigan Press, 1994, p. 312.

11 See, for example, Janet Spence, *Gender Issues in Contemporary Psychology*, London, Sage, 1993, p. 5.

12 Helen Thompson, 'A Review of Recent Literature on the Psychology of Sex', *Psychological Bulletin*, vol. 7, 1910, pp. 335–42. See also R. W. Connell, *Gender and Power*, Cambridge, Polity Press, 1987, p. 30.

13 Eleanor Maccoby and Carol Jacklin, *The Psychology of Sex Differences*, Oxford, Oxford University Press, 1974.

14 Kay Deaux, 'From Individual Differences to Social Categories: Analysis of a Decade's Research on Gender', *American Psychologist*, vol. 39, Feb. 1984, p. 107.

15 Stephen Jay Gould, *The Mismeasure of Man*, New York, Norton, 1981; Carole Tavris, *The Mismeasure of Woman*, New York, Simon & Schuster, 1992.

16 See, for example, Diane Halpern's exhaustive 1990s overview, *Sex Differences in Cognitive Abilities*, 2nd edn, Hillsdale, NJ, Lawrence & Erlbaum, 1992; see also A. Feingold, 'Cognitive Gender Differences Are Disappearing', *American Psychologist*, vol. 43, 1998, pp. 95–103; J. S. Hyde and M. C. Linn, 'Gender Differences in Verbal Ability: A Meta-Analysis', *Psychological Bulletin*, vol. 104, 1988, pp. 53–69; Janet K. Swim, 'Perceived Versus Meta-Analytic Effect Sizes: An Assessment of the Accuracy of Gender Stereotypes', *Journal of Personality and Social Psychology*, vol. 66, no. 1, 1994, pp. 21–36.

17 Alice Eagly, 'On the Advantage of Reporting Sex Differences', *American Psychologist*, vol. 45, 1990, pp. 560–2. Carol Jacklin, ed., *The*

Psychology of Gender, Aldershot, Edward Elgar, 1992. Those who think we should stop sex difference research include Roy Baumeister, 'Should we Stop Studying Sex Differences Altogether', *American Psychologist*, vol. 43, 1988, p. 1093, and the contributors to Rachel Hare-Mustin and Jeanne Marecek, eds, *Making a Difference: Psychology and the Construction of Gender*, New Haven, Yale University Press, 1990.

18 See Celia Kitzinger ed., 'Special Feature: Should Psychologists Study Sex Differences?', *Feminism and Psychology*, vol. 4, no. 4, November 1994.

19 Michael Messner, *Politics of Masculinity: Men in Movements*, London, Sage, 1997, p. xiv.

20 Nigel Edley and Margaret Wetherall, *Men in Perspective: Practice, Power and Identity*, London, Prentice Hall, 1995, p. 30.

21 Sahorta Sarker, *Genetics and Reductionism*, Cambridge, Cambridge University Press, 1998.

22 See Celia Kitzinger, 'Editor's Introduction to "Psychology Constructs the female": A Reappraisal', *Feminism and Psychology*, vol. 3, no. 2, 1993. Naomi Weisstein received a standing ovation after delivering 'Psychology Constructs the Female' to the American Studies Association at the University of California, Davis, in 1968.

23 Rhoda Unger and Mary Crawford, *Women and Gender: A Feminist Psychology*, New York, McGraw Hill, 1992.

24 Leonore Tiefer, 'Retrospective: At the Age of 20 we are Old Enough to Learn from Our Past', paper presented to the 14th Annual Research Conference of the Association for Women in Psychology, Newport, RI, March 1989.

25 Unger and Crawford, *Women and Gender*, p. 624.

26 Jennifer Wicke, 'Celebrity Material: Materialist Feminism and the Culture of Celebrity', *South Atlantic Quarterly*, vol. 93, no. 4, Fall, 1994, p. 761; see also Lyn Mikel Brown and Carol Gilligan, *Meeting at the Crossroads: Women's Psychology and Girls' Development*, Cambridge, Mass., Harvard University Press, 1992.

27 Shirley Prendergast and Simon Forrest, '"Hieroglyphs of the Heterosexual": Learning about Gender in School', in *New Sexual Agendas*, ed. Lynne Segal, Basingstoke, Macmillan, 1997; Helen Wilkinson, *No Turning Back*, London, Demos, 1994; Helen Wilkinson and Geoff Mulgan, *Freedom's Children*, London, Demos, 1995.

28 Esther Rothblum, 'The Stigma of Women's Weight: Social and Economic Realities', *Feminism and Psychology*, vol. 2, no. 1, 1992, Helen Mason, *The Thin Woman*, London, Routledge, 1997.

29 Jane Ussher, 'Research and Theory Related to Female Reproduction: Implications for Clinical Psychology', *British Journal of Clinical Psychology*, vol. 31, 1992, pp. 129–51.

30 Pauline Bart and Eileen Moran, eds, *Violence against Women: The*

Bloody Footprints, London, Sage, 1993.
31 Kum-Kum Bhavnani and Ann Phoenix, eds, *Feminism and Psychology: Special Issue on Shifting Identities Shifting Racism*, vol. 4, no. 1, 1994.
32 Rozsika Parker, *Torn in Two: The Experience of Maternal Ambivalence*, London, Virago, 1995.
33 Mary Crawford, *Talking Difference: On Gender and Language*, London, Sage, 1995.
34 Ibid., p. 12.
35 See, for example, Michelle Fine, 'Reflections on a Feminist Psychology of Women: Paradoxes and Prospects', *Psychology of Women Quarterly*, vol. 9, 1985, pp. 167–83; Mary Jane Parlee, 'Feminism and Psychology', in *Psychology of Gender*, ed. Gergen and Davis.
36 Lynne Segal, *Is the Future Female?: Troubled Thoughts on Contemporary Feminism*, London, Virago, 1987.
37 James Harrison, 'Roles, Identities, and Sexual Orientation: Homosexuality, Heterosexuality, and Bisexuality', in *A New Psychology of Men*, ed. Ronald Levant and William Pollack, New York, Basic Books, 1995, p. 375.
38 Dimen, 'Deconstructing Difference', p. 339.
39 Jessica Benjamin, *Like Subjects, Love Objects*, New Haven, Yale University Press, 1995; Nancy Chodorow, *Femininities, Masculinities, Sexualities*, London, Free Association Books, 1994; Jane Flax, *Thinking Fragments*, Berkeley, University of California Press, 1990.
40 Prendergast and Forrest, in *New Sexual Agendas*, ed. Segal, p. 187; Harriet Bjerrum Nielson and Monica Rudberg, 'Gender Recipes Among Young Girls', *Young-Nordic Journal of Youth Research*, vol. 2, no. 3, 1995.
41 Michael Roper, *Masculinity and the British Organization Man since 1945*, Oxford, Oxford University Press, 1994.
42 Parker, *Torn in Two*; Wendy Hollway and Brid Featherstone, *Mothering and Ambivalence*, London, Routledge, 1997; Susan Kippax et al., *Surviving Safer Sex: Gay Community Responses to Aids*, London, Falmer, 1993; Michael Kauffman, *Cracking the Armour: Power, Pain and the Lives of Men*, Toronto, Viking, 1993.
43 Harry Brod, 'A Case for Men's Studies', in *Changing Men: New Directions in Research on Men and Masculinity*, ed. Michael Kimmel, London, Sage, 1987.
44 Office for Standards in Education and Equal Opportunities Commission [Ofsted/EOC], *The Gender Divide: Performance Differences between Boys and Girls at School*, London, HMSO, 1996.
45 Lloyd and Wood, eds, *What Next for Men*.
46 R. W. Connell, *Masculinities*, Cambridge, Polity Press, 1995, pp. 82–6; Sian Griffith, ed., *Beyond the Glass Ceiling*, Manchester,

Manchester University Press, 1996; Natasha Walter, *The New Feminism*, London, Virago, 1998, pp. 10–25.

47 John Charlton et al., 'Suicide Deaths in England and Wales: Trends in Factors Associated with Suicide Deaths', *Population Trends*, no. 71, Spring, 1993.

48 The Commission on Children and Violence, *Children and Violence*, London, Calouste Gulbenkian Foundation, 1995.

49 These media programmes and newspaper articles are discussed in Debbie Epstein et al., 'Schoolboy Frictions: Feminism and 'Failing' Boys', in *Failing Boys: Issues in Gender and Achievement*, ed. Epstein et al., Buckingham, Open University Press, 1998, p. 6. In this essay they point to similar rhetoric in other Western states.

50 Ibid., pp. 11–12.

51 Madeleine Arnot, Miriam David and Gaby Weiner, *Educational Reforms and Gender Equality in Schools*, Manchester, Equal Opportunity Commission, 1996.

52 See Michèle Cohen, 'A Habit of Healthy Idleness: Boy's Underachievement in Historical Perspective', in *Failing Boys*, ed. Epstein et al.; Tony Sewell, *Black Masculinities and Schooling: How Black Boys Survive Modern Schooling*, Stoke-on-Trent, Trentham Books, 1997.

53 Girls have always outperformed boys in school up until the age of eleven; due to official attempts to keep a gender balance, in Britain in the 1950s and 1960s girls therefore had to score higher than boys to enter grammar schools. See Epstein et al., in *Failing Boys*, ed. Epstein et al., p. 5.

54 Roger Horrocks, *Masculinity in Crisis: Myths, Fantasies and Realities*, London and Basingstoke, Macmillan, 1994, p. 1.

55 Ronald Levant and William Pollack, eds, *A New Psychology of Men*, Basic Books, 1995. This collection includes examples of most of the recent work being done on the psychology of masculinity in the USA; see also S. Oskamp and M. Costanzo, eds, *Gender Issues in Social Psychology*, London, Sage, 1993; R. C Barnett, N. L. Marshall and J. Pleck, 'Men's Multiple Roles and their Relationship to Psychological Distress', *Journal of Marriage and the Family*, vol. 54, no. 2, 1992.

56 Joseph Pleck, *The Myth of Masculinity*, Cambridge, Mass., MIT Press, 1981; Pleck, 'The Gender Role Strain Paradigm: An Update', in *Psychology of Men*, ed. Levant and Pollack.

57 Levant and Pollack, 'Introduction', in *Psychology of Men*, ed. Levant and Pollack, p. 1.

58 See T. Brooks-Gunn and W. Mathews, *He and She: How Children Develop their Sex-Role Identity*, Englewood Cliffs, NJ, Prentice Hall, 1979.

59 Robert Weiss, *Staying the Course: The Emotional and Social Lives of Men who Do Well at Work*, New York, Fawcett, Columbia, 1990,

quoted in Schwalbe, *Unlocking the Iron Cage*, New York, Oxford University Press, 1996, p. 27.

60 Joseph H. Pleck, Freya Lund Sonenstein and Lighton C. Ku, 'Masculinity Ideology and its Correlates', in *Gender Issues in Social Psychology*, ed. Oskamp and Costanzo, London, Sage, 1993.

61 Andrew Ross, 'The Great White Dude', in *Constructing Masculinity*, ed. Maurice Berger et al., London, Routledge, 1995, p. 172.

62 Some feminists, and gender theorists, have objected to discourses of 'patriarchy', except in terms of its literal meaning 'power of the father', on the grounds that it suggests a universal and unchanging structure of male dominance, diverting attention from the multiplicity of ways in which gender operates. Its shifting usage seems clear enough to me, but I prefer the notion of 'men's dominance' as a more precise description of the overall pattern of gender relations in modernity.

63 Connell, *Masculinities*, p. 211.

64 See Susan Faludi, *Backlash: The Undeclared War against Women*, New York, Crown, 1991.

65 Lynn Raphael Reed, ' "Zero Tolerance": Gender Performance and School Failure', in *Failing Boys*, ed. Epstein, et al., p. 65.

66 Michael Kimmel, *Manhood in America: A Cultural History*, New York, The Free Press, 1996; J. A. Mangan and James Walvin, eds, *Manliness and Morality*, Manchester, Manchester University Press; Michael Roper and John Tosh, eds, *Manful Assertions: Masculinities in Britain since 1800*, London, Routledge, 1991.

67 See *What Next for Men*, ed. Lloyd and Wood.

68 Will Hutton, 'Why the Workplace is No Longer a Man's World', *The Observer*, 8 Dec. 1996, p. 26.

69 See Sandy Ruxton, 'Boys Won't Be Boys: Tackling the Roots of Male Delinquency', in *What Next for Men*, ed. Lloyd and Wood, p. 89; Peter Moss, 'Increasing Men's Involvement with their Children, in *What Next for Men*, ed. Lloyd and Wood, p. 250.

70 Judith Butler, *Gender Trouble*, London, Routledge, 1990; Lynne Segal, *Straight Sex: The Politics of Pleasure*, London, Virago, 1994.

71 Homi Bhabha, 'Are You a Man or a Mouse?', in *Constructing Masculinity*, ed. Berger et al., p. 58.

72 Robert Reid-Pharr, 'It's Raining Men', *Transitions: An International Review*, vol. 6, no.1, 1996, p. 38.

73 Ibid.

74 Connell, *Masculinities*; Messner, *Politics of Masculinity*; Jeff Hearn, Mac an Ghaill, ed., *Understanding Masculinities*, Milton Keynes, Open University Press, 1996; John MacInnes, *The End of Masculinity*, Milton Keynes, Open University Press, 1998.

75 See Jeffrey Weeks, *Invented Moralities: Sexual Values in an Age of*

Uncertainty, Cambridge, Polity Press, 1995; Edward King, *Safety in Numbers: Safer Sex and Gay Men*, London, Cassell, 1993; Thom Gunn, *The Man with Night Sweats*, London, Faber & Faber, 1992; Mark Doty, *Heaven's Coast: A Memoir*, London, Jonathan Cape, 1996.

Chapter 6 Cautionary Tales: Between Freud and Feminism

1 Lesley Caldwell, 'Editorial', *New Formations: Psychoanalysis and Culture*, no. 26, Autumn, 1995, p. vii.
2 Juliet Mitchell, 'Twenty Years On', in *New Formations: Psychoanalysis and Culture*, no. 26, Autumn, 1995, p. 124.
3 Mari Jo Buhle, *Feminism and its Discontents: A Century of Struggle with Psychoanalysis*, London, Harvard University Press, 1998; see also Lisa Appignanesi and John Forrester, *Freud's Women*, London, Weidenfeld & Nicholson, 1992.
4 Emma Goldman quoted in Buhle, ibid., p. 2.
5 Charlotte Perkins Gihman, discussed in Buhle, ibid., p. 48.
6 H. J. Eysenck, 'Emote Controls', *Times Higher Education Supplement*, 17 May 1996, p. 24.
7 One of the most recent, highly polemical efforts along these lines can be found in Judith Rich Harris, *The Nature Assumption: Why Children Turn Out the Way They Do*, London, Bloomsbury, 1998.
8 Jacques Derrida, '"To Do Justice to Freud": The History of Madness in the Age of Psychoanalysis, *Critcal Inquiry*, vol. 20, Winter, 1994, p. 239.
9 Rachel Bowlby, 'Still Crazy Afer All These Years', in *Feminism and Psychoanalysis*, ed. Teresa Brennan, Routledge, 1989, p. 42.
10 Mitchell, 'Twenty Years On', p. 125.
11 Jane Gallop, *The Daughter's Seduction: Feminism and Psychoanalysis*, Ithaca, NY, Cornell University Press, 1982, p. xii.
12 Sigmund Freud, *Three Essays on the Theory of Sexuality* [1905, footnote added 1915], Penguin Freud Library, vol. 7, Harmondsworth, 1977, pp. 141–2.
13 Norman Mailer, *Advertisements for Myself*, London, Putnam, 1959, p. 222.
14 See Elisabeth Roudinesco, *A History of Psychoanalysis in France 1925–1985*, trans. Jeffrey Mehlman, London, Free Association Books, 1990, pp. 404–6.
15 Cited in David Macey, *Lacan in Contexts*, London, Verso, 1988, p. 208.
16 Cited in Roudinesco, *Psychoanalysis in France*, p. 423.
17 Cited in Stephen Heath, 'Difference' [1978], in *The Sexual Subject: A*

Screen Reader in Sexuality, ed. M. Merck, London, Routledge, 1992, p. 63.

18 Jacques Lacan, 'The Signification of the Phallus', in *Lacapo, Ecrits: A Selection*, pp. 281–91.

19 Lacan, 1957–8, quoted in *Feminine Sexuality*, ed. Juliet Mitchell and Jacqueline Rose, trans. Rose, London, Macmillan, 1982, p. 39.

20 Luce Irigaray, *Speculum of the Other Woman*, trans. Gillian Gill, Ithaca, NY, Cornell University Press, 1985, p. 83.

21 Slavoj Žižek, ' "Postscript" to Slavoj Žižek and Renate Salec "Lacan in Slovenia" ', in *A Critical Sense: Interviews with Intellectuals*, ed. Peter Osborne, London, Routledge, 1996, p. 42.

22 See Ann Rosalind Jones, 'Editors' Introduction', in Catherine Clément, *The Weary Sons of Freud*, London, Verso, 1987, p. 4.

23 Drucilla Cornell, *Beyond Accommodation: Ethical Feminism, Deconstruction and the Law*, London, Routledge, 1991, p. 199.

24 Drucilla Cornell, 'Feminism, Deconstruction and the Law: Drucilla Cornell Interviewed by Peter Osborne', *Radical Philosophy*, no. 73, Sept.–Oct. 1995, p. 30.

25 Judith Butler, 'Against Proper Objects', *More Gender Trouble: Feminism Meets Queer Theory*, special issue of *Differences*, vol. 6, nos 2–3, 1994, p. 19.

26 Juliet Flower MacCannell, 'Language', in *Feminism and Psychoanalysis: A Critical Dictionary*, ed. Elizabeth Wright, Oxford, Blackwell, 1992, p. 213.

27 See Jacqueline Rose, *Why War: The Bucknell Lectures in Literary Theory*, Oxford, Blackwell, 1993, p. 245.

28 David Macey, 'Phallus: Definitions', in *Feminism and Psychoanalysis*, ed. Wright, p. 319.

29 See Jean Laplanche, *New Foundations of Psychoanalysis*, trans. D. Macey, Oxford, Blackwell, 1989; John Fletcher and Michael Stanton, eds, *Jean Laplanche: Seduction, Translation, Drives*, London, Institute of Contemporary Arts, 1992.

30 See John Fletcher, 'Introduction: Psychoanalysis and the Question of the Other' in Jean Laplanche, *Essays on Otherness*, London, Routledge, 1999, pp. 44–5.

31 John Fletcher, 'Phallocentrism and the General Theory of Seduction', unpublished.

32 Philippe Van Haute, 'Fatal Attraction: Jean Laplanche on Sexuality, Subjectivity and Singularity in the work of Sigmund Freud', *Radical Philosophy*, vol. 73, Sept.–Oct., 1995, p. 10.

33 David Macey, 'On the Subject of Lacan', in *Psychoanalysis in Context*, ed. Anthony Elliott and Stephen Frosh, London, Routledge, 1994, p. 81.

34 John Brenkman, *Straight, Male, Modern*, London, Routledge, 1993.

35   Gayle Rubin with Judith Butler, 'Sexual Traffic', *More Gender Trouble: Feminism Meets Queer Theory*, special issue of *Differences*, vol. 6, nos 2–3, 1994, p. 69.

36   Teresa de Lauretis, *Technologies of Gender: Essays on Theory, Film and Fiction*, London and Basingstoke, Macmillan, 1987, p. 2.

37   Teresa de Lauretis, *The Practice of Love: Lesbian Sexuality and Perverse Desire*, Bloomington, Indiana University Press, 1994.

38   Judith Butler, 'Desire', in *Critical Terms for Literary Study*, ed. Frank Lentricchia and Thomas McLaughlin, Chicago, University of Chicago Press, 1995, pp. 385; Butler, 'Against Proper Objects', p. 20.

39   Elizabeth Grosz, 'The Labors of Love. Analyzing Perverse Desire: An Interrogation of Teresa de Lauretis's *The Practice of Love*', *Differences*, vol. 6, nos 2 and 3, 1994, p. 275.

40   Jacqueline Rose, 'Introduction', in *Feminine Sexuality*, ed. Mitchell and Rose, p. 57.

41   Rose, *Why War*, pp. 243–4.

42   Mikkel Borch-Jacobsen, 'The Oedipus Problem in Freud and Lacan', trans. Douglas Brick, *Critical Inquiry*, vol. 20, Winter, 1994, p. 277.

43   Peter Dews, 'The Early Lacan and the Frankfurt School', in *Psychoanalysis in Context*, ed. Elliott and Frosh, p. 61.

44   Dews, ibid., p. 60; Borch-Jacobsen, 'Oedipus Problem', p. 282; emphasis added.

45   Žižek, 'Postscript', in *Critical Sense*, ed. Peter Osborne, p. 42.

46   Ethel Person, 'The Influence of Values in Psychoanalysis: The Case of Female Psychology', in *Essential Papers on the Psychology of Women*, ed. Claudia Zanardi, New York, New York University Press, 1990, pp. 314–15.

47   Lacan, 'Seminar of 21 January 1975', in *Feminine Sexuality*, ed. Mitchell and Rose, p. 170.

48   Otto Kernberg, 'Boundaries and Structures in Love Relations', in *Internal World and External Reality*, New York, Jason Aronson, 1980, p. 279.

49   Hanna Segal interviewed by Jacqueline Rose in *Women: A Cultural Review*, vol. 1, no. 2, Summer, 1990, p. 207.

50   Michael Balint, 'Perversion and Genitality', in *Primary Love and Psycho-Analytic Technique*, London, Tavistock, 1965, p. 136.

51   Cited in Susie Orbach, 'Beware the Prejudiced Analyst', *Guardian Weekend*, 29 April 1995.

52   Freud, *Three Essays*, pp. 56–7.

53   Janine Chasseguet-Smirgel, 'Being a Mother and a Psychoanalyst', in *Representations of Motherhood*, ed. D. Bassin et al., New Haven and London, Yale University Press, 1994, p. 125.

54   M. Eglé Laufer, 'The Female Oedipus Complex and the Relationship to the Body', in *The Gender Conundrum*, ed. D. Breen, London,

Routledge, 1993, p. 76.

55   Laufer, ibid.; see also Chasseguet-Smirgel, 'Freud and Female Sexuality: The Consideration of some Blind Spots in the Exploration of the "Dark Continent"', in *Gender Conundrum*, ed. Breen.

56   Adam Jukes, *Why Men Hate Women*, London, Free Association Books, 1993, p. 317.

57   Freud, *Three Essays*,' p. 160. See also Alain Gibeault, 'On the Feminine and the Masculine: Afterthoughts on Jacqueline Cosnier's Book, *Destins de la féminité*', in *Gender Conundrum*, ed. Breen.

58   Sigmund Freud, 'Analysis Terminable and Interminable' [1937–9], Standard Edition, vol. xxiii London, Hogarth, 1964, p. 252.

59   Monique Schneider, interviewed in *Women Analyze Women*, ed. E. H. Baruch and L. J. Serrano, New York, New York University Press, 1988; emphasis added.

60   Dana Breen, 'General Introduction', in *Gender Conundrum*, ed. Breen, p. 35, citing Joyce McDougall.

61   Jessica Benjamin, 'The Omnipotent Mother', in *Representations of Motherhood*, ed. Bassin et al., p. 132.

62   Virginia Goldner, 'Towards a Critical Relational Theory of Gender', *Psychoanalytic Dialogues*, vol. 1, no. 3, 1991, p. 249. See also Muriel Dimen, 'Deconstructing Difference: Gender, Splitting, and Transitional Space', *Psychoanalytic Dialogues*, vol. 1, no. 3, pp. 335–52.

63   Benjamin, in *Representations of Motherhood*, ed. Bassin et al., p. 130.

64   Juliet Mitchell, 'Commentary on "Deconstructing Difference: Gender, Splitting and Transitional Space', *Psychoanalytic Dialogues*, vol. 1, no. 3, 1991, pp. 353–7.

65   Jessica Benjamin, 'An "Over-inclusive" Theory of Gender Development', in *Psychoanalysis in Context*, ed. Elliott and Frosh, p. 120.

66   Kaja Silverman, *Male Subjectivity at the Margins*, London, Routledge, 1992, p. 65.

67   Adam Phillips, *Terrors and Experts*, London, Faber & Faber, 1995, p. 86.

68   Ibid., p. xvi.

Chapter 7   Only Contradictions on Offer: Feminism at the Millennium

1   Joan Scott, *Only Paradoxes to Offer: French Feminists and the Rights of Man*, Cambridge, Mass., Harvard University Press, 1996.

2   Caroline Glendinning and Jane Miller, eds, *Women and Poverty in Britain: The 1990s*, London, Harvester, 1992; Sylvia Bashevkin, *Women on the Defensive: Living through Conservative Times*, Chicago, University of Chicago Press, 1998.

3 Bashevkin, ibid. p. 95.

4 Harold Bloom, cited in Sandra M. Gilbert, 'Presidential Address 1996: Shadows of Futurity: The Literary Imagination, the MLA, and the Twenty-First Century', *Proceedings of the Modern Language Association*, vol. 112, no. 3, May, 1997, p. 3.

5 See Lynne Segal, *Straight Sex: The Politics of Pleasure*, London, Virago, 1994.

6 These figures come from the Incomes Data Service, 77 Bastwick Street, London, EC1V 3TT, Feb. 1999.

7 See Marlene Kim, 'Comments', in *Women and Unions: Forging a Partnership*, ed. Dorothy Cobble, New York, International Labour Review Press, 1993.

8 B. Bagilhole, *Women, Work and Equal Opportunity*, Aldershot, Avebury, 1994, p. 1.

9 See Suzanne Franks, *Having None of It: Women, Men and the Future of Work*, London, Granta, 1999.

10 Joni Lovendeski, 'Sex, Gender and British Politics', *Parliamentary Affairs*, vol. 49, no. 1, Jan. 1996, p. 10; Bashevkin, *Women on the Defensive*, p. 120.

11 Reported in Mary McIntosh, 'Dependency Culture? Welfare, Women and Work', *Radical Philosophy*, no. 91, Sept.–Oct., 1998, p. 5.

12 Sue Lees, *Carnal Knowledge: Rape on Trial*, London, Penguin, 1996; Bashevkin, *Women on the Defensive*, pp. 60, 116.

13 Information from *Social Focus on Women*, quoted in *Who's Afraid of Feminism Seeing through the Backlash*, ed. Ann Oakley and Juliet Mitchell, London, Penguin, 1997, p. 7.

14 Manuel Castells, 'The End of Patriarchalism: Social Movements, Family, and Sexuality in the Information Age', in *The Information Age: Economy, Society and Culture*, vol. 11: *The Power of Identity*, Oxford, Blackwell, 1998, pp. 165–70.

15 Suzanne Franks, 'Vital Statistics', *The Guardian*, 11 Jan. 1999, p. 7.

16 The declaration condemns violence against women, especially systemic rape in warfare, and encourages assistance for female victims of violence; recommends enactment of legislation to guarantee the right of women and men to equal pay for equal work; supports the promotion of businesses run by women and women's media networks; calls for women's equal participation in governments; promotes research on women's health, and so on. See a variety of reports from the Beijing conference in *Signs*, vol. 22, no. 1, 1996, pp. 181–226.

17 Charlotte Bunch, cited in Barbara Crossette, 'Women See Key Gains since Talks in Beijing', *New York Times*, 8 March 1998.

18 Rachel Blau DuPlessis and Ann Snitow, 'A Feminist Memoir Project', in *The Feminist Memoir Project: Voices from Women's Liberation*, New York, Three Rivers Press, 1998, p. 4.

19 For example, Leslie Heywood and Jennifer Drake, eds, *Third Wave Agenda: Doing Feminism, Being Feminist*, Minneapolis, University of Minnesota Press, 1997; Special Issue: Third Wave Feminisms, *Hypatia: A Journal of Feminist Philosophy*, ed. J. Zita, Summer, 1997.

20 Eleanor Rathbone, quoted in Susan Pedersen, 'The Failure of Feminism in the Making of the British Welfare State', *Radical History Review: The Women's Story*, vol. 43, Winter, 1989, pp. 86–110 (86).

21 Nancy Fraser and Linda Gordon, 'A Genealogy of "Dependency": Tracing a Keyword of the U.S. Welfare State', in Fraser, *Justice Interruptus: Critical Reflections on the "Postsocialist" Condition*, New York and London, Routledge, 1997; Moynihan quoted in ibid., p. 138.

22 'News in Brief: Midwives to Look for Abuse of Women', *The Guardian*, 29 Dec., 1997, p. 8.: 'There seems to be evidence of violence starting or being exacerbated when a woman is pregnant or postnatally, with the violence directed towards her stomach, breasts and genitals'.

23 Carolyn Steedman, 'Landscape of a Good Woman', in Steedman, *Past Tense: Essays in Writing, Autobiography and History*, London, Rivers Oram Press, 1992, p. 36.

24 Liz Heron, *Truth, Dare or Promise: Girls Growing Up in the Sixties*, London, Virago, 1985, p. 6.

25 Castells, 'The End of Patriarchalism', p. 235.

26 McIntosh, 'Dependency Culture?', p. 5.

27 See Katherine McFate et al., eds, *Poverty, Inequality and the Future of Social Policy*, New York, Russell Sage, 1995.

28 Lawrence Mead, ed., *The New Paternalism: Supervising Approaches to Poverty*, Washington, DC, Brookings Institution Press, 1997; Susanne MacGregor, 'Welfare, Neo-Liberalism and New Paternalism: Three Ways for Social Policy in Late Capitalist Societies, *Capital and Class*, no. 67, Spring, 1999.

29 Tony Cutler and Barbara Waine, *Managing the Welfare State*, Oxford, Berg, 1997.

30 Alan Finder, 'Evidence Is Scant that Workfare Leads to Full-Time Jobs', *New York Times*, 12 April 1998, pp. 1, 30.

31 Judith Stacey, 'Families against the Family', *Radical Philosophy*, no. 89, May–June 1998; *In the Name of the Family: Rethinking Family Values in the Postmodern Age*, Boston, Beacon Press, 1996, ch. 4.

32 Lillian Rubin, *The Transcendent Child: Tales of Triumph over the Past*, New York, HarperCollins, 1997.

33 Judith Williamson, 'This Life: Careless Talk Costs Lives', *The Guardian*, 20 Dec. 1997.

34 Quoted in Carol Gilligan, 'Getting Civilized', in *Who's Afraid of Feminism*, ed. Oakley and Mitchell, p. 15.

35 David Popenoe, *Disturbing the Nest: Family Change and Decline in*

Modern Societies, New York, Aldine, 1988; *Rebuilding the Nest: A New Commitment to the American Family*, ed. David Blakenhorn, Jean Bethke Elshtain and Steven Bayme, Milwaukee, Family Service American, 1991; David Blakenhorn, *Fatherless America: Confronting our most Urgent Social Problem*, New York, Basic Books, 1995.

36 Barbara Ehrenreich, 'When Government Gets Mean: Confessions of a Recovering Statist', *The Nation*, 17 Nov. 1997, p. 12; emphasis added.

37 See Anna Marie Smith, 'Feminist Activism and Presidential Politics: Theorizing the Costs of the "Insider Strategy" ', *Radical Philosophy*, no. 83, May–June, 1997; Zillah Eisenstein, *Hatreds: Racialized and Sexualized Conflicts in the 21st Century*, London, Routledge, 1996, p. 118.

38 Wendy Brown, *States of Injury Power and Freedom in Late Modernity*, Princeton, NJ, Princeton University Press, 1995, p. x. In this book I do not address the influential strand of anti-pornography feminism, though I have done so frequently elsewhere, because I believe it has served primarily to reinvigorate the moral right, rather than any progressive left politics. See Segal, *Straight Sex*; Segal and McIntosh, eds, *Sex Exposed: Sexuality and the Pornography Debates*, New Brunswick, NJ, Rutgers University Press, 1992.

39 See, for example, McIntosh, 'Dependency Culture?', p. 2.

40 Ibid., p. 3.

41 Paul Pierson, *Dismantling the Welfare State? Reagan, Thatcher and the Politics of Retrenchment*, Cambridge, Cambridge University Press, 1995.

42 Harvey Levenstein, *Paradoxes of Plenty: A Social History of Eating in Modern America*, New York, Oxford University Press, 1993, p. 81.

43 Franks, 'Vital Statistics', p. 7; Franks, *Having None of It*.

44 For the fullest overview see Castells, 'The End of Patriarchalism'.

45 Toril Moi, 'Psychoanalysis, Feminism, and Politics: A Conversation with Juliet Mitchell', *Materialist Feminism*, special eds Toril Moi and Janice Radway, *South Atlantic Quarterly*, vol. 93, no. 4, Fall, 1994, p. 937.

46 Patrizia Romito, ' "Damned if You Do and Damned if You Don't": Psychological and Social Constraints on Otherhood in Contemporary Europe', in *Who's Afraid of Feminism*, ed. Oakley and Mitchell; Adriana Cavarero, 'The Politics of Sexual Difference', paper delivered to *Radical Philosophy Conference: Torn Halves: Theory and Politics in Contemporary Feminism*, School of Oriental and African Studies, University of London, 9 Nov. 1996.

47 See Rita Felski, 'The Doxa of Difference', *Signs*, vol. 23, no. 1, Autumn, 1997.

48 Cora Kaplan reminded me of Mitchell's argument in her talk at the conference entitled *At the Millennium: Interrogating Gender*, Harkness Hall, London University, London, 9 Jan. 1998.

49 Juliet Mitchell, 'Reflections on Twenty Years of Feminism', in *What is Feminism?*, ed. J. Mitchell and A. Oakley, Oxford, Blackwell, 1986, pp. 47, 48, 45.

50 Norman Mailer, quoted in David Denby, 'The Contender', *New Yorker*, 20 April 1998, p. 70.

51 See, for example, Judith Stacey, *Brave New Families: Stories of Domestic Upheaval in the Late Twentieth Century*, New York, Basic Books, 1990.

52 For a detailed and stimulating account of women and men working in the upper echelons of banking in the City of London, see Linda McDowell, *Capital Culture: Gender and Work in the City*, Oxford, Blackwell, 1997.

53 Cynthia Salzman, *In the Shadows of Privilege: Women and Unions at Yale*, forthcoming; Hank Johnson and Bert Klandermans, eds, *Social Movements and Culture* (Social Movements, Protest, and Contention, vol. 4), Minneapolis, University of Minnesota Press, 1995.

54 Andrew Ross, *Real Love: In Pursuit of Cultural Justice*, New York, New York University Press, 1998, pp. 5, 216.

55 Jane Gallop, *Around 1981: Academic Feminist Literary Theory*, London, Routledge, 1992, p. 4.

56 Hazel V. Carby, 'The Multicultural Wars', *Radical History Review*, vol. 54, 1992, pp. 7–18.

57 Heidi Hartmann et al., 'Bringing Together Feminist Theory and Practice: A Collective Interview', *Signs*, vol. 21, no. 41, 1996.

58 Temma Kaplan, *Crazy for Democracy: Women in Grassroots Movements*, London, Routledge, 1997, p. 1.

59 Patricia Williams, *The Alchemy of Race and Rights*, Cambridge, Mass., Harvard University Press, p. 149. See also John Anner, ed., *Beyond Identity Politics: Emerging Social Justice Movements in Communities of Color*, Boston, South End Press, 1996. Reporting on the wave of black and immigrant-based struggles in the USA over the last decade, in all of which women have played a critical role, Anner similarly points to the need for shared political ideals to forge bonds between diverse 'identities' and communities of interest.

60 See Etienne Balibar, 'Ambiguous Universality', *Differences*, vol. 7, no. 1, 1995.

61 For example, see Barbara Epstein, 'Why Post-structuralism is a Dead End for Progressive Thought', *Socialist Review*, vol. 25, no. 2, 1995.

62 See Paul Hirst and Grahame Thompson, *Globalization in Question*, Cambridge, Polity Press, 1996; Simon Bromley, 'Globalization', *Radical Philosophy*, no. 80, Nov.–Dec. 1996.

63 Paul Hirst and Grahame Thompson, 'Globalization: Ten Frequently Asked Questions and some Surprising Answers', *Soundings*, no. 4, Autumn, 1996, p. 62.

64 Kim Moody, *Workers in a Lean World*, London, Verso, 1997.

65 Theresa Ann Sears, 'Feminist Misogyny; or, What Kind of Feminist Are You?', in *Generations: Academic Feminists in Dialogue*, ed. Ann Kaplan and Devoney Looser, Minneapolis, University of Minnesota Press, 1997, p. 269.

66 Kathleen Hulley, 'Interview with Grace Paley', *Delta: Grace Paley*, no. 14, May 1982, p. 32.

67 Jean-François Lyotard, *The Postmodern Condition: A Report on Knowledge*, trans. Geoff Bennington and Brian Massumi, Minneapolis, University of Minnesota Press, 1984.

68 See the many interesting essays along these lines in Elizabeth Long, ed., *From Sociology to Cultural Studies*, Oxford, Blackwell, 1997.

69 Cary Nelson, 'Manifesto of a Tenured Radical', New York, New York University Press, 1997, p. 51. See also Peter Osborne and Lynne Segal, 'Culture and Power: Interview with Stuart Hall', *Radical Philosophy*, no. 86, Nov.–Dec. 1997.

70 Barbara Johnson, *The Wake of Deconstruction*, Oxford, Blackwell, 1995, pp. 94, 85.

71 See Judith Butler, 'Merely Cultural', *Social Text*, nos 52–53, Fall–Winter, 1997.

72 Alan D. Sokal, 'Transgressing the Boundaries: Towards a Transformative Hermeneutics of Quantum Gravity', *Social Text*, nos 46–7, Spring–Summer, 1996. For insightful discussion, see Ellen Willis, 'My Sokaled Life', *Village Voice*, 25 June 1996, pp. 22–3.

73 Martha Nussbaum: 'The Hip Defeatism of Judith Butler: The Professor of Parody', *New Republic*, 22 Feb. 1999, pp. 37, 43.

74 Ferdinand Mount, 'Death and Burial of the Utopian Feminist', *Sunday Times*, 14 Dec. 1997, p. 15.

75 See, for example, Debbie Epstein et al., ed., *Failing Boys: Issues in Gender and Achievement*, Milton Keynes, Open University Press, 1998.

76 David Collinson and Jeff Hearn, eds, *Men as Managers, Managers as Men: Critical Perspectives on Men, Masculinities and Managements*, London, Sage, 1996.

77 In the late 1990s in Britain Susie Orbach and Andrew Samuels founded the pressure group Antidote, aiming to put the insights of psychotherapy to various political uses, ranging from the classroom to informing government policy.

78 David Sexton, 'Time to Dump the F-word', *Evening Standard: Features*, 2 Feb. 1999, p. 23.

79 Such sentiments were expressed by several feminists when interviewed by Nicci Gerard for the newspaper feature 'Where are they Now?', *Observer Review*, 21 Dec. 1997, p. 5.

80 Mitchell, in Moi, 'Psychoanalysis, Feminism, and Politics', *Materialist Feminism*, special eds Moi and Radway, p. 945; emphasis in the original.

81 Natasha Walter, *What is the New Feminism?*, London, Little, Brown, 1998, p. 4.
82 Ibid., pp. 34, 9.
83 Helen Simpson, 'Lentils and Lilies: A Story', in *On the Move: Feminism for a New Generation*, ed. Natasha Walter, London, Virago, 1999, p. 111. In her introduction (p. 3), Walter refers to Jade Beaumont as providing 'a heroine for our time'.
84 Sue Himmelweit, 'Not Much of a Choice', *Red Pepper*, Oct. 1996, p. 25.
85 For example, Sadie Plant, *Zeroes and Ones: Digital Women and the New Technoculture*, London, Fourth Estate, 1997.
86 Juliet Schor, *The Overworked American: The Unexpected Decline of Leisure*, New York, Basic Books, 1991; WFD/Management Today survey, London, May 1998.

Index

abuse 125, 131, 143, 210; *see also* child abuse; child sexual abuse
academics, memoirs 6
activism 10, 53–4, 67, 218, 271n59
adaptationism 78, 87–8, 91, 100, 103
Adolescent Family Life Act 73
adolescents 74–5, 155, 158, 160
AIDS 55–6, 67, 172–3
Aitkenhead, Decca 244n92
Alpert, Jane 44
Altman, Dennis 67–8
altruism 90, 98
American Psychiatric Association 119, 145
American Psychological Association 151
American Psychologist 88
American Sociology Association 152
American Women in Psychology 155
amnesia 119
Amos, Valerie 23
androgyny 40
Anner, John 271n59
anthropology 96–7, 114, 122
anti-pornography 28, 46, 270n38

anti-statism 211
Anzaldúa, Gloria 47
Archer, John 87, 88
Argentina, Mother of the Plaza de Mayo 54
Armstrong, Louise 147–8
Arnot, Madeleine 162
Asian women strikers 25–6
autobiographical material 5–6, 118, 143, 146–7
Avise, John 104

baboons: *see* primatology
Balibar, Etienne 220
Balint, Michael 190, 192
Barash, David 83, 85
Barrett, Michèle 12, 234n6
Barthes, Roland 78–9
Bartlett, Frederick 134
Bashevkin, Sylvia 202
Baudrillard, Jean 66, 73
Baxandall, Rosalyn 10
Beer, Gillian 221
behaviour: cultural causes 89; gendered 159; genetics 104, 108, 110, 154; memory 133–4; phenotypes 107; universalism 91
Beijing Declaration 204, 268n16
Bem, Sandra 40
Benefit Integrity Project 212–13

Benjamin, Jessica 69, 158, 197, 198
Benn, Melissa 25
Bertram, Corrine 151
Beyene, Yewoubdar 114
Bhabha, Homi 171
Billig, Michael 122
binary oppositions 12, 42
biology 85; absolutism 99; culture 110–11, 112–13, 114; diversity 81; psychology 115; sociobiology 85, 93
biotechnology 85–6, 109–10
black activism 10
black culture 219
black feminism 10, 23, 25, 31, 47, 48, 218
Blair, Tony 208, 209, 212, 230
Blakemore, Susan 111
Blakenhorn, David 210, 211
Bleier, Ruth 96
Bloom, Harold 202
body: ambiguities 59–60, 75, 246n122; castration 194; female 44, 196–7; mapping 12; materiality 70; pregnancy 113–14; prosthetic 64–5; reclaimed 30, 31; as site of resistance 60
Bolin, Anne 60–1
Bollas, Christopher 140
Borch-Jacobsen, Mikkel 188, 189
Bornstein, Kate 60
Bowlby, Rachel 176–7
boys 148, 160, 162–3; *see also* mother–child relationships
Braidotti, Rosi 52–3
breast cancer 112
Breen, Dana 196
Bronfen, Elizabeth 221–2
Brown, Wendy 212
Brownmiller, Susan 125, 177
Bruner, Jerome 121
Buhle, Mari Jo 174
Bunch, Charlotte 204

Burman, Erica 136
Business Week 83
Buss, David 87, 88, 89, 90
Butler, Judith: bodily ambiguities 59; cultural studies 224; drag 58, 62; feminist theorizing 13, 14, 29, 235n12; gender as performance 33, 57–8, 242n66; gender/sexuality 73; Lacan 183–4, 188; pregnancy 70; transgenderism 62–3

Cade, Toni 23
Campbell, Bea 2
cancer 112
capitalism 20–1, 65, 216–17
Carby, Hazel 218
care-based ethic 227
career/mothering conflicts 3, 213–14; *see also* work
Castells, Manuel 214
castration 127, 178, 184, 185, 194
Cavarero, Adriana 216
Charcot, Jean-Martin 126
Chasseguet-Smirgel, Janine 193–4
cheater detection 91, 100
Chenevix-Trench, Anthony 123–4
child abuse 117, 119, 122–3, 129
child sexual abuse 203, 250n78; cultural backlash 141–2; feminism 7, 124–5, 131–2; Freud 122–3, 125, 177; incest 99, 117; memory 117, 131–2, 135; Woolf 144–5
childcare, single mothers 212
childhood: care/gender 72; domestic violence 210; Freud 120; memory 116, 117, 143–4, 146–7; psychic life 191, 197; sexuality 126, 128, 131, 141, 193; trauma 119–20, 130; *see also*

childhood (*Cont'd*)
adolescents; boys; girls; infants
Chodorow, Nancy 45, 158,
190–1
Chomsky, Noam 91
Christian, Barbara 31
Cixous, Hélène 30, 50, 180, 182
class: feminism 23; oppression
34; and race 218; rape
acquittals 85; trade unions
218; welfare benefits 207
Clément, Catherine 182
Clinton, Bill 208, 209, 211–12
Clough, Patricia 15
cognitive differences 45
cognitive psychology 121, 135–7
Cohen, Michèle 163
collective action 11, 14, 52
commodification, body 64–5
competitiveness 83, 162
Connell, Bob 43, 70, 167, 168
consciousness-raising 125, 204,
226, 235–6n31
Conway, Martin 136–7
Cornell, Drucilla 51, 183
Cosmides, Leda 87, 91, 93
Coward, Rosalind 7
Crawford, Mary 155, 156
Crews, Frederick 120, 132–3,
141
Crick, Francis 104
cross-dressing 42, 63
cultural feminism 28, 44, 58,
181
cultural narrative 118, 119
cultural studies 110, 223–5
culture: behaviour 89; and
biology 110–11, 112–13, 114;
black 219; gender 173; and
genetics 93; oppression 34;
and politics 199;
psychoanalysis 138–9;
sexuality 61, 93, 223–5
cyberspace 114, 230

Daly, Martin 87, 90, 92

Darwin, Charles 79, 81–2,
101–3
Darwinism 78, 80, 82–3, 94–5,
100, 249n42
Davies, Michele 148
Dawkins, Richard 79, 80, 83,
84, 97–8, 101, 111
de Beauvoir, Simone 39, 40–1,
43–4
de Jong, Looren 91
de Lauretis, Teresa 187
de Salvo, Louise 144
de Saussure, Ferdinand 49, 184
de Vore, Irven 97
de Waal, Frans 95
Deaux, Kay 152
deconstruction 27, 32, 49, 215
deferred action 136, 139–40,
186
Deleuze, G. 53
Demos 80
Dennett, Daniel 111
dependence 3, 206, 208; *see also*
welfare dependency
depression gene 104–5
Derrida, Jacques 29, 31, 49, 176
desire 22, 63, 65, 128–9, 170–1,
187, 188
deviance, sexual 59
Dews, Peter 189
Didion, Joan 26
différance 49
difference: cognitive 45; gender
38–9, 44, 45; and identity
217–18; politics 2, 48,
238n74; *see also* sexual
difference
difference theory 30, 31–2, 47,
52–3, 215
Dimen, Muriel 22, 69, 71, 150,
158, 197, 200
disabled, welfare 213
discourse and practice 217
disease, genetics 108–9, 110,
112
dissidence, sexual 57–8, 68

DNA 86, 104, 105–6, 108, 110
DNA testing 108, 109
Dollimore, Jonathan 65
domesticity 26–7, 43, 203; *see also* family life
domination: institutionalized 88; language 19; male 210–11, 214, 236n35, 263n52; sexual 46
Douglas, Mary 134
drag 58, 61, 62
Duckworth, Gerald and George 144–5
Dunant, Sarah 149
Dunbar, Robin 98–9
DuPlessis, Rachel 11
Dworkin, Andrea 27, 28, 29

Eagleton, Terry 35, 223
Eagly, Alice 153
Ebbinghaus, Hermann 133, 134
economy, feminized 204
Edelman, Gerald 134
educational performance, gender 160, 162–3, 262n53
Educational Reforms and Gender Equality in Schools 162
Ehrenreich, Barbara 211, 212, 224
Einon, Dorothy 90
Eisenstein, Zillah 212
Eissler, Kurt 133
Eldredge, Niles 100, 101
Elshtain, Jean Bethke 1, 227
employment 169, 201, 204; *see also* work
employment training 209
environmental pollutants 111, 112
Epstein, Barbara 224
Equal Rights Amendment, USA 47
equality feminism 180–1, 215, 219
ethnicity 31, 218; *see also* race
Etzioni, Amitai 209

eugenics 81, 101, 111
evolutionary biology 79–80, 91, 93–4, 98
evolutionary psychology 80, 86–7, 92, 98–9
experience 19, 71–2, 120, 139–40
Eysenck, Hans 104, 119, 175
Eysenck, Michael 104–5

Fairbairn, Ronald 190
false memory 132–3, 135, 141–2, 144
False Memory Syndrome Foundation 133
family background 116, 117, 119, 175
family life: conservatism 192; dysfunctional 119; gender relations 210–11, 214; sexual abuse 131; state 21; structure 188, 230; values 209–11; welfare 202
fathers 194, 202, 203, 210
Fedigan, Linda 95, 97
Felski, Rita 51–2
femininity 27; anxieties 150; Freud 178; identification 198; imaginary 51, 182; and masculinity 27, 166, 170, 173, 178; mothering 190–1; oppression 39–40; otherness 49, 51–2; power 161; psychic 69–70; social construct 38, 44, 155–6; stereotypes 155–6
feminism 2, 3–4, 10–12, 14–15; anthropology 96–7; capitalism 216–17; child sexual abuse 7, 124–5, 131–2; class 23; collective action 14; conflicts within 1, 9, 10, 13, 200–1, 235n14; cultural backlash 141–2, 229; Darwinism 83–4, 94–5; deradicalized 52–3; discourse/practices 15, 215, 217; exclusions 22, 23–4;

feminism (*Cont'd*)
  Foucault 56–7; Freud 125–6,
  174, 177; Lacan 29, 179–80,
  181; metaphors 221–2;
  object-relations theory 190,
  191–2; politics 231; and post-
  structuralism 5, 27, 200–1,
  215; psychoanalysis 69, 148,
  174, 176–7, 197–9;
  psychology 151, 154–5;
  psychotherapy 227; sexuality
  59; societal transformation
  15–16, 20, 35, 232; solidarity
  24–5; subjectivity 187
feminisms 2, 12, 27, 231–2;
  academic 27, 29, 150–1, 221,
  222–3; black 10, 23, 25, 31,
  47, 48, 218; cultural 28, 44,
  58, 181; difference-based 205;
  equality 180–1, 206, 215,
  219; ethnic minority 31;
  French 30, 50–2, 180–1,
  186–7, 237n58; Italian 216;
  Kristeva 16; lesbian 22, 58–9;
  liberal 41; materialist 47–8;
  modernist 13; post-modern
  13; post-structuralist 200–1;
  power 228–9; radical 45–6,
  203, 211; second-wave 4–5, 9,
  17, 35–6, 38, 44; seventies 12;
  socialist 11, 16, 17, 20, 21–2,
  28, 34, 37, 180–1, 215–16,
  232; third wave 205; Third
  World 218
feminist literary criticism 41
feminist publishing 3, 28
feminist studies 15, 221, 222–3
feminist theorizing 13–15, 29,
  220, 235n12
feminization of economy 204
Le Figaro 106
Fine, Michelle 151
Firestone, Shulamith 44
First, Elsa 197
Flanders, Laura 36
Flax, Jane 43, 158

Fletcher, John 185
Fliess, Wilhelm 128, 139
Flockhart, Calista 6
folk psychology 120, 122
Fonagy, Peter 138–40, 141–2
Foot, Paul 123, 124
Foucault, Michel 29, 32–3, 56–7
Fouque, Antoinette 180, 181
France: *see* French feminism
Frankfurt School 189
Franklin, Rosalind 104
Franks, Suzanne 204, 214
Fraser, Nancy 206
Fraser, Sylvia 132
French feminism 30, 50–2,
  180–1, 186–7, 237n58
Freud, Anna 131
Freud, Sigmund 132–3, 227;
  child sexual abuse 122–3,
  125, 177; childhood 120;
  deferred action 136, 139–40,
  186; femininity 178; feminists
  125–6, 174, 177;
  homosexuality 193; hysteria
  126, 140–1, 254n21; *The
  Interpretation of Dreams*
  121–2, 126; loving/working
  80; masochism 195; memory
  7, 117, 138; Oedipus complex
  126–7; seduction theory 126,
  127–8; self-deception 124;
  self-exploration 118, 134;
  sexual desire 128–9; sexual
  difference 125, 126, 195;
  subjectivity 176
Friedan, Betty 177
Friedman, Susan Stanford
  235n14
fundamentalism 25, 78, 79, 80,
  82–3

Gagnon, John 76
Gallop, Jane 6, 177, 218
gay gene 104, 112
gay studies 32, 55–6; *see also*
  queer theory

gay subculture 172, 210; *see also* homosexuality
Geertz, Clifford 122
gender 2, 3, 36, 43, 156–7; behaviour 159; child sexual abuse 131–2; cultural dynamics 173; difference 38–9, 44, 45; educational performance 160, 162–3, 262n53; evolutionary theory 88; identity 6, 52, 54, 60, 63, 69, 150, 178–9; inequity 68; not transcended 54; observer 94, 95; oppression 34; passing 68; as performance 33, 57–8, 242n66; and power 42, 43; psychology 41; and race 48; Scott 42–3; and sex 38–40, 46, 75, 170–1; and sexuality 55, 72, 73, 75–7; social construct 38, 75, 155, 157, 158–9; social relations 224; social sciences 41–2; subjectivity 41, 149; symbolic construct 40–1; transgressions 61
gender anxieties 2, 148–9, 157–8, 168–9, 178
Gender Identity Disorder 41–2
gender relations 19; changing 225; family 210–11, 214; justice 172, 200; masculinity 163–4; modernity 253n52; politics 159; social movements 159; transformed 168; work 75
gender roles 83, 84, 203
gender theory 42–3, 71–2, 172
gene splicing 85–6
genetic predispositions 111
genetics 103, 104–5, 106–7; behaviour 104, 108, 110, 154; cancer 112; and culture 93; determinism 6–7; disease 108–9, 110; gender roles 83, 84; homosexuality 112;

politics 115; research 86
genital ambiguities 59–60, 75, 246n122
Gibson, Suzanne 36
Gilbert, Walter 104
Gilligan, Carol 45, 155, 227
Gilman, Charlotte Perkins 174–5
girls, adolescent 155, 158
globalization 25, 34, 220–1
Glover, Edward 131
Goldman, Emma 174
Goldner, Virginia 69, 197
Goodall, Jane 95
Gordon, Linda 10, 206
Gornick, Vivian 24
Gould, Stephen Jay 78, 88–9, 100, 101, 102–3, 152
Greer, Germaine 7, 46, 177
Grosz, Elizabeth 188
growth hormone 110
Guntrip, Harry 190

Haaken, Janice 142, 149
Hacking, Ian 134, 137–8, 140, 145, 146
haemophilia 107, 110
Halberstam, Judith 61
Haldane, J. B. S. 101
Hall, Stuart 223
Hamer, Dean 112
Haraway, Donna 31–2, 73, 99–100, 114
Harris, Adrienne 197
Harris, Arlene 69
Harris, Judith 119
Heilbrun, Carolyn 10
Herman, Judith 130
Heron, Liz 207
heterosexuality 65, 191–2; coercive 57; compulsory 45; gender identity 63; Greer 7; marriage 210; masculinity 63
Hibbert, Christopher 123–4
Hinshelwood, Bob 142
history 10–12, 14–15, 80
Hochschild, Arlie 27

homicide 90
homophobia 192
homosexuality 112, 172, 193,
  210; *see also* gay subculture;
  lesbianism; queer theory
Horkheimer, Max 189
Horrocks, Roger 163
Hrdy, Sarah Blaffer 95
Hubbard, Ruth 107, 108, 112
Human Genome Project 86,
  104, 105–6, 109
human rights 36, 219–20,
  238n74
Huxley, Aldous 109
Huxley, Julian 101
hysteria 126, 140–1, 254n21

identity 1, 53; desire 65; and
  difference 217–18; gender 6,
  52, 54, 60, 63, 69, 150, 178–9;
  politics of 48, 218; post-
  modern 240–1n35; sexual 57,
  158; social construct 158;
  unconscious 50; vulnerable
  147
ideology 111
imaginaries 34, 51, 182
incest 99, 117, 127, 147–8, 210
Independent 162
individualistic ethic 229
industrial action 25–6
infanticide, female 72
infants 197; genital ambiguity
  59–60, 75, 246n122; sexuality
  126, 128, 193
International Women's Day
  march 17
interpersonal skills 166–7, 226
Intersex Society of North
  America 59–60
Irigaray, Luce 30, 50, 52, 180,
  182, 183
Italian feminism 216

Jacklin, Carol 152, 153
Jacobus, Mary 51

Janet, Pierre 141
Johnson, Barbara 223
Jones, Steven 91–2, 110, 111
Jukes, Adam 194–5

Kaplan, Cora 270n48
Kaplan, Temma 219–20
Keller, Evelyn Fox 110
Kenrick, Douglas 93
Kernberg, Otto 191
Kessler, Suzanne 75, 246n122
Kevles, David 112
Kierkegaard, S. 118
Kimmel, Michael 168–9
kin selection 90
Kinsey report 157
Klein, Melanie 131, 188, 190,
  192
Koshland, David 109
Kristeva, Julia 16, 50, 52, 180
Kuhn, Thomas 87

labour divisions 26–7, 43
Lacan, Jacques: Butler on
  183–4, 188; feminism 29,
  179–80, 181; memory/truth
  130, 140; patriarchy 179–80;
  phallocentrism 183, 184, 188,
  189–90; sexual difference
  49–50, 188–9; symbolic
  181–2, 184, 187, 189; women/
  lack 182, 184
Lancaster, Roger 62–3
language 19, 53, 91, 188–9,
  215–16
Laplanche, Jean 128, 129,
  139–40, 184–5
Latin America, transgenderism
  62
Laufer, Eglé 194
Lee, Hermione 145
Lee, Richard 97
left wing 20, 80, 218; *see also*
  socialist feminism
leisure 230
Lemoine-Luccioni, Eugénie 181

lesbian feminism 22, 58
lesbian theorizing 32–3, 44–5, 55–6
lesbianism: castration 194; desexualized 58–9; desire 188; as dissidence 68; genetics 112; primates 96; rights 210; *see also* queer theory
Levant, Ronald 163, 165
Levenstein, Harvey 213
Levine, Judith 74
Lévi-Strauss, Claude 181, 187
Lewis, Gail 23
Lewontin, Richard 94, 101, 103, 107–8
liberalism 41, 165
Loftus, Elizabeth 135
Lorde, Audre 47

MacCannell, Juliet Flower 184
Maccoby, Eleanor 152
McDowell, Deborah 31
Macey, David 186
McGuffin, Peter 105
machismo 167
McIntosh, Mary 21, 207–8, 212
MacKinnon, Catharine 28, 29, 45–6, 203, 212, 224
Mailer, Norman 26, 178, 216
mallard ducks 85
Mama, Amina 23
managers, skills 166–7, 226
Marcus, Laura 121
marriage 26, 210
Mars-Jones, Adam 123–4
Martin, Biddy 76–7
masculinity: as abstraction 165–6; Bhabha 171; in crisis 160–1, 163–4, 194–5; and femininity 27, 166, 170, 173, 178; gender relations 163–4; heterosexual 63; inferiority 225; liberalism 165; men's anxieties 150, 153, 163; phallic 52; power 161; psychic 69–70; reforming 164–5, 166–7, 172–3; shoring up 168; and women 160–1, 169
masochism 195
Masson, Jeffrey 125, 127, 128, 129–30, 140–1, 147
mating strategies 89–90, 100
meaning and representation 32–3
memes 111
memoirs, academics 6
memory 133–7; affective 120, 142; and amnesia 119; behaviour 133–4; child sexual abuse 117, 131–2, 135; childhood 116, 117, 143–4, 146–7; cognitive psychology 135–7; false 132–3, 135, 141–2, 144; as fiction 140–1; Freud 7, 117, 138; and history 10–11; psychoanalysis 134, 139; repressed 119; storage/ retrieval 137; trauma 7, 145–6
men: competition 83, 162; dominance 10–11, 211, 214, 236n35, 263n52; gender anxieties 52, 148, 149–50, 157–8, 168–9, 178; as managers 166–7, 226; mother–son relationship 164, 190–1, 194–5; patriarchy 167; power 36, 42, 43, 143, 196; self-esteem 164–5; sexuality 157, 196; social inequality 162, 166, 167, 170; suffering 161–2; as universal 41; violence 46, 85, 88, 90–1, 203, 207, 229, 249n42; vulnerabilities 3, 7, 8, 52; Wright 82–3; *see also* masculinity
men's studies 160, 163
mentors 168
Merck, Mandy 62
mestiza 47

midwives, reports on violence 90–1, 207, 269n22
Miller, Alice 125
Miller, Jacques-Alain 179
Million Man March 171
mimesis 183
misogyny 44, 166, 205, 229
Mitchell, Juliet 125, 174, 177, 179, 188, 197, 216, 228
Mitchell, Stephen 140
Mohanty, Chandra 48, 240–1n35
Moi, Toril 16, 215
monkey studies: *see* primatology
Morgan, Robin 27
Morrison, Toni 92
mother–child relationships 164, 190–1, 194–5
motherhood 44, 45, 190–1, 204, 216; *see also* single mothers
Mothers of the Plaza de Mayo 54
Moynihan, Daniel 171, 206
Mulhern, Francis 223
multinationals 67, 86, 221
Multiple Personality Disorder 119, 145–6
murder, husband–wife 90
Mysterud, Iver 98

National Black Feminist Organization 23
National Cancer Institute 112
National Children's Home Action 210
National Organization of Women 4
natural selection 82, 85, 91, 100–1
nature and history 80
nature/nurture 109–10
Nelson, Cary 223
neo-Darwinism 86, 101
neo-liberalism 208
Nestle, Joan 22, 59
Netherlands, pregnancy 73

neuropsychology 134, 136
New York Times Book Review 26
non-adaptationism 103
Nussbaum, Martha 224

Oakley, Ann 39
object-relations theory 50, 140, 179–80, 190, 191–2
observer, gender 94, 95
Oedipus complex 126–7, 185, 186, 189, 199
oncogenes 112
oppression 34 ; femininity 39–40; state 212; women 19, 20, 186–7, 234n6
Orbach, Susie 226
other 40, 49, 51–2, 180

Paglia, Camille 2, 29
Paley, Grace 222
Parmar, Pratibha 23
passing, gender 68
paternalism 143, 202, 208; *see also* fathers
patriarchy 21, 167, 177, 179–80, 189, 214, 263n62
Patton, Cindy 59
pederasty 123
Peel, Mark 124
penis 181, 198
penis envy 127
Perelman, Rosine Josef 150
performance 33, 57–8, 242n66
Person, Ethel 191, 192
personal, and political 227–8, 231
Peterson, D. 95
phallocentrism 50, 183, 184, 189–90, 198
phallogocentrism 53, 182
phallus 50, 52, 178, 181–2, 188, 198
phantasy 131, 132
phenotypes, behaviour 107
Phillips, Adam 65, 199
Phillips, Anne 12, 35

phyletic gradualism 101
Pinker, Steven 91, 92, 99
Pleck, Joseph 164, 166
Plomin, Robert 109
Plotkin, Henry 111
Plummer, Ken 56, 75–6
Policy Studies Unit 203
politics 2, 4; and culture 199; of
    difference 2, 48, 238n74;
    feminism 231; gender
    relations 159; genetics 115;
    identity-based 48, 218; and
    personal 227–8, 231;
    psychoanalysis 177; queer 58,
    59; sex 172
Pollack, William 163, 165
Pollitt, Katha 224
Pontalis, J.-B. 116, 128, 139–40,
    143, 147
Popenoe, David 210
population control 111
pornography 28–9, 212
Porter, Roy 149
post-modernism 29, 67,
    240–1n35
post-structuralism: Anglo-
    American response 35;
    Derrida 31, 49; and feminism
    5, 27, 200–1, 215; Foucault
    32–3; identity 33–4; state
    36–7
Post-Traumatic-Stress-Disorder
    145–6
poverty 23, 25, 202, 203, 208–9
power: abused 143; and gender
    36, 42, 43, 143, 196;
    masculinity/femininity 161;
    phallic 181–2; sexuality 67;
    societal 19
pregnancy 70–1, 91, 113–14,
    207, 269n22
pregnancy prevention 73–4
pre-Oedipal attachments 51,
    180, 190, 197
primatology 94–7, 99–100
promiscuity 84, 89, 90

Prosser, Jay 63, 65–6, 243–4n89
psychic life 69, 117–18; analysis
    140; child 191, 197;
    masculinity/femininity 69–70;
    particularities 157; sexuality
    187; and social 193–4
psychoanalysis: cultural context
    138–9; feminism 69, 148,
    174, 176–7, 197–9; gender
    identity 178–9; memory 134,
    139; men's power 196;
    political need 177; psychology
    117, 120, 175; sexual
    difference 158, 176–7, 179;
    women practitioners 175
psychobisexuality 196
psychology: biological 115;
    cognitive 121, 135–7; fear of
    the mind 115; feminism 151,
    154–5; gender 41; genetics
    104–5; neo-Darwinism 86;
    and psychoanalysis 117, 120,
    175; quantitative/qualitative
    studies 122, 151–2, 153–4,
    175–6; social 122
psychotherapy 43, 192, 227
public school life 123–4

queer politics 58, 59
queer self-presentations 61
queer theory 56, 58, 65, 67–9,
    243–4n89

race: activism 271n59; and class
    218; feminism 23–4; and
    gender 48; oppression 34;
    post-modernism 241n35;
    poverty 202; school
    performance 163
racism 25, 92
radical feminism 45–6, 203, 211
rape 3, 85, 125, 203
rape-adaptation hypothesis 84–5
Raphael-Leff, Joan 150
Rapping, Elayne 148
Rathbone, Eleanor 205–6

Reagan, Ronald 208
Redbook 26
Reed, Lynn Raphael 168
Reid-Pharr, Robert 171
representations 32–3, 231
reproduction 44, 70, 80, 113
resistance 5, 60, 220–1, 222
responsibility, personal 230
Rich, Adrienne 3, 44, 58
Ricoeur, Paul 137
Riggs, Marlon 62
right wing 21–2, 208, 209
Riley, Denise 38, 54
Robbins, Bruce 238n74
Romito, Patrizia 216
Romney, Patricia 10
Roper, Michael 158
Rose, Hilary 107–8
Rose, Jacqueline 50, 120, 184, 188
Rose, Steven 100, 102, 106, 134, 135
Rosen, Ruth 224
Ross, Andrew 86, 167, 218
Rowbotham, Sheila 9, 17–21, 26
Rubin, Gayle 40, 55, 72, 73, 187
Rush, Florence 125, 127, 177

Samuels, Andrew 149–50, 226
Schacter, Daniel 135
schizophrenia 92
Schneider, Monique 196
school failure, gender 160, 162–3, 262n53
Schor, Juliet 230
Schreber, Daniel Paul 129–30
Science 109
scorpionflies 84
Scott, Joan 13, 14, 19–20, 42–3, 200
Sedgwick, Eve Kosofsky 55
seduction theory 126, 127–8
Segal, Hanna 192
Segal, Lynne 28, 61, 63

self-deception 124
self-esteem 164–5
self-exploration 118, 134
self-help books 204, 206, 226
selfish gene 97–8
sex 28; desire 22, 128–9, 170–1; domination 46; and gender 38–40, 46, 75, 170–1; identity 57, 158; politics 172; and reproduction 70, 80, 113; roles 39, 165
sex education 73–4, 211–12
sex-reversed species 98
sexual abuse 125, 131; *see also* child sexual abuse
sexual difference: cultural analysis 61, 93, 223–5; feminism 1, 30–1; French feminists 51; Freud 125, 126, 195; Lacan 49–50, 188–9; language 188–9; psychic life 49–50; psychoanalysis 158, 176–7, 179; similarities 152, 153, 157–8; social context 152; stereotypes 152–3
sexual harassment 83, 88
sexual selection 82, 92
sexuality: ambiguous 59–60, 61, 75, 246n122; childhood 126, 128, 131, 141, 193; culture 61, 93, 223–5; deviance 59; dissident 57–8, 68; Foucault 32–3; and gender 55, 72, 73, 75–7; lesbian 58–9; male 157, 196; passivity 185, 195; pleasure 90; power 67; psychic/social relations 187; transgressive 66–7
Showalter, Elaine 41
Shulman, Alix Kates 26
signifiers 181, 212
Signs 219
Silverman, Kaja 198
Silverstein, Louise 96
Sinason, Valerie 132, 142
Sinfield, Alan 65, 68

single mothers 23, 201–2, 206, 207–8, 212
Sinsheimer, Robert 104
sisterhood 20, 22, 23–4
skin colour 92
Small, Meredith 95, 99
Smith, Anna Marie 212
Smith, Barbara 24, 47, 68
Smuts, Barbara 95
Snitow, Ann 11, 28–9, 44, 53–4
Socarides, Charles 192
social constructionism:
    femininity 38, 44, 155–6;
    gender 38, 75, 155, 157, 158–9; identity 158;
    psychology 154–7
social contexts 96–7, 109, 152
social inequality 229;
    adolescents 74–5; gender relations 19; men 8, 162, 166, 167, 170; race 25;
    women 2, 25
social justice 34, 220
social learning theory 87
social movements 1, 9, 159
social role theory 87
social sciences 41–2, 43, 222, 223
social transformation 15–16, 20, 35, 232
socialist feminism 16, 17, 28, 37, 215–16, 232; and equal rights 180–1, 215–16; and right wing 21–2; social transformation 20, 34, 232
sociobiologists 85, 93
Sokal, Alan 224
solidarity, feminist 20, 24–5
Spence, Donald 140
Sperling, Susan 97, 114
Spivak, Gayatri 31, 32, 51
Stacey, Judith 210, 217
state 21, 36–7, 169, 212, 236n35
Steedman, Carolyn 207
stereotypes 39, 152–3, 155–6

Stern, Daniel 197
Stoller, Robert 41–2, 60
Strobel, Margaret 10
subcultures 159, 172
subjectivity 14, 41, 149, 176, 187, 231
subordination 167, 215–16; *see also* oppression
survival 80, 82, 148
Sutherland, Stuart 119, 141
Swaab, Dick 244n92
Sweden, as social democracy 208
symbolic, Lacan 181–2, 184, 187, 189
Symons, Donald 83

Tavris, Carole 152
Tax, Meredith 11
Terr, Leonore 135–6
Thatcher, Margaret 208
Thornhill, Randy 84
Tiefer, Leonore 155
Tooby, John 87, 91, 93
Toynbee, Polly 3
transgenderism 60–3
transgression 61, 66–7
transsexualism 60–2, 63, 64, 65–6, 244n92
transvestism 42, 63
trauma 7, 119–20, 130, 136, 140, 145–6
Trivers, Robert 84
Trost, Melanie 93
Trowell, Judith 132

UN Fourth World Conference on Women 204
unemployment 162
Unger, Rhoda 155
universalism: behaviour 91; false 47, 151; masculine 41; models 121; truths 78–9
USA: culture wars 202; Equal Rights Amendment 47; feminism 13, 24, 28–9, 205,

USA (*Cont'd*)
219; incest 147–8; leisure
230; masculinity 163–4, 171;
memory/trauma 145–6; men/
universal 41; National
Organization of Women 4;
sex education 73–4; sexual
abuse 125; welfare reforms
211–12; Women's Liberation
10; women's studies 45

Van Der Steen, W. J. 91
Van Haute, Philippe 185
Village Voice 24
violence: domestic 3, 21, 210;
male 46, 85, 88, 90–1, 203,
207, 229, 249n42; against
women 90–1, 207, 268n16,
269n22

wage levels 3, 203
Wald, Elijah 108, 112
Walker, Alice 47
Walter, Natasha 228–9
Walter, Suzanna 68
war veterans, trauma 145–6
Warner, Michael 59
Watney, Simon 67
Watson, James 104, 105,
111–12
Weinberg, Simon 131
Weiss, Robert 166
Weisstein, Naomi 154–5
welfare benefit cuts 7–8, 201–2,
207
welfare dependency 206–7,
209
welfare entitlements 207, 213,
220–1
welfare reform 203, 206,
211–12, 212–13
welfare-to-work 209
Wexler, Nancy 106, 109
Williams, Patricia 220

Williams, Raymond 223
Williamson, Judith 210
Wilson, E. O. 83, 84
Wilson, Elizabeth 21, 68
Wilson, Margo 87, 90, 92
Winnicott, Donald 131, 190
Wittig, Monique 41, 57
women 97, 200–1; divisions 47;
empowering 200; gender
issues 150, 203; human rights
issues 36; independence 214;
lack 20–1, 182; and men 36,
90–1, 169; oppressed 19, 20,
186–7, 234n6; Other 40;
paid/unpaid work 26–7, 204,
213–14; reproductive cycle
113, 114; resistant to change
5; social status 2, 25, 160–1
Women's Liberation 4, 9–10,
24, 201; and feminism 14;
Ruskin College conference 18;
social transformation 15–16,
17; social-feminism 21–2
women's movement 4, 5
women's studies 45
Women's WORLD 11
Woolf, Virginia 144–5
work: flexibility 2; hours 230;
labour division 26–7, 43, 75;
paid/unpaid 3, 26–7, 204,
213–14; *see also* employment
work ethic 230
work incentives 213
workfare 209
Wrangham, R. 95
Wright, Robert 82–3, 98
Wyngaarden, James 105

Young, Allon 146

Zebrowitz, Leslie 92
Zihlman, Adrienne 97
Zita, Jacqueline 72
Žižek, Slavoj 182, 189